Tascha Boychuk-Spears, Ph.D., RN

Children Who Witness Homicide and Other Violent Crimes

A PRACTICAL GUIDE FOR LAW ENFORCEMENT, CHILD SERVICES AND MENTAL HEALTH PROFESSIONALS

A Practical Guide Series
By Specialized Training Services

San Diego, California

Published by Specialized Training Services
(An imprint of Specialized Training Services, Inc.)
9606 Tierra Grande, Suite 105
San Diego, CA 92126

Editor: Drew Leavens

Library of Congress Cataloging-in-Publication Data

Boychuk-Spears, Tascha
    Children Who Witness Homicide and Other Violent Crimes /
    Tascha Boychuk-Spears.
      p. 239
    Includes bibliographical references (p. 231-237)
    ISBN 0-9703189-2-8

Library of Congress Control Number: 2002102780

*T*his book is meant for professionals and families whose lives have been marked forever by exposure to the tragedies of human violence.

It is for those on the front lines – police, paramedics, and child protection specialists confronted with interviewing children amidst the shock that accompanies the investigation of a violent crime.

This book is for every nurse, physician and mental health practitioner charged with the care and healing of children in the aftermath of violence.

It is for criminal justice personnel who see both victims and perpetrators of violence on a daily basis and yearn for just, moral and ethical solutions.

And with gratitude, this book is for those who looked violence in the face and survived to tell their stories.

For these profound accounts remind us not to trivialize violence but instead call us to research and service.

The Specialized Training Services Practical Guide Series:

Children Who Witness Homicide and Other Violent Crimes
    Tascha Boychuk-Spears, Ph.D., R.N.

School Violence Threat Management
    Kris Mohandie, Ph.D.

Violence Risk and Threat Assessment
    J. Reid Meloy, Ph.D.

*For information on these and other books, tapes, and videos offered by
Specialized Training Services, contact us at:*
Specialized Training Services, Inc.
9606 Tierra Grande, Suite 105
San Diego, CA 92126
(858) 695-1313, (858) 695-6599 (fax)
or visit our website at: www.specializedtraining.com

TABLE OF CONTENTS

Acknowledgments

It was the efforts of many that created this book. My deepest thanks to the children and families who were my teachers about life in the aftermath of violence. Your courageous struggles are the threads that weave and bind this book. Another group of teachers were police – more than I could possibly name or thank. The case material for this book spanned many states and nations. Investigative knowledge, imparted with humor while working on cases in the wee hours of the morning was invaluable. Many colleagues, attorneys and judges in criminal and civil proceedings also shared their judicious efforts to address the complex circumstances of children who witness violent crimes. Thanks as well to seminar coordinators and conference participants in workshops throughout Canada, Europe and the United States. This book is designed as a practical guide based upon many of your suggestions.

I am also grateful to my mentors, among them, my friend, Phil Esplin, Ed.D., who long ago introduced me to the possibility that children could be interviewed competently yet compassionately. His deep interests in the tragedies of life and our lively debates have always kept me honest. Kathleen Ferraro, Ph.D., a pioneer in the study of violence against women, has always encouraged my endeavors. Thank you to Caryl Ainley, Ph.D. and Egan "Butch" Artichoker who later shared integrative healing techniques for those who have survived the cruelest forms of suffering. Cindy, Mimi, Mary, and all my nursing colleagues, your friendship sustained me through the joys and sorrows of many days.

My appreciation to editor, Drew Leavens for his careful reading of the manuscript and thoughtful feedback.

A bouquet of gratitude to my family, particularly my mother who sadly did not get to see the publication of this book but left our family with a precious legacy in the field of education. To my Dad and sisters, thanks for your love, support and continuous laughter in the face of adversity.

My heartfelt thanks to my husband and friend, Mitch, who believed in me and encouraged me to speak from the deepest place in my heart. Words can not express my gratitude and love.

My final acknowledgement is to the readers – I am honored you have chosen this book.

Prologue

Entering The World Of Children's Grief

The girl stared at her mother's hand, swollen beyond recognition. Bruises discolored the once perfectly shaped fingers. Steady breathing...in and out. Her mother rested peacefully. The girl was oblivious to the medical equipment that kept her mother alive. Instead, she focused on the gravest of possibilities. Somehow, one of the bullets struck the most delicate and unique aspect of her mother. She closed her eyes as the ache in her heart grew.

In her mind's eye, she could see her mother playing the piano. Fingers keenly poised on the ivories, she recalled the moment of anticipation before melodies floated throughout the house. Laughingly, her father would state, "there is no one in the world who has such beautiful hands!" She loved to sit quietly beside her mother watching the careful application of pale pink polish to neatly trimmed nails.

But there was no color now on the nails, chipped and peeling from the fluid that weighted each nail bed. The girl was there when her mother took one last breath. The child's tears fell silently, like water from the roof of a cavern, to a puddle on the hospital floor. The girl lingered, eyes fixed on the bed. For a long time, the distorted hand remained the single most salient image of her mother. I know this story. I listened to this girl.

The mother of this child died from multiple gunshot wounds. In an effort to defend herself from the assailant, she raised her hand and one of the bullets shattered her wrist. It was this injury that the girl focused on during the brief hospital visit prior to her mother's death. The girl was seven years old.

From the hospital, the girl was accompanied to the police department. She was the only witness to the attack on her mother. A concerned and nervous detective began to take down the facts. The last thing he wanted to do was cause this little girl harm. The way her story would be told depended upon his skill along with the nature, timing and place of the interview.

For many children who witness violence, the disclosure, or "telling of the event" will initially occur in a law enforcement setting during an investigative interview. After the investigation, it may be any number of people who provide an array of formal and informal support services for children and families. In the aftermath of violence, children will be affected by the interplay of dynamics related to their stage of development, personal experiences of the violence and responses following the event.

Following her mother's murder, the seven-year-old girl lived a quiet and lonely life with her father. Grief-stricken, the child's father could not bear to speak about his beloved wife. The girl was not allowed to talk about her mother. No pictures of her mother were displayed in the home.

I share this girl's story with you to illustrate how a child's experience of an untimely and violent death is personal and unique. When I heard this child's sorrow over ten years ago, I was taken aback by the most vivid image she stored about her mother, who by all accounts was a highly accomplished and compassionate woman. We know that unlocking the specific and unique recollections of children is critical to their recovery from traumatic experiences. But for children who witness the homicide of a loved one, loss and grief intermingle with trauma.

To grieve effectively one must remember a loved one over time. For a child, recalling even favorable memories of the deceased may lead to a flood of violent images related to the crime. The disturbing images can exacerbate symptoms of distress that lead some children to avoid remembering at all costs. The price paid for blocking out thoughts and feelings can indeed be high. We are all too familiar with the eyes of the walking wounded, the depressed and those who self-medicate with drugs and alcohol. In contrast, what do we know about children and families who develop extraordinary strategies for survival.

Ours is a relatively new field when it comes to studying children and violence. It wasn't until the Chowchilla kidnapping in 1976 that twenty-six children, imprisoned for thirty hours, were studied following their release. In spite of early reports by a psychiatrist that their mental health was unaffected, Dr. Lenore Terr reported serious long-term effects in the children, families and community eight months after the rescue. More researchers began concerted efforts to examine children following stressful events. In addition, clinicians began identifying adverse effects of violence and therapies were developed to moderate symptoms that altered children's physical and mental health.

Amidst this work, media frenzy in the 1980's drew our attention to investigations involving child victims and witnesses. Interview strategies used with children reporting a particular type of violence, sexual abuse, were increasingly being scrutinized during criminal and civil proceedings. Attacks, primarily by defense attorneys, focused on the reliability and credibility of children's statements during investigations. The emphasis gradually changed from challenging children to those who interviewed them. Interviewers, in general, were portrayed as unskilled primarily due to the use of coercive, leading or suggestive questions. At the heart of the debate was the distinct difference between counseling and investigative methods.

The purpose of this book is to describe investigative interview strategies used with children who witness violence. In addition, counseling methods for traumatized children are also provided. The book is designed with case studies offering highly personal accounts from children, families, police, counselors and child service providers. Practical interview and counseling techniques are woven through the stories in an effort to consider the wisdom that comes from experience along with the findings of science.

Organization of the Book

The book includes twelve chapters. The foundations of investigative interviewing are found in Chapter one. Chapter two provides a case history where the use of basic interview principles was not effective with school age witnesses who were coerced to provide inaccurate eyewitness accounts. The children required modifications to the interview protocol. Flexibility with interview design is also necessary for very young children.

Chapter three focuses on the capacities of preschoolers using two case histories of children who witnessed the homicide of their mother. Chapter four describes the plight of foster children, abandoned or abused by their own parents and placed with those who would kill another. Their unique circumstances require thorough and thoughtful investigations.

Likewise, cold case homicides present numerous issues for those interviewing child witnesses. Chapter five provides suggestions for interviewing children after several years have passed since the commission of the crime. Some witnesses in cold case investigations have symptoms of distress that have gone untreated for years. They may present with hypervigilance, anxiety or difficulty attending to questions. Managing highly active children during an investigative interview is the focus of chapter six.

Given the diverse circumstances involving children who witness homicide, it is imperative to examine if certain types of investigative questions are more useful than others in eliciting crime scene facts. Chapter seven provides preliminary research findings from a study involving school age children who witnessed the homicide of a family member. Crimes involving family members are complex given the relationships between the child witness, the victim and the offender. Nowhere is this more evident than in cases of domestic violence. Chapter eight offers investigative techniques and crisis intervention strategies for children who witness conflict at home.

Related to domestic violence are issues of custody and visitation. Extreme quarrels about custody sometimes result in the abduction of children by non-custodial parents. Assessment methods used with abducted children who have been recovered are described in Chapter nine. In addition, ideas for interviewing children who may have knowledge about child abductions by strangers are also provided. Stranger abductions at times result in appalling experiences but children can also be witness to unimaginable horrors in their own communities. Chapter ten describes techniques used to interview two children exposed to inconceivable types of violence.

Children who have witnessed extreme cruelty require specialized therapy. Specific activities used during counseling sessions of children who witnessed severe violence are provided in Chapter eleven. Finally, Chapter twelve identifies the concept of compassion fatigue. Suggestions are offered for taking care of those who provide services to children and families.

As you can see, the primary focus of this book is not the presentation of theory and formidable research findings. Instead, the book evolved from years of professional forensic and clinical work. It is designed to be of practical use to the reader and relies heavily on lessons learned in actual cases.

For every story told here, there are a thousand others heard by police, prosecutors, counselors and families throughout the world. These were chosen, not only for the triumphant and unique children involved in the investigations, but for the unforgettable accomplishments and mistakes that were made along the way. Hopefully the book will encourage you to examine the combination of skills and kindness necessary to provide competent care to traumatized children. May it also inspire you to reflect on the transformed lives of children who witness violence.

CHAPTER ONE

Foundations of Child Investigative Interviews

In nations throughout the world, police investigators or their authorized agents conduct investigative interviews of witnesses to crimes. Many detectives, individually knowledgeable in criminal investigations, despair about effectively interviewing witnesses who are children. One of the biggest fears is worsening the plight of a child in the turmoil and aftermath of a horrific event. The recent advent of Children's Advocacy Centers, however, now enables police to collaborate with other professionals regarding child witness interviews.

Children's Advocacy Centers typically provide child-friendly environments where professionals from a variety of disciplines collectively determine the most effective manner of proceeding with an investigation involving a child. In these settings, police, child protection specialists or forensic mental health practitioners may interview children who witness violent crimes. Irrespective of which professional conducts the interview, an investigative interview protocol is necessary to collect evidence from children.

Investigative interviews are those conducted with the intent of collecting accurate information about an alleged crime. The investigator approaches the child interview without a preexisting bias about the alleged event. In other words, one keeps an open mind about what did or did not happen. In the past two decades, investigative interview techniques have come under intense scrutiny based largely upon researchers who have emphasized how easily young children can be mislead by suggestion.[1] Fewer researchers have focused on accurate information that children provide when interviews are conducted well.[2] In addition to study findings, rulings by a number of Supreme Courts emphasized methods employed during investigative interviews of children.

The highly publicized "McMartin Preschool" case in the 1980's focused on interview methods used with young children reporting sexual abuse. The "McMartin" case was soon followed by the "the Little Rascals Daycare" case, which resulted in the overturned conviction of Margaret Kelly Michaels, a preschool teacher accused of molesting children in New Jersey. The conviction was overturned in large part due to challenges about the investigative interviews of the children. Five years after Michaels' conviction, the New Jersey Court of Appeals noted:

> "We therefore determine that a sufficient consensus exists within the academic, professional, and law enforcement communities, confirmed in varying degrees by courts, to warrant the conclusion that the use of coercive or highly suggestive interrogation techniques can create a significant risk that the interrogation itself will distort the child's recollections of events, thereby undermining the reliability of the statements and subsequent testimony concerning such events..." [3]

The Court went so far as to indicate that if the prosecution wanted to retry the case a pretrial taint hearing would be required. The taint hearing placed a burden on the state to prove the reliability of the children's statements by clear and convincing evidence. The issue to be addressed at the taint hearing was the reliability of the evidence, not the competence or credibility of the child witness.

While the Michaels decision applied only to New Jersey, a 1995 decision in California overturned the conviction of Donna Sue Hubbard when the 5th District Court of Appeals in Fresno concluded:

> "the interrogating techniques used in this case were suggestive and coercive, and there is a substantial likelihood that the children's resulting trial testimony was false and thus unreliable in violation of her constitutional right to due process of law..." [4]

The Courts' decisions may have been safeguards for defendants, but they also perpetuated cynicism about the competency of interviewers and the reliability of children's testimony. Since all interviews have some element of suggestiveness in them, under which situations can children's descriptions of violent crimes improve? The answer lies largely in the interview protocol itself.

Interview Protocols For Child Witnesses

An interview protocol designed for children who witness violence must be flexible in nature. At a minimum, it must:

1) contain questions that maximize the accuracy of information,
2) be adaptable for differing emotional presentations,
3) work with children of different developmental stages, and
4) provide for those children that may have difficulty in organizing or retrieving their memories.

In an ideal world, the interview method that most enhances the recall of adults is known as the Cognitive Interview Technique (CI). Described in 1985 by Geiselman, Fisher, Mackinnon and Holland, the central technique involved having an adult victim restate the context of a criminal event.[5] The victim was then asked to recall the incident in reverse order. The main principle of the CI was that memory for an event has several retrieval paths. Witness information that was not accessible with one technique may be accessible with another. Since there may be several retrieval paths to memory, some basic information about memory is important to comprehend.

How a Child's Memory Works

While I leave a comprehensive discussion about memory to scholars such as Schacter[6] or van der Kolk,[7] a basic understanding of how memory works is important to understanding the interview process. Memory can be characterized in terms of three basic components: encoding, storage and retrieval. There are age-related issues in all three components. Encoding of information, or the preserving of an event, is related to selectivity in a child's attention and perception – both of which improve with age. Situational factors such as how interesting an event was to the child also influences the encoding of an event.

Once encoded, the information can be stored in short term or long term memory or it may decay. No research is available to date on the decay theory with respect to child witnesses of violence. The retrieval process begins when questions are asked of children and ends when children terminate search of their memory. The way questions are worded in an interview can direct children to certain retrieval paths.

Open-ended questions generally lead children to a complex form of memory known as free recall. When children access free recall, they are telling you about their experiences in a series of uninterrupted sentences versus a single word response. In laboratory studies of children, researchers suggest that information found in free recall has a high degree of accuracy in comparison to other forms of memory such as recognition memory. Interview questions that direct children to free recall, therefore, are desirable in investigative interviews.

The request, "tell me about everything that happened" is open-ended and directs a child to recall an event. In contrast, a direct question such as, "who did something to your mother" usually results in single word responses, most often accessed from recognition memory.

Recognition memory develops early in childhood between the ages of two and three years and requires the most basic form of memory retrieval.[8] This type of retrieval requires that the child recognize something such as a person, object or place. For example, recognition memory is evident when preschool children identify pictures of objects in storybooks. Children as young as three years old, therefore, are able to specify persons, places and specific acts they have witnessed.

Suspect identification in a witness lineup is one example of a child accessing recognition memory during a criminal investigation. Pictures are usually selected for the lineup based upon the likelihood of triggering identification of the suspect who committed the crime. Inaccuracy can occur if several of the pictures too closely resemble the suspect and the child fails to "recognize" the correct individual.

Needless to say, accuracy of information is critical to the investigation of any crimes, including those witnessed by children. If free recall is generally more accurate than recognition memory, what type of interview protocol will allow for narrative portions of speech?

Most researchers and clinicians agree that interview methods encouraging children to talk freely about their experiences are most effective.[9] In 1987, German psychologist, Max Steller and an international group of colleagues used principles of the cognitive interview to develop an interview schedule for children reporting abuse.[10] The main component of the interview method involved eliciting narratives from children about their experiences. The interview strategy suggested for use with children who witness violence is similar in nature.

A Modified Cognitive Interview Method – "The Diamond"

The modified cognitive interview can best be understood using the analogy of a diamond. The interviewer's goal is to produce crystal clear interviews, like the best quality of diamond. Unfortunately, many end up being diamonds in the rough. Others appear to be muddied but upon closer examination the interview is actually clean.

"Clean," as it's known in the profession, means that at least three key issues critical to the integrity of the interview have been considered. First, the interview is conducted in a developmentally appropriate, non-leading fashion. Second, the amount of accurate information obtained about the crime is maximized. Finally, and of equal importance, the child's mental health is considered at all times during the interview.

The interview components, reflected in the shape of a diamond, include:

- developing rapport
- assessing language style
- eliciting a narrative
- directing to an episode
- using cue questions
- using direct questions
- neutral closure

An illustration of the interview components is found below.

Figure 5. Components of Modified Cognitive Interviews

5

Interview components found at the peak ends of the diamond tend to yield the least amount of investigative information. The categories depicted in the center of the diamond are designed to have children elaborate about the event, thereby producing the most investigative information. All of the components are necessary in an investigative interview.

Developing Rapport

Since an interview is an interaction between two people, the quality of the information will be affected not only by the interview method but also by the relationship between the child and the individual asking the questions. If a child feels comfortable with an interviewer, the quality of the interview can be greatly enhanced. The purpose of building rapport, however, involves more than establishing the comfort level of the child. Rapport-building also sets the stage for children to provide narratives later in the interview. In addition, during this early interview phase one can assess the language style of a child prior to introducing emotionally laden topics.

In contrast to therapy, investigations usually involve only one or two contacts with a child witness so rapport needs to be established quickly. While developing rapport sounds easy enough, there is a skill to establishing children's comfort levels in a short period of time. In addition to the time constraints of investigations, child witnesses can be highly distressed which makes rapport building a challenging task. The following suggestions can facilitate the development of rapport with child witnesses:

• Be gentle but confident with your words and actions.

• Prior to accompanying a child into the interview room, inquire regarding basic comforts such as the need to use the restroom or whether the child might be thirsty or hungry.

• Arrange the seating in the interview room so that you and the child are at the same level.

• Sit at an angle to the child. Sitting squarely in front of children gives the impression of confrontation.

• Be conscious of the distance between you and the child. Younger children require less space between themselves and an adult. Adolescents have space boundaries that require more distance between the interviewer and themselves.

• Compliment the child on his or her appearance. In particular, pointing out the unique color of a child's eyes not only boosts self-esteem, it quickly facilitates eye contact. Directing attention to children's eyes should not be used with those whose cultural beliefs include avoidance of eye contact.

• Explain who you are and the purpose of the interview. Tell children that it is okay to say that they don't know the answer to a particular question. Ask children to inform you if a question is not understood. Instructions such as these minimize children's anxiety about "performing" well in an interview.

• Minimize the sense of isolation a child may experience in the interview. Statements such as, "I talk with many boys and girls who have a mother that died" make children realize that they are not the only ones who have been interviewed in a criminal investigation.

• During the initial phase of the interview, converse with the child about neutral topics such as pets, school or hobbies. During this exchange, design a question that assesses the child's language skills. This is such an important part of developing rapport that it has been more thoroughly described below.

Assessing Language Style

There are several reasons for assessing the language style of the child with whom you are communicating. First, it is helpful to know the child's usual manner of conversing. For example, does the child typically answer questions with narratives or single word responses? Second, the child's capacity to provide narratives about a neutral topic indicates his or her ability to provide descriptions of emotionally laden events. Finally, if children are given the opportunity to retrieve information from free recall about a neutral event, they will be more likely to use this memory retrieval strategy to access information about the crime.[11]

Understandably, many investigative interviews begin with the collection of demographics such as the child's age and grade level in school. Questions strictly about demographics may imply to the child that the interview will proceed with direct questions that require short, limited responses. Offering children the opportunity to elaborate in the rapport building phase can encourage children to provide narratives later in the interview.

Determining a child's language style is easily accomplished by requesting a narrative early in the interview about a neutral topic. Begin the request with, *"tell me about."* The assessment should be part of the normal flow of conversation during the initial phase of the interview. Note the following exchange between the interviewer and a ten year-old child:

Interviewer:	You have such a pretty ribbon in your hair.
Child:	Thanks, my mom did it right before school.
Interviewer:	Well, tell me about school.
Child:	It's good. I'm gonna pass this year. We're going to have tests this week because school is almost out and then we get to go on a year end field trip. We're going to the IMAX – you know where they have those 3-D movies...

The child in this interview provided several sentences of uninterrupted speech. Clearly she has the capacity to provide a description about the witnessed event. The ability to provide a narrative should not be confused with "willingness." A child may be capable of talking about neutral topics but reluctant to elaborate upon traumatic events. Obtaining a narrative about the witnessed event, however, is the central component of the modified cognitive interview.

Obtaining A Narrative

Questions designed to obtain a narrative about a crime are those that allow a child to mentally reconstruct the context of a witnessed event. Children are asked to recall the event by thinking about the auditory, tactile and other sensory sensations that surround the experience. This is based on the assumption that one can obtain more information from children when they are directed to the physical and personal meaning of the event.

Aspects of the crime that are meaningful differ among children. For example, sounds of people arguing may be more important to one child than another. Similarly, smells such as gunpowder may be more or less salient to individual children. Encourage children to describe the crime with original sounds, smells, and tactile conditions of the scene, along with their feelings and thoughts at the time. The instruction about reconstructing the context is administered immediately prior to asking what happened. Here is an example of how a narrative was elicited from eight year-old Jake.

Interviewer:	I understand that something happened to your mom. I want you to think of what happened – everything about it...the sounds, smells...what

	you were thinking, what you felt. Tell me about it as best you can.
Jake:	Well...my mom was cooking and I well...my dad was on the patio and I heard this car – like the tires...and I went to see. I seen this blue Camaro and this guy jumped out the side and he had a rifle and then my dad – there was blood everywhere he was shooting in his back and my mom screamed. And then my mom grabbed me and ran in the room and locked us in the room. And then the guy was pounding on the door and my mom was...I was scared and he kicked it in – the door and I seen him shoot her in the head...and that's all...

As you can see, Jake was able to offer a rich narrative with details about the crime. The violent acts were embedded in the context of his routine that day. Direct questions would still be necessary to satisfy basic investigative elements. Interruptions, however, in the midst of a narrative are discouraged. Allow the child to continue with a narrative until he or she is done. If the child's narrative does not appear to reach a logical conclusion, prompt the child to continue by stating, *"and then what happened?"* Once a child has completed his or her description, proceed with clarifying questions. Clarifying questions come in a number of formats. The least suggestive of these is the directive to an episode.

Directives To Episodes

Questions that direct children to an episode are typically used when the violence that is witnessed is likely to be chronic in nature. Isolated events such as a homicide committed by a stranger or a school shooting would not involve directives to an episode since the crime was the single incident in question. In contrast, crimes of domestic violence, physical maltreatment or sexual abuse often occur more than once prior to a child's report. Because of the similarity in the way perpetrators commit these offenses, children can develop scripted accounts of chronic violence.

Scripted accounts are those in which a child has blended together violence that has occurred on several different occasions.[12]

9

For example, if a child's father batters his mother in a similar manner on different days, the child may develop a script of how the acts usually occur. Little information will be available for chargeable offenses since specific acts will not be provided in the context of time, place and person.

If a child has developed a script of the violence, he or she will need assistance from the interviewer in relating one specific episode at a time. Phrases that direct children to specific episodes are:

    a) tell me everything about <u>the last time</u> something happened,

    b) tell me about <u>a time that you remember most clearly</u>, and

    c) tell me everything about <u>the first time</u> something happened.

Inquiring if the violent acts occurred in different settings can also direct children to specific events. If violent acts occurred in the bedroom, garage and kitchen, have the child recall what happened in one particular room. For example, the statement, *"tell me about the time when something happened in the kitchen,"* facilitates retrieval of information about an episode in one location. Once the child has described specific incidents, proceed with questions intended to clarify information. One format for clarifying information is cued recall.

Cue Questions

    As the title suggests, these questions are used to cue retrieval of specific information about the crime. The "cue" is one word placed in the question to help a child recall or retrieve information about a particular topic. The cue word can be selected from any number of sources such as crime scene photos, other evidence or earlier portions of the child's interview. The most common source for the development of cue questions is the child's narrative provided early in the interview.

A child's initial narrative can provide features of the crime that require further explanation. For example, if a child stated, "my dad hit my mom with his fist and then she tried to run but he grabbed her," the interviewer could design a cue question using the word "grabbed." A statement by the interviewer such as, "you said someone was grabbed. Tell me more so I understand," would cue recall.

Another source for developing cue questions is the crime scene itself. Examination of crime scene photos may reveal items that are not understood. For example during one homicide investigation the photos revealed a telephone cord that appeared to be severed. The child could be cued to discuss this topic by stating, "Something happened to the telephone. Help me understand about that."

If the cue is selected from a source other than the child, pick something that appears peripheral in nature. One would not want to cue a child with suggestions about key elements of the crime such as an alleged perpetrator, violent acts, nature of the victim's injuries or murder weapon. Cue questions about seemingly innocuous details can provide a wealth of information that was not originally offered or clarified by the child. Clarification can also be accomplished with the use of direct questions. In contrast to cue questions, direct questions are considered more suggestive in nature.

Direct Questions

Direct questions are necessary in all investigative interviews. They are part of normal conversation and clearly present during the rapport building and neutral closure phases of an interview. Who, what, where, when, and how questions are required in order to charge an offense. Irrespective of where direct questions are used in an interview, minimize their suggestive nature. For example, it would be less suggestive to ask, "who did something to your mom?" than "did your mom's boyfriend hurt her?" To further minimize the effects of suggestion, request a narrative once the child has responded to a direct question. If a child indicates, "Sam did something to my mom." request an elaboration by stating, "tell me everything that Sam did."

Since most direct questions are based upon unique circumstances of the crime, a standard bank of questions is of little utility. Certain direct questions, however, prove useful in most situations involving child witnesses. For example, reproduction of conversation that occurred between the crime victim and offender can yield valuable information for the investigator. In particular, ask the child "what words" the victim said during the crime. Inquire as well about the suspect's statements. The exchange often provides investigators with motives for crimes. For example, during one investigation, the following question and response revealed the motive of a homicide:

I: What words did daddy say to mommy?
C: Him said he thought she loved Phil so he shot Phil and then he shot himself.

The motive of the killer in this situation was jealousy over an alleged affair between his wife and best friend.

11

In addition to questions that require children to reproduce conversation, direct questions that begin with "how" are highly effective. Inquiries that begin with "how" are not readily answered with one word. For example, "how did your mom get hurt?" requires a child to elaborate. As the interview draws to a close, direct questions will be part of the normal conversation that occurs when terminating an interview.

Neutral Closure

Investigative interviews are concluded by answering any questions the child may have. Be honest in your responses. Once the child's questions are answered, end the interview with conversation about a neutral topic so that children are not leaving the interview distressed. Inquire what plans the child has for the rest of the day. Encourage children to tell you about something fun they like to do. Do not leave a child with the impression that the interviewer simply needed something and got it with little regard for the child's interests.

Other Critical Factors Affecting the Interview

Duration of the Interview

Be conscious of children's needs during the interview. It is easy to become so focused on the questions that one loses track of time. Placing a clock on the wall in view of the interviewer is helpful to monitor the duration of the interview. Interviews with preschool children average approximately twenty to thirty minutes. School-age children have greater attention spans. Their interviews range from forty to fifty minutes. While these are general guidelines, highly distressed children or those with other special needs may require interviews that are shorter.

The Interview Environment

Investigative interviews of children are recommended in child-friendly environments. This does not exclude police department interview rooms, but rather, refers to the nature of the room versus the building in which a room is housed. Child-friendly interview rooms are those that provide comfortable furniture along with décor that minimizes the typically stark appearance of an interrogation room. In police departments, "soft rooms" serve well as investigative interview rooms for children. Soft rooms, however, do not mean play rooms filled with toys.

While toys are recommended for waiting areas or counseling

rooms, they are not advised for investigative interview rooms. The primary focus of an interview is conversation. For a child, listening to and answering questions can be difficult if toys are in view. Activities and toys are best kept in waiting areas and counseling rooms. Many police departments and child advocacy centers around the country have given special consideration to the layout and design of waiting areas, interview rooms and those areas allocated for monitoring a child's interview.

A model for centers nationally and internationally, the City of Mesa Center Against Family Violence was the first advocacy center in Arizona developed and run by law enforcement. The Center specializes in investigations of crimes involving children and families. Staff consists of detectives from child abuse, domestic violence, elder abuse and missing persons units. In addition, forensic interviewers, child protection specialists, victim advocates, medical and administrative personnel participate in the investigation of crimes involving child victims and witnesses. The following photos are courtesy of the City of Mesa Police Department.

Figure 1. Lobby

As seen in the photograph, the lobby is inviting and comfortable for child witnesses and the adults who accompany them. Adolescents may chose to wait here as opposed to the playroom available for younger children.

Figure 2. Play Room/Waiting Area

In contrast to the playroom, the interview room is child-friendly, yet free from toys that can distract children. Crayons, paper or other aids the interviewer may need during the interview are strategically placed so that the interviewer has access to them when deemed necessary.

Figure 3. Interview Room

While play therapy can be an effective method of counseling, it is not desirable during an investigation where the purpose is to obtain facts in order to fully develop an understanding of a crime. Play therapy that relies primarily upon interpretation of children's behaviors can be dangerous during investigative interviews and more often than not, leads to incorrect and unreliable investigative information.

In contrast to play, the other end of the interview continuum yields techniques that mirror an interrogation style. With these extreme methods, investigator's words or actions can assume the threatening posture of an interrogation. Since interrogations are designed to elicit incriminating responses from suspects, they can frighten children thereby compromising the investigation and emotional well-being of the child. Given educational programs for both law enforcement and mental health professionals, both of these unbalanced interview styles are less evident today than during the past decade. In addition, investigative interviewers today have others to help monitor an interview style that gets out of hand.

The use of monitor rooms allows observers to provide feedback to interviewers during breaks. Questioning techniques can then be adjusted and interviewers are reminded of how long the interview has been in progress. Individuals such as physicians, child protective service specialists and co-investigators can observe the interview through a television monitor so that their presence is not obtrusive to the child. The monitor room affords a number of professionals the opportunity to obtain necessary information while minimizing secondary trauma to children that can come from multiple interviews. The following is an example of a monitor room where two videotapes record the interview along with a backup audiotape. Headphones are available to hear the interview in the event that other monitors in the room are being used. Larger centers with multiple interview rooms have several monitors available.

Figure 4. Monitor Room

As you can see, the interview environment is a critical component to the success of the overall interview. Children who have witnessed violence are often anxious and distressed already. Giving some thought to the interview environment can assist in providing a comfortable yet efficient setting for investigative interviews.

Paracommunication Techniques

Nonverbal skills such as the use of silence, hesitation or nodding of one's head are all paracommunication techniques. Investigative interviewers need to be aware of their own body language, which may affect children's responses. Criticisms have been leveled at interviewers who frequently nod their heads while children are talking during an interview. On the other hand, gestures are a natural part of communication between two people and can be a prompt for the child to continue. Evaluating one's own videotaped interviews can provide a wealth of information about both verbal and nonverbal communication.

How To Evaluate The Interview

Given the adversarial nature of most legal proceedings, questions often flood an interviewer's thoughts even before attorneys for both sides have their tape recorders plugged in. Was the interviewer conscious of the child's well-being? Was the interview conducted in a non-leading manner? Were investigative methods versus therapy techniques used? Did the child provide forensically relevant information? Were the questions developmentally appropriate? How many sentences did the interviewer speak in contrast with how many sentences the child spoke? In other words, who did most of the talking? This is only the beginning of scrutiny by oneself, attorneys and the triers of fact. The wrath, however, typically generated by the defense, often falls upon the "messenger," the "bearer of news," otherwise known as the interviewer.

Even though many investigators conduct interviews of a high quality, the words "going to trial" generate feelings in the gut known to anyone who has ever been in the witness chair during criminal or civil proceedings. In some cases, the "chair" can get awfully hot. As a friend of mine once lamented during trial, "the chair was hotter than the hinges of hell." It is most helpful, therefore, to be prepared. Prior to trial, there are a number of ways to examine your own interviews. Careful and routine analysis of one's interviews is valuable in order to fully examine information offered by child witnesses. Such scrutiny also contributes to one's development as an effective interviewer. The following steps can systematize the process of evaluating investigative interviews.

1. Transcribe the interview in its entirety. Line by line, examine both the questions and responses.

2. Identify each question for its type or purpose. For example, "developing rapport, language sample, cue question" and so forth.

3. Indicate which of your questions are suggestive. A suggestive question does not necessarily have negative consequences. In fact, if your question suggested an answer to a child and he or she did not incorporate any of your words into the response, the child has resisted suggestion. While interviewers have become extremely cautious and sometimes defensive about asking suggestive questions, I know of no honest interviewers who state that they conduct perfect interviews.

4. Count how many words you spoke and how many belong to the child. Some children are extremely talkative. Others are reluctant witnesses or have limited language skills. Irrespective of the type of child one interviews it is helpful to assess who did most of the talking. Count the words only in the substantive part of the interview, since rapport building and closure of the interview more closely resembles conversation. While the number of words may not be a fair representation of an interview with a reluctant, mentally challenged, or depressed child, it will give you a fair estimate of who did most of the talking during an interview with an average school age child.

5. When you have finished examining the written transcript of the interview, watch the videotape and note any visible signs of distress or behaviors that have caught your attention. This may refresh your recollection about why you may have changed topics or asked questions in the manner in which you did.

6. Note your own body language and any effects it had on the child's responses.

7. Calculate the time that the interview took and determine if it was developmentally appropriate for the child being interviewed.

8. Identify the strengths in the interview as well as weaknesses. Did the weaknesses impact major components of the interview? For example, if there were suggestive questions at times, assess whether they affected the overall quality of the statement provided by the child.

9. Do not offer your opinion about the veracity or truthfulness of the child. Those decisions are the province of a judge or jury.

10. Learn from your mistakes. Strive to conduct an even better interview.

These steps were applied in an assessment of an interview with eleven year-old Sandra. Sandra's mother, returning home from work during the wee hours of the morning, was brutally murdered while Sandra and her sister were inside the residence. After seven hours of captivity by the suspect, it was Sandra who planned the children's escape and made her way to a neighbor for help. Nearby residents immediately called police. When law enforcement arrived, they found Sandra's mother with multiple stab wounds, ceremoniously laid out on the floor of the children's bedroom. A key chain with the name of her new boyfriend had been placed on her chest. Investigators knew that Sandra would be their most informative witness. Sandra's transcript in its entirety is analyzed below.

Investigative Interview of Sandra

I: Interviewer
S: Sandra
Age of Sandra: 11 years 2 months
Date of Interview: January 12, 1990
Date Police Responded to Scene: January 7, 1990

I: Sandra, come on in and have a seat. Let me tell you what we're going to do today. My name is Tascha and what I do all day long is talk with girls who have a mom that died. I know that you talked with a really nice policeman a little bit but we're going to talk a bit more today. **I'm going to tape what we talk about so that I don't have to write things down...I can listen to you better. If I ask you a question you don't understand, let me know. If I make a mistake about anything, please correct me cause I want to make sure I get things right. But first I need to know a bit about you.** What's your whole name?

S: Sandra _____

I: What a nice name. And how old are you?

S: Eleven

I: Eleven and when is your birthday?

S: December 27th.

I: Just after Christmas. And what grade are you in?

S: Fifth at Carson.

I: And what do you like to do at school?

S: Math.

I: Well, what do you have here?

S: It's a necklace from Jazz On the Rocks.

Developing Rapport

I: Oh, how pretty. **Tell me about jazz on the rocks.**

S: It's this concert they have outside. And there's lots of music and it was a lot of fun. We had tons of food. My Aunt took me and my sister and there was a pretty sunset and I wished it didn't end so early.

Assessing Language Style

I: Was this the concert in Sedona?

S: Yes.

I: It is a beautiful place for a concert. Maybe you can go again sometime. Right now, though, we're going to go ahead and get started talking about what happened.

Sandra's Narrative About A Neutral Topic

I: **I understand that something happened to your mom. I want you to think of what happened – the sounds, smells...everything you remember. If you do not remember, please do not make anything up. Just tell me about everything as best you can.** ━━━━━━━━━━━━━▶

> Eliciting Narrative & Encouraging Context

S: Um...what...um...

I: **Tell me everything that happened so I can understand.** ━━━━━━━━▶

> Second Request For Narrative

S: Yeh...my mom went to work and me and my sister were home watching Toy Story and we had just turned off the lights and I woke up about 3:30 in the morning and he came in the room and I was kind of sleeping and kind of not and my mom's exboy-friend, Johnny walked in the room and my sister opened her eyes and he had a gun in his hand and so he grabbed her by the neck and threw her down on the ground and started choking her. And I just like asked, begged him not to kill her and I yelled at him and he finally let my sister go and he told us not to say anything. Well, first he tied us up and I asked him to be untied cause I had to throw up and I went like this. And I threw up and he took one of my mom's shirts and put it here so he wouldn't get throw up on him and then he tied us up again. And then my mom walked in and he shut the door. And then she just started screaming and eighty bucks flew out of her purse into the bedroom. And he tackled her into the bar stools by our counter and she started saying stuff like "it's not worth it. I don't want to die." And he said, "it's too late for that now." And I got untied and I went into my mom's room and he had drug my mom into our bedroom and I ran in there and I walked in there and he...like he tied her arms behind her back. And he like hung her from the railing and he saw me. And he gave me a bad look and I ran back onto the

> Sandra's Narrative About The Homicide

20

bed. And some time went by and we were about to try and climb out the window and he came in and saw us and put a gun here and said "I'm going to kill you and your sister but I'm going to kill your sister and your mom first." And um he put us in the bathroom and um tied the door shut with like these shirts to other objects and he locked us in. And he said "don't come out." Finally, I tried to pull on the door but it wouldn't open so I stuck a lotion bottle in the door and I reached out and opened it. And we heard the dog jump off the bed and we ran out the door quietly cause we didn't know if he was still there. And we ran to our friend's house and told her what happened and all the news came and the cops and stuff and that's all.

I: **OK, You've told me a lot of things but let me ask you some questions so that I can understand better. You said you woke up at about 3:30 and how did you know it was 3:30?** ➤ *Direct Question (Clarifying using "how")*

S: Um there is an alarm clock right next to my bed and I saw it.

I: OK and then you said Johnny was choking your sister...

S: And he let my sister go on the bed and um well he tied us up cause I don't know he just tied us up with cloth and I threw up on him and he grabbed one of my mom's shirts and then he untied me so I could go to the bathroom.

I: **And then what happened?** ➤ *Encouraging Narrative*

S: We stayed on the bed and then he came into the bedroom and he said whatever we hear not to scream or make noises and about half an hour to an hour my mom walked in the door and he was in our bedroom which is behind the main door and he came out with a gun to her head and she turned around and started screaming and she threw her purse...and right before he put us in the bathroom

21

he made me write a note... and then my mom has a door right here and her bed goes past the door and I could see perfectly out.

I: **And what exactly did you see when you were looking out?** ⟶

S: He had the gun to her head and she turned around cause she didn't know. And she got really scared and she threw her purse and he had tackled her into the bar stools.

> Direct
> Question
> (Clarifying)

I: **And then what happened very next...that you saw?** ⟶

S: He started choking her and he didn't let her go. He didn't let her sit up – he was on top of her like this...he had her pinned down and he was like...and she was "it's not worth it I don't want to die" and he said "it's too late for that now" and he started dragging her into the bedroom and that's when I untied myself and I saw him hang her up from the railing.

> Encouraging
> Narrative

I: **From the railing...** ⟶

S: My mom has like a King Size bed and say here is the bed and I could see she wasn't moving and he had tied her up like this and then he turned and looked at me and so I turned and ran back to the other room and so um then he came after me. And he had heard when I tried to get out the window screen. And he put the gun to our heads and wanted to know if we yelled to anyone down there and if we told anybody down there but when we were calling no one heard us.

> Encouraging
> Narrative

I: **Now when you say Johnny tied her up, I'm confused about exactly how he did that.** ⟶

S: When you can hang people with ropes. Well there was one just like that. He had tied it so on the bunk bed railing he put her neck in it and her arms were tied behind her back and I don't know if her feet were tied or not.

> Feigning
> Confusion

22

I: **Did she have clothes on at that time**?

S: Yes.

                                              ➤
> *Direct Question (Suggestive)*

I: **Tell me more about the clothes**.

S: I don't know...she was wearing a shirt and some short pants...that's when I first saw her but then I got scared and ran out.   ➤
> *Attempt to Minimize Effect of Suggestive Question*

I: Where was Johnny when you ran out?

S: We have a desk by the bunk bed and he was right there standing up. My mom... she wasn't looking then and I don't know....

I: **Then what happened next?**

S: He told us to get in the closet and we stayed in there for a while and then he put us in the bathroom...   ➤
> *Encouraging Narrative*

I: **Then what happened next?**

S: We laid on the floor and he gave us cereal and I told him I didn't want any and he dumped it out and he came with water and I said I didn't want any.

I: **Then what happened next?**   ➤
> *Encouraging Narrative*

S: I asked him if we could go lay on the bed and he said "no" and he tied me and my sister's hands together and after awhile he left us again. And he shut the door and he tied the strings to other things and the closet door. And we couldn't get out for a lot of hours and he said he was going to take my mom and him on a trip. And um so I got a shampoo bottle in the door and I reached out my hand and untied the knot so we could squeeze out and we ran into the living room and the dog jumped off the bed. And we didn't know if he was there cause her collar has licenses and it makes a sound and we thought it was him so we ran out the door. And that's what happened.

I: **Sandra, earlier you said something about a note. Tell me about that.**   ➤
> *Cue Question*

S: Oh, yeh he had me write a note...mmm he made me write, I don't know...he told me what words to write and I was on my mom's bed....I can't...

I: **OK, we'll go really slowly. What were the words?** ⟶ | Note Distress of Sandra

S: I can't.

I: Just give me an idea of what the note was about.

S: It said, to whom this may concern. It's time for the pied piper to stop piping meaning her new boyfriend to stop leading her away from him. And she broke our trust and now I must do this. I treated her like a queen and I treated her kids like queens and I bought her everything and she went back to her boyfriend who supposedly beats her...which is not true. And other stuff bad about her...and he signed it.

I: **That part about the pied piper, how did you know what that meant?** ⟶ | *Direct Questions (Clarifying)*

S: Cause that was all he would talk about all night over and over.

I: **Where did he put the note?**

S: I don't know, he took it with him when he left the room.

I: **You know, you look like you might be getting a bit tired.** ⟶ | Child Tired

S: I'm Okay.

I: **Okay...maybe a few more questions and then we stop for today. I was wondering, at any time through the night, did you hear your mom say anything?** ⟶ | *Direct Question*

S: Yeh.

I: **Tell me about that.** ⟶ | *Encouraging Narrative after Direct Question*

S: When she walked in the door she started screaming and when he tackled her into the bar stools she said, "it's not worth it. I don't want to die" And then he started choking her and then she said, "please I

24

don't want to die" and he said "it's too late for that."

I: **And then you said somehow he got her into your room.** ➔ | Clarifying

S: Yeh, he dragged her by her feet cause I could see through the door.

I: **Was she moving in any way at this time?**

S: No, she was still. He had done something to her when he tackled her in the hallway – like he was hitting her with something in his hand but I couldn't see what it was. ➔ | **Direct Question**

I: **Now, during this entire time, did anyone else come into the house besides Johnny?**

S: No just my three pets were there. ➔ | **Direct Question** (*Rule out other suspects*)

I: **Oh, what are your three pets?**

S: Two cats and one dog.

I: **What are your cats' names?**

S: Sweety and Sky. ➔ | **Leading to Termination of Interview**

I: **And your dog?**

S: It's a Cocker Spaniel.

I: **That's pretty – I have a collie.**

S: I like collies.

I: **Me too. What we're going to do Sandra is finish for today. We may have to meet for about half an hour tomorrow. Is that okay?**

S: Yeh, my Aunt can bring me.

I: **I've been asking so many questions – do you have any questions for me?**

S: Um...yeh – are you married?

I: **Well yes, I am.**

S: Oh, that's all I was wondering.

I: **What are you doing the rest of the day?** ➔ | **Neutral Closure**

S: I don't know. I think we might go pick up my sister. And then my Aunt might take us to get some clothes cause our clothes are still in the house.

I: Well, I better get you going so you can get some

25

nice things. Any other questions for me?

S: Do a lot of girls have a mom that died?

I: Well, I see quite a few girls whose moms died.

S: Do they say things at her funeral cause I said a speech at her funeral and said how much I miss her.

I: You must miss her very much. I bet it was a beautiful speech. If you feel like writing down the parts you remember and bringing it tomorrow, I'd like to see it.

S: OK

I: Let's go and see if your Aunt is back yet.

Evaluation of Sandra's Interview

Word Count In Substantive Part of Interview

Number of words spoken by interviewer: 272
Number of words spoken by child: 1,306

Duration of Interview: 41 minutes

Preservation of Interview: Videotape and audiotape

Interview Environment: Children's Center

Overall Quality of Interview:

The majority of the interview questions were open-ended. The child offered several lengthy narratives. She identified both central elements and unique, peripheral details of the crime. The child was visibly anxious with her feet and hands constantly moving. Her speech was pressured. The interview was terminated early given her level of anxiety.

Conclusion of Sandra's Case

Sandra and her sister now live with their maternal Aunt. The defendant was charged with first-degree murder, three counts of kidnapping, two counts of aggravated assault, one count of sexual assault and armed burglary. Following the investigation the girls attended counseling regularly. The girls would need to relive their experience two years later in the upcoming criminal proceedings. On the eve of trial, the prosecutor, defense attorney and the defendant acknowledged that putting the girls on the stand was not in their best interest. An agreement was reached to submit all of the evidence to the Judge for consideration. After careful review of the evidence, including Sandra's interview, the Judge found the defendant guilty on all counts.

As you can see from her transcript, Sandra was able to provide extensive and detailed information about the homicide. In other circumstances, children who provide extensive narratives are challenged about the accuracy of their descriptions. In recent years there has been a concern about misleading effects on children's testimony, commonly referred to as post-event contamination. In other words, children can be subject to suggestions or misinformation from persons or events they come in contact with after the crime. Researchers are now examining whether the cognitive interview can be effective if witness behavior has been manipulated. For example, can situational pressure affect the type of information provided by children in a narrative? Chapter two provides a case illustrating how complex circumstances may require modification of basic interview principles.

CHAPTER TWO

When The Basic Principles Don't Work

The modified cognitive interview relies purely on verbal accounts from children. There are times, however, when verbal tasks alone are not effective in helping us to obtain a full account of what the child witnessed. In the past, interviewers of children reporting sexual abuse have come under attack for using props such as anatomically correct dolls or dollhouses to help children describe what happened.[13] It was felt by some that props could be suggestive to young children. These criticisms appear to have created an over reliance on verbal skills at the expense of using developmentally appropriate tasks such as drawing or writing during interviews of child witnesses. Consider the case of Katie and her sisters.

Katie was a bright and energetic eight year-old who lived in an upper class subdivision with her parents and two sisters. Katie was the middle child. She was close to both of her sisters given their proximity in ages. Her older sister was nine and the youngest was seven years of age. Katie was an A student and she, along with her sisters, worked hard at school and play. The children of Vietnamese immigrants, the girls mirrored the disciplined work ethic of their parents. Upon arrival in America, Katie's father became an engineer. He was employed at an electronics company in a nearby suburb. Katie's mother stayed home to care for the children.

According to their teachers, the children were well mannered, neatly dressed and perfectionists at school. The family kept largely to themselves but did occasionally visit with their friends next door. For folks in the neighborhood, there was no reason to believe that April 4th would be different than any other day, until the yellow crime scene tape cordoned off Katie's home. The neighbors heard that a body had been found in the room that the family used as a Buddhist shrine. It was the body of Katie.

The Crime Scene

When police arrived at the scene they discovered the girl stiff and cold, with obvious signs that she had been dead some time. Crime scene photos revealed massive bruising to multiple areas of the body. On the following photo, once can see the extensive bruising on the child's right leg. No one who responded to the scene had ever seen the degree of bruising that covered Katie's thigh. It was as though every inch of skin on her leg was discolored. The darkened areas on her legs were similar to lividity. Large bruises were also found on Katie's torso and arms.

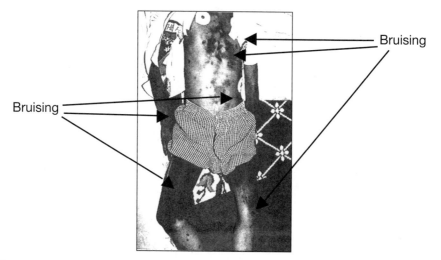

Figure 5. Katie's Bruises

Struck by the severity of the child's injuries, one officer at the scene later acknowledged that he broke down and cried when he finally got home. He could not believe that so many bruises and cuts could cover a 4'5" tall child who weighed only ninety pounds.

As with all homicide investigations, the methodical task of collecting and investigating information had already begun. A note written in blood was found above the altar next to Katie's head. Deciphered from Vietnamese, the writings prayed for "compassion, love and kindness." In as sensitive a manner possible, detectives quickly separated the parents and children.

Child Protective Services had arrived to begin their assessment of safety for the surviving children. A review of their records would later indicate that a school nurse reported signs of physical abuse towards the children on four previous occasions. A black eye and bruises on the children's legs and arms had been explained to Child Protection Specialists as accidents or injuries sustained while playing. During the prior investigations, all three of the girls denied any type of abuse. The history of this child's death began to unfold as follows.

Interviews of the Adults

Katie's father reported that he left for work at 7:00 a.m. and returned home at about 5:00 p.m on April 4th. At 7:04 p.m., Katie's mother called a non-emergency police number to report that her daughter had stopped breathing. Katie's father felt that the cause of death was related to a beating that Katie sustained the day before at a construction site. He felt that the beating might have been racially motivated, although no other acts of violence had been directed at the family in the past. Katie's father stated that according to his other children, all three of the girls had been playing at a construction site near the neighborhood park. Katie's sisters returned home earlier, leaving Katie to play a bit longer. Reportedly, when Katie did arrive home, she appeared disheveled with scrapes and bruises. Katie was also incoherent. The family thought that she had been attacked, however, no one knew who might be the perpetrator.

Katie's mother independently gave the same account as her husband. She added that prior to calling law enforcement, she called an adult cousin who told her to call the police immediately. Katie's mother instead bathed the child and rubbed her wounds with oil. She then took her into the shrine room to pray. The next morning, Katie was not breathing. Katie's father stated that he tried to revive her with CPR. She did not respond. The parents waited fourteen hours to call police, stating that their religion required them to keep the child in the shrine.

Interviews of the Children

Detectives briefly interviewed the two girls. Each corroborated their parent's account of the past two days. The girls were interviewed separately using an interview style that allowed each to provide an account in their own words. During the interview of the nine-year old sister, the following inquiry was made. "Something happened to your sister. Tell me as best you can what happened." The child responded as follows:

"On Thursday we went for a walk to school and then we took a shower. And when we came home from school my mom let us go outside. My sister didn't want to go so me and my other sister said okay and we're leaving. Where we're living they're building a school so we walked around. And there were other people walking – like adults walking their dogs but it was getting late and I don't know what time it was and I was getting tired and hungry and I wanted to go home. And she said, "no we haven't been there that long." And when I got home my mom said where is Katie and she started yelling that I left her alone…and then we were about to eat and my sister came home and rang the front doorbell. She was dirty so she took a shower and we saw bruises on her chest and neck and my Katie was drowsy. And she mumbled and then after we took her up to the praying room and we have this special oil that we rub on bruises and that night my dad came home and he saw my mom was crying. And then she was tired so me and my sister did our homework and my mom and dad stayed with Katie. But before I went to bed I said goodnight to my sister and hugged her and she just mumbled – and another person might not know what she said but I know she said good night. And at 5:15 in the morning my sister woke me up and she said "wake up mom's crying" and my – when I came closer I saw she was dead and my mom said she was dead and not to cry but to pray for her and my dad said…"no she's not ever coming back.""

The child was then asked follow-up questions to further clarify the information. In response to all of the questions, the girl remained adamant that someone had hurt her sister between the construction site and the family home. Katie's youngest sister reported a similar account of the events. To the seasoned detective, perhaps the accounts were just too similar.

Careful to examine every possible lead, officers began to comb the park and construction site inch by inch for some evidence of Katie's attacker. By nightfall of the second day, the search yielded nothing. Typical of the high volume of cases brought to coroners in large urban areas, the medical examiner's report was not yet complete. The exact cause of death was still unknown. On April 9th, five days after the discovery of her body, Katie was buried. The family was in mourning.

Preliminary Findings

The day after Katie was buried, detectives requested another videotaped interview of Katie's sisters. Additional information had come in the form of the medical examiner's report. The medical findings indicated blunt force trauma to the abdomen. The liver had been lacerated from the force of the blows. With such an injury, there was no possible way that Katie could have walked from the site to her home. In fact, the medical examiner stated that she wouldn't have been able to walk anywhere. Given the extent of her other injuries, Katie would have died a slow and painful death. The truth was beginning to reveal itself through physical evidence. But what about the original statements provided by the children? Their accounts were lengthy and detailed.

Review of the early interviews conducted with the girls revealed that they had been provided several opportunities through the use of open-ended questions to describe what they knew. Leading or suggestive questions were not of major concern. Why then, was their account inconsistent with crime scene facts? The interviewer had not suggested any incorrect information to the children. Had someone else coerced the girls? Perhaps in their follow-up interviews the girls would explain.

Preparation For Follow-up Interviews

The interviews were scheduled two days after Katie's memorial services. The girls were still in the care and custody of the state child welfare program. All available data about the girls was reviewed, along with the crime scene evidence. After reviewing the information, the following hypotheses were considered:

1. A stranger injured Katie.
2. Katie was injured by her mother.
3. Katie was injured by her father.
4. A sibling injured Katie.
5. Katie was injured by a non-family member but someone known to her.

With regard to the alternative hypotheses, it was possible that one or both sisters had knowledge of the events. Alternately, it was possible that neither girl knew what happened to their sister. So the question arises, how does one proceed with follow-up interviews if a modified cognitive interview resulted in descriptions of acts that could not have been possible?

Alternative Strategies

In determining an alternate strategy to a modified cognitive interview, one could turn to current research findings from studies of children's memory. The dilemma is that most researchers indicate that interview strategies that allow for lengthy narratives are the technique of preference. Information found in lengthy narratives has been deemed to be more reliable than that found in limited responses of children to direct questions. Most of the studies that generated these conclusions, however, were conducted in laboratory settings – quite different than studying memory in real world contexts. In contrast to laboratory studies, reliability of information provided by child witnesses is best determined by corroborating facts and evidence related to the crime, not by the length of a child's response to questions.

Researcher, Ray Bull and his colleagues suggest both interview technique and rapport with the person conducting the interview undoubtedly affects memory performance.[14] But was the issue with Katie's sisters really one of memory performance? Could there be other reasons for the children's lengthy and confusing statements?

Since both girls had good language skills, the dilemma was whether or not to proceed with yet another modified cognitive interview. If interviews were not conducted, would the decision place the children in harm's way? If the children were re-interviewed, would the strategy selected produce forensically relevant material and could it withstand the scrutiny that would surely follow? In light of all of the evidence, a decision was made to re-interview the girls.

The Second Investigative Interviews

Given the children's cognitive and linguistic abilities, one more "limited" attempt at obtaining a narrative was warranted. Katie's oldest sister was interviewed first. Following some rapport building the typical open-ended directive was offered. "Tell me about what happened to Katie so I would understand. " The nine year-old immediately launched into a lengthy response similar to the one provided in her first interview. Since this description once again involved Katie's walk home from the construction site, this method of interviewing was fruitless. It was apparent that a change of tasks was required to one that would include something other than talking. The task involved having each girl independently complete the following sentences:

1. The cuts and bruises were put on Katie by: _____.
2. The cuts and bruises were put on with a _____.
3. I was at _____ when Katie was hurt.
4. I saw _____.
5. I heard _____.

While these questions were not all inclusive, they might provide a starting point for further elaboration. The forms were completed as follows. The italicized, underlined sections are those filled in by each child.

9 year old
1. The person who put the cuts and bruises on Katie is *little Tommy*
2. The cuts were put on with a *scratch from his finger*.
3. I was *at the kitchen cooking with my mom* when Katie was hurt.
4. I saw *the scratches but they were not bleeding at the time.*
5. I heard *Katie say, "Mom, Tommy scratched me."*

---

7 year old

1. The person who put the cuts and bruises on Katie is *mom and dad*.

2. The cuts were put on with a *belt*.

3. I was *at there* when Katie was hurt.

4. I saw *what happened to Katie*.

5. I heard *her cry*.

As you can see, we forgot one hypothesis in our original list – both parents could have inflicted the injuries.

Clarifying The Information

The next step was to obtain a more comprehensive description from the seven year-old since her limited responses in writing appeared to make some sense. In fact the medical examiner had photographed linear injuries on Katie that resembled markings from a belt. While this child indicated that both parents put cuts and bruises on Katie, no date, time or location was obtained in her written statement. Since most children have poor concepts of time, one of the parents could have hurt Katie on a different occasion. In addition, it was not certain which parent inflicted the injuries that eventually lead to Katie's death. Therefore, each written response was addressed with the youngest child by asking her to elaborate about each answer. Katie's seven year-old sister explained that Katie lied about returning home late from the park so mom hit her with a belt. The beating occurred in the living room of the family house. When dad came home from work, he continued to hit Katie:

> "since Mom was tired because she was pregnant.
> Dad went on for about two more minutes but I
> didn't count how many times he hit her..."

Later, the children's mother had the seven year-old put the belt back in the master bedroom closet. During the beatings, both of

36

Katie's sisters had to stand there because:

> "...like if me or my sister lied, we'd have to do
> the same thing. My mom put two sheets in the
> room and we were sitting on the sheets. The
> family rule is if one of us does something
> wrong...all of us have to stay there to keep us to
> restrain yourself from misbehaving...and after...
> Katie said she was sorry for what she did...but
> she couldn't say anything else because we're not
> allowed to say anything else when we are being
> punished..."

Katie then needed help getting up the stairs. Her father and sisters assisted her. Once upstairs, Katie's mother combed the child's hair, bathed her and laid her down in the prayer room. The two girls then heard Katie crying. The next morning, Katie wasn't moving at all. Katie's mother then called her cousin and told him the story about Katie going for a walk. The girls were also present during the mother's telephone call.

In an attempt to clarify the youngest child's account, a series of direct questions were asked based upon the information that she had already provided. Many questions that may have resulted in a more complete picture of the crime went unasked. Fretfulness and apprehension were beginning to be evident in the seven year-old. Reporting about one's own parents quickly led to inevitable fatigue. Katie's sister slumped down in the chair and her posture clearly indicated that the interview should be terminated. The interview had lasted about forty minutes.

At the conclusion of the interview it was apparent that both parents struck Katie with a belt. It was uncertain, however, which parent yielded the blow that eventually killed her. While the question may be important in a criminal context, in the overall scheme of things, clearly, both parents contributed to Katie's death. There still remained the problem of the girls' original stories. Their inconsistent statements would be the first of many obstacles to be overcome in the ensuing criminal and civil matters.

Inconsistent Statements

Inconsistencies in children's statements are dilemmas faced by any investigator, prosecutor, defense attorney or mental health professional that has ever conducted or evaluated interviews of children. In many instances careful scrutiny of a child's statement will indicate an appearance of inconsistency when in fact the central elements of the crime remain consistent. Few children, or adults for that matter, are able to relate an event in exactly the same way over time. Peripheral details may change and the sequence of the description may be altered during the telling of an event. In this matter, however, the whole account differed from one statement to the next.

When inconsistencies exist, ask the child about the difference in the accounts. One way to inquire about inconsistencies without appearing confrontational is to feign confusion, placing the burden on oneself versus the child. For example, statements such as, "I'm confused...I heard you say X earlier and this time Y. Did I misunderstand something?" Begin clarifying questions with "how" rather than "why" in order to refrain from implying a sense of blame on the child. For example, in order to clarify the inconsistencies in Katie's case, her sister was asked:

> "How was it that you decided to say Katie walked home from the park when Officer John first talked with you?"

The child provided a plausible response:

> "I was afraid that if I told what happened the police would take my mom and dad away to jail. So mom said to tell that story – if somebody asked."

A follow-up question ruled out the possibility that the new statement was the result of coercion. In response to, "what made you decide to tell about this today?" the child stated:

> "...I didn't get to walk up to the box to see her – only mom and dad. I couldn't see what she was wearing. Her favorite thing to wear was her Tweety Shirt...Katie will be put into ashes after the funeral...she still needs to get some books from school...I need to help her...I saw what really happened..."

Stress and Coercion

Whether it was the stark and solemn memorial service or a realization that she might return home to a similar fate, something prompted Katie's sister to divulge what really happened. Her older sister, however, did not reveal information for several weeks. She stood by her implausible account of Katie's death.

It is understandable that some children will provide inaccurate accounts of a violent crime. Such statements are given for a variety of reasons, one of which is to protect themselves or someone dear to them. In some situations, incorrect statements are simply a matter of a child's need to physically or emotionally survive. For example, it would be dangerous for a child to talk about a parent who killed a sibling if the child remained in the custody of that parent. Other children may offer information that was based upon suggestion from outside sources, including interviewers. Still others provide information they think was correct but in fact was observed incorrectly. And finally, in rare situations, children who do not know what happened can make up statements and attempt an explanation. Katie's older sister, however, did witness the homicide. Like many other children, her disclosure occurred in bits and pieces over time.

Disclosure Is A Process

It is helpful to remember that disclosure about a violent event is a process. It is not a single isolated event. Children share information when they are ready and during times that they feel comfortable. The disclosure is often in fragments and appears unstructured in nature. Katie's oldest sister eventually revealed what happened in the household. Her initial statement reflects the concept of a fragmented account:

> "I don't remember all of what happened but mom told my sister to get the belt and then my mom hit Katie with the belt...then dad came home and hit her...then we helped wash her and prayed over her in the prayer room. We prayed all day Friday and mom laid down cause she was tired. That evening mom called my Auntie in California and my cousin in Glendale...he told us to call the police."

During another instance, she related the following:
> "you pray over a dead person for forty nine hours and then cremate them so you do not take up room on this earth – especially room that poor people could use...it is the greatest honor to die and be with Buddha...I miss my mom and dad. They hit us too but we didn't die..."

By reading these statements, one can almost hear this child's confusion and anguish regarding the violence that occurred in her home. Not only did she lose her sister but her parents as well. The following letter, penned to her parents indicated her distress about causing them harm.

> *Dear Dad and Mom:*
>
> *How are you doing? Have you been getting enough rest lately Mom and Dad? We stayed in the shelter and now are in a foster home...it's a pretty nice place...How was everything in court Mom and Dad? If there is anything that I did wrong, I do ask for your forgiveness with my full heart...*
>
> *Your Daughter, _____*

It is no wonder that it took more time for the oldest child to talk about Katie's death. As the eldest, she assumed responsibility not only for the welfare of her siblings but her parents as well. And now, all of her family was lost to her. Fortunately, the foster family who cared for her encouraged her to resume the role of a little girl. Over time, the eldest child revealed even more details than her younger sister.

Experienced investigators understand that time is often on their side. Pressuring or coercing a child to talk will generally create a windfall of problems for the investigation as well as for the child. Following a criminal investigation, there will be many who muddy the waters, trying to create phantom problems in addition to those that legitimately exist. Nowhere in the criminal justice and mental health fields does there seem to be such an explosive issue as investigative practices involving interviews with child victims or witnesses. In its aftermath, this case was no different.

The Aftermath

Three months after the discovery of Katie's body, cumulative evidence supported the arrest of her parents. Eventually, Katie's youngest sister testified at a juvenile court hearing about her experiences during the seven years of her young life. She calmly stated that both her mother and father beat Katie to death. In my opinion, she adequately explained her initial inaccurate statements to detectives. Her mother had created the story. Rehearsal of the account was necessary so that everyone gave the same information to police. The girls, extremely intelligent, had retained the story well.

Both girls also spoke of physical and sexual abuse. Not a surprising discovery, since for decades researchers have posited that where one form of violence exists, it is likely that you will find another. And amidst all of this horror, the girls were repetitively instructed not to tell because there was honor to be upheld in the family. Perhaps the real honor was best reflected by the courage of the two sisters. It was not an easy task to respond to criticisms about their reliability. But they withstood the scrutiny, as did investigators. Children, investigators and witnesses, however, face similar circumstances across the country.

Challenges To Investigative Interviews

During any given week, one can turn on the television or read in print media about a criminal matter involving child witnesses. Local, national and international debates rage about the reliability of children's recollections and interviewer methodologies. As you can see by this newspaper clipping, it didn't take long for the interview methods used in Katie's investigation to be scrutinized privately and publicly.

Figure 6.
Newspaper Clipping

Most attorneys in criminal and civil matters carefully analyze child witness interviews and rightfully so. It has been my experience, however, that even when information has been obtained in developmentally appropriate and non-leading styles, interviewers are still subject to attack. Unfortunately, this has been the trend across the country. This type of backlash has its roots in early psycho-legal tenets indicating that children are not reliable witnesses to crimes.[15] There is no point in debating such a dogma. It's only certainty lies in the fact that this belief, similar to history, is repeating itself.

During the investigation of Katie's death, arrays of criticisms were leveled about the investigative interview strategy. The major condemnation involved an inaccurate representation by a defense attorney regarding the use of writing versus talking in order to obtain investigative information from a child. The technique was misrepresented as a "sentence completion test" and news reporters were incorrectly informed that the first sentence provided to the child was, "your mom and dad hurt Katie."

While media representations often sensationalize investigations, erroneous information is more disturbing when provided to jurors. In this case, the interviews were preserved on videotapes and the actual writings of the children were secured in evidence. One professional involved in the case indicated that having children write was an "improper investigative interview procedure." In this particular case, protocols did need to be modified to meet the individual needs of fragile children who had been threatened by their parents.

Interview strategies can be creatively adapted using theoretically sound judgment and developmentally appropriate methods. Effective interviewers are flexible in their approaches in order to afford children every opportunity to describe their experiences. Accommodations for child witnesses are not only helpful, but also necessary during the investigation of violent crimes. Nowhere are modifications required more often than during interviews of preschool children. Chapter three reveals the perils of interviewing very young children who witnessed the homicide of their mother.

CHAPTER THREE

Interviews With Preschool Children: *Two Dynamic Cases*

Interviewing preschool children is a daunting task for even the most experienced investigators. Young children are highly distractible and many have limited attention spans. Interviewers are concerned about whether the child really comprehends the questions being posed. Responses may be difficult to understand since preschool children do not have fully developed language skills. In addition, some researchers have suggested that preschoolers are more likely to go along with suggestions from an interviewer, particularly about the meaning of an event.[16] Others have countered that young children may be swayed about meaning, but can provide accurate reports of witnessed events.[17]

Amidst the debates about suggestibility, interviewers wonder about the practicalities of interviewing preschool children. What is the best way to question a preschool child? How long can young children attend to interview questions? Do preschool children have adequate witness abilities? Are there circumstances where preschool children have contributed valuable information to investigations? The following two cases are used to illustrate individual differences among preschool children who witnessed homicides.

Four Year-Old Billy

Bob Spoerry was the kind of guy you would want on your case. A veteran detective, Bob served his first twelve years with an urban police department working a variety of squads from motor cop to sex crimes. His next seventeen years were devoted to the Lake Havasu City Police Department where he investigated homicides. Havasu was famous for being the new home to the London Bridge, purchased when the British put it up for sale because it was falling into the

Thames River. Surrounded by forty-seven miles of shoreline, Lake Havasu City was home to about 40,000 people. Close enough to Las Vegas, crime slunk in daily and kept the police department busy. Havasu was a haven for felons who wanted to hide in a community bustling with tourists and water sports enthusiasts.

The Crime Scene

It was 7:15 a.m. on Monday morning when Detective Spoerry responded to the scene of a possible suicide. Patrol officers had already secured the scene. Earlier, a police officer driving by the residence had noticed two young children standing out on the road near their mailbox. The boys were four and three years of age. The officer was the uncle of the boys. When he pulled up next to them, he asked where their mother was. The oldest boy, Billy, said, "mommy is dead."

The boys' Uncle entered the home and found the victim on the living room floor with part of a rope around her neck. A similar frayed piece of rope dangled from the ceiling. The Uncle immediately phoned the police and exited the building. He waited for police with the children in the back seat of his car. Detective Spoerry immediately assigned an individual to transport the children to the local advocacy center to be interviewed.

Detective Spoerry surveyed the scene. The victim, a twenty five year-old white female, lay on the living room floor in front of a large picture window. She was wearing a pink tank top with gray shorts. A rope was around her neck with what appeared to be a break in the rope along the right side of her neck. Lividity was present in the lower extremities of the body and was consistent with her position. She was slumped over her knees, almost in a fetal position.

The living room had a couch and it appeared as though the victim had recently been doing laundry. Folded clothes were stacked up on the couch as well as on the floor. Laundry baskets lay against the wall under the picture frame. A mattress was lying in the middle of the living room floor and the victim's head just touched it's edge. Directly above the victim, a red hook was noted in the ceiling. A rope hung from the hook with what appeared to be a breakage at the lower end of the rope. The rope was similar to the one on the victim's neck.

As Spoerry looked closer at the rope, he wondered how the ends had broken in the particular spot that they did. As the evidence technician bagged the items, he once again focused on the rope

Something wasn't quite right here. He looked about the rest of the house. There were several red hooks bolted into the ceilings of various rooms in the house. It was clear they weren't hooks for plants. About this time the victim's mother, Mrs. Jay, arrived.

Preliminary Statements

Clearly horrified at the scene before her, the victim's mother said she had just been over helping her daughter clean the house all day yesterday. She repeatedly stated there was no way that her daughter would commit suicide. And she definitely wouldn't kill herself in front of her boys. Mrs. Jay, however, did admit that the victim had been despondent over the loss of her two month-old daughter two weeks ago. The infant had died from an immune disorder. This was the second child of the victim's that had died from the same disorder. The first death occurred approximately four years ago. The victim's mother stated that since the death of the child, the victim had not felt up to cleaning much so Mrs. Jay came over to help. Both mother and daughter cleaned and cooked on the day prior to the victim's death.

The victim and her boyfriend had been together for approximately one year. Mrs. Jay last saw him during the afternoon that she was cleaning with her daughter. The victim had told her mother that she had broken up with her boyfriend, Sean. The only reason that he was on the property was to put a motor on his boat so he could tow it out of her garage. Mrs. Jay reported that Sean came in the house once to get a drink of water and left. He did not return to the residence while she was there. Clearly shaken, Mrs. Jay was escorted home, agreeing to provide more information to detectives as needed.

It was 9:35 a.m. when Detective Spoerry received the telephone call from the Advocacy Center where the interviewer had spoken with the victim's four year-old son. Although he had a speech impediment, the interviewer reported that one of the few understandable statements the child made was, "daddy rope – mommy's neck." This put a whole new light on the investigation.

The Follow-Up Interview of Billy

While the investigation continued, a follow-up interview with 4 year-old Billy was requested. Prior to interviewing Billy, the original videotaped interview of Billy was reviewed. Overall, it was a good interview. The interviewer was patient but given Billy's speech impediment, she had a hard time understanding the little boy's responses. The clearest statements were "daddy put rope" and "mommy's neck." After a four-hour drive, the child arrived for the interview tired and crying. Things were not starting out well. The first task was to get Billy to accompany the interviewer into the interview room.

Interviewing An Upset Preschool Child

After some cajoling, Billy entered the interview room. Once inside, however, he began crying. Distraction, by offering him crayons or toys, did not stop his crying. He wailed, "I don't want to draw." In addition, his articulation was so poor that he was barely understandable. The difficulty of the situation was apparent. How could one proceed?

Several options exist when interviewing a visibly distressed, crying child. Depending upon the level of distress:
1. stop the interview,
2. discuss neutral topics and then try to get back into the substantive material,
3. take a break and then resume the interview a few minutes later, or
4. provide the child with Kleenex and carry on if the crying is not debilitating to the child.

This last option is frequently used with adolescents who are old enough to understand the gravity of what happened to the victim. Generally, if children are not crying profusely, but rather, are tearful, it is recommended that the interviewer continue. Be wary of stopping an interview because of your own discomfort. It is understandable that some children will cry when discussing emotionally laden events.

At the other extreme, avoid taking on the role of a therapist by spending a lot of time addressing the crying. Statements such as "why are you crying" tend to exacerbate crying. Even adults react poorly to this inquiry. Most women understand this concept. If you are upset and your husband asks you why you are crying, in general, you tend to cry more. Instead, with an older child, you might state, "is there something I can do to make it easier for you?" With a younger child, "would it help you if I explained better what we are going to do today" or "Is there something that you're thinking about that is making you upset?"

Statements that place a subjective interpretation on crying are counterproductive. Interviewer comments such as "this is really hard for you" or "I know this must be scary" may be incorrect interpretations or a projection on the part of the interviewer. Crying can be related to all kinds of things during an investigation, including but not limited to fear, physical exhaustion, sadness, thinking one is in trouble, lying, telling the truth, or recollection of emotionally disturbing content. It can be extremely difficult to sit with a person in pain and not reach over to try and fix it. If you aren't certain what to do when a child cries during the interview, make a judgment call that errs on the side of the child's best interest and stop the interview.

In Billy's situation, the crying may have been a by-product of a four-hour drive for a preschooler. It could also have been his recollection of just having participated in an interview for an hour the previous evening. Or perhaps it was the overall turmoil of his life and the unfamiliarity of the current setting. Although he was staying with his grandparents, Billy had been displaced from his own room, toys and family comforts. And of course, he also missed his mother.

Given Billy's emotional state, it was not productive to spend more time engaging him with toys or art supplies. Early in the interview, he did not respond well to being given choices such as a selection of crayons or favorite colors of paper. He simply stated, "I don't want those." More structure needed to be part of the interview. In these types of situations, short and specific directives are required. Billy was directed to the simple task of drawing a picture of his mother. Within about thirty seconds, he started scribbling. As Billy calmed himself he began to draw more carefully. He also began to answer questions about his mother. Billy's diminished anxiety while drawing is an important effect to note.

There exists a misconception that it is terribly traumatic for children to relate the events of a violent crime. While there will be some children whose anxiety is increased when discussing a horrific event, there will be others whose anxiety is diminished by the opportunity to draw or talk. It is almost as though one can see the relief that comes when the talking begins. Such was the case with Billy. As Billy talked, he drew the following picture:

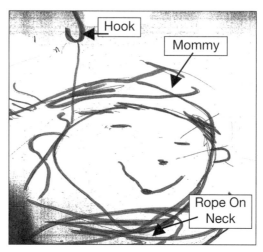

Figure 7. Billy's Drawing

As the interview progressed, Billy kept saying "on mommy neck." He stated that "Daddy Sean" put the rope on mommy's neck. Billy then added that Daddy Sean "put mommy on the hook." At this point in the interview, Billy steadily drew the hook, coloring it in darkly. Billy further stated that his daddy then went out the door and went to work.

Billy immediately flipped the page over and spontaneously started drawing a picture of his "daddy, Sean." He drew a man with a baseball hat, clearly identifying the hat Sean regularly wore. Upon completion of his drawing, Billy gripped the pencil and started poking the eyes out of the picture. The action was so repetitive that he needed to be diverted and eventually have the paper placed to the side. As you can imagine, Billy's therapist would have her work cut out for her. In spite of one's desire to address the behavior, the purpose of this interview was not therapy. Instead, clarification of the investigative information was required.

Clarifying Information With Direct Questions

Although Billy made some specific statements, the information he provided was limited. There were still several concerns with regard to the hook. Certainly one possibility was that Billy's mom and her boyfriend were in the process of engaging in sexual practices where individuals are hung from hooks. It certainly wouldn't be the first time that this was the reason there were several hooks in strange places throughout the house. And then again, perhaps the residents really did like plants or hanging lamps in the oddest of places. Given this child's limited language capacity and poor speech, it would be difficult to ascertain the context of what was happening at the time that the victim was placed on the hook.

Attempting to clarify the context of what occurred during a complex event is difficult when the child is a preschooler with limited language capacity. You are left with the necessary task of asking direct questions. There is no way around it. Ever since the McMartin and Little Rascals Daycare Cases, however, there has been tremendous fear among interviewers with regard to asking young children direct questions. But given the average expressive and receptive language skills of preschoolers, direct questions must be asked.

Language Skills of Preschoolers

Expressive language skills are those words that the child is able to express or verbalize. Receptive language is words that a child "receives" or hears from others and is able understand. Children between the ages of three to four years, have an average of 800 words in their expressive vocabulary.[18] They can understand about 1,000 words. The average mean length of their responses is 4.3 words. Children who are four to five years of age do slightly better. Their expressive language skills average around 1,000 words with receptive skills ranging from about 1,200-1,500 words. Their mean length of response, however, is only about five words. With this in mind, please be reassured. Direct questions must be asked of preschool children during the investigation of a criminal case.

Developing Direct Questions

Since direct questions can be leading, develop the questions to minimize their suggestive nature. For example, "what happened to mommy" is less suggestive than "did daddy hurt mommy?" Every crime scene is unique so ask questions that are most relevant to your investigation. Remember, however, that preschool children are in a preoperational state of cognitive development. The main characteristic of this stage is the ability to understand simple concepts and verbally symbolize the environment by naming objects. Preschool children will attend to physical characteristics of objects versus making inferences. In other words, children will describe what they see and hear without ascribing connotations about meaning.

In Billy's case, if the adults were engaged in sexual activity, it would appear likely that at some point their clothes or some portion of their clothes would be off. Conversation between the victim and suspect prior to death might also reveal the motive of the crime. In this instance both of those areas were addressed. Billy reported that his mother had her clothes "on" when daddy put her on the hook. In addition, when asked, "what words" mommy was saying Billy replied, "she was crying." In response to the question about "what words" daddy was saying he answered, "Daddy was mad." It didn't appear that this was a bondage scene gone bad. After about twenty minutes of talking, Billy said he was done. He left the interview room calmly and proceeded to the play area where his grandma waited. The family made their way back to Havasu and Detective Spoerry continued with his investigation.

Detective Spoerry was persistent in his search for information. He obtained a second opinion about the cause of the victim's death, eventually described by the Chief Medical Examiner as, "asphyxia due to ligature strangulation." Other multiple contusions were noted on the victim. The manner of death was listed as homicide.

In addition to the medical findings and multiple statements from witnesses, Spoerry compiled a binder of drawings that he found in Sean Ward's residence. Mr. Ward, it seemed had a propensity for drawing nude women hanging from ropes. All neatly compiled, the case was submitted to the prosecutor. It was well into the following year when Sean Ward, the victim's ex-boyfriend, faced charges of second-degree murder.

The Trial

During the trial, predictably the defense suggested that the questions posed of Billy were leading and suggestive. The expert hired by the defense indicated that the first interview of Billy suggested to the child who his daddy was. In addition, criticism of the follow-up interview included a lack of obtaining a preliminary developmental assessment from the crying child. It seemed evident that Billy, sobbing when he entered the interview room, did not want to recite his ABC's. The videotapes and drawings were presented to the jury to formulate their own opinions. But it was Billy's own testimony that was a critical part of the trial. Prosecutor, Matt Smith posed the questions.

The parenting of his own young daughter and years of trial

experience gave the prosecutor some insight into Billy. But perhaps it was simply his confidence in Billy that ultimately led the child to do so well. As you can see from the following headlines, the defense countered, stating, that a five year old should not be believed.

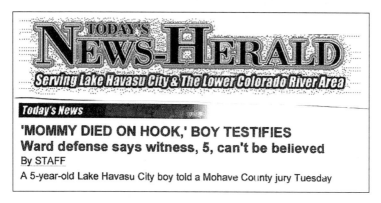

Figure 8. Newspaper Article

Even though he was a year older at trial, Billy still had a speech impediment. Jurors, however, clearly heard him state, "Sean put the rope on mommy's neck." The Judge agreed that Billy was difficult to understand, however, indicated that the child "was unequivocal about what happened to mommy and who did it to mommy." He left the weight of the testimony to be decided by the jury. During the course of the trial, jurors also heard from the defendant.

In six hours of testimony, Sean Ward related his woes about his relationship with the victim. He testified that she had affairs with other men and that without explanation she broke up with him two days prior to her death. He took back his engagement ring and went back for his boat the day before she died. Ward stated that police who came to his workplace told him about the death.

When asked about his sex life, Ward admitted that he used ropes and other items of bondage. He spoke of his sexual practices with the victim, which included the use of swings, ropes, and handcuffs hanging from hooks on the ceiling and walls. He also videotaped some of the acts in order to sell them on the Internet. Ward admitted to drawing the sketches of nude women hanging from ropes, some of them distorted and bleeding. The problem, he stated, was that the victim became "sharp" and "nasty" after the death of their child. According to Ward, she probably committed suicide.

51

The jury eventually convicted Sean Ward of second-degree murder. He was sentenced to twenty-two years in prison. If not for the careful criminal investigation that included interviews of a four year old child witness, the case may have been ruled a suicide. In spite of his distress and delayed development, Billy was able to tell us who killed his mother. In another jurisdiction, a trial with much different dynamics was underway. In this case as well, a preschool child's reports were a critical piece of a larger puzzle.

In Memory Of Judy

It was an early morning for a veteran detective, arriving at the scene of a possible suicide. The victim, Judy, was only thirty years old. Judy had two children, ages three and five, a boy and girl respectively. The girl I will refer to as Rosey. Both Rosey and her brother were at home when their father arrived at 5:30 a.m. following a night of gambling at the casino. According to the children's father, he arrived home to find his wife laying in a fetal position on the bathroom floor. She was not breathing.

The children's nanny was awoken by the distraught man, who had begun CPR on his wife. He directed her to call 911. In the background of the 911 tape, one can hear him frantically saying, "Judy don't do this to me. I can't raise these two kids on my own."
Paramedics and police arrived to find the victim on the floor of the master bathroom. A tongue blade and washcloth were next to the victim's head. Blood was dripping out of her nose. The victim, a white female, was laying on her back with one leg propped up against the bathroom cupboard. The rest of her 5'8" frame was stretched out on the floor. Her legs were blue from lividity. It looked like all 108 pounds of her were in rigor.

The Crime Scene

When the detective arrived at the upscale residence, the children were in the care of the neighbors. Officers had already secured the scene. As he examined the house, the detective noted that there was no forced entry or disturbance of the residence that would indicate a robbery. The master bedroom was intact, other than a blanket that was crumpled up on the bed as though someone had used it for a cover. As you can see from the photo, the bedroom was immaculate.

Figure 9. Bedroom of the Residence

The master bathroom where the victim was found was also free of clutter. The victim's makeup bag was resting on the bathroom vanity. Next to the victim on the floor were a hairbrush, several hair elastics, a comb and a tongue blade. The victim was clothed in blue boxer shorts and a printed T-shirt.

The remainder of the house appeared similarly intact with no disturbances noted in the children's rooms or the nanny's bedroom. The victim's purse was found on the kitchen counter. It did not appear to be ransacked. A pager without batteries lay next to her purse. Nowhere in the home did there appear to be signs of a struggle.

Preliminary Statements

Outside the home, detectives were obtaining preliminary statements from the nanny and Judy's husband. The nanny stated that she saw Judy at about 8:00 the previous morning. Shortly thereafter, the nanny left for college and church classes. After class, she went out with some friends and did not return home until 1:00 a.m. When she entered the home, the door was unlocked and she proceeded to her bedroom. The nanny did not notice anything unusual in the house when she went to bed.

Judy's husband stated that he and Judy were home all day. He wasn't feeling well and she was cleaning. His friend came over at about 10:00 p.m. and they left to go the casino. The friend entered the residence but stated that he did not see Judy at the time. Judy's husband said his wife was in the bedroom watching videos with the children. Police later found out that the last person to see Judy was a neighbor who spotted her outside while he repaired his roof. Judy waved to him and went back into her house. The time was approximately 9:00 p.m. Somewhere between 9:00 p.m. and 5:30 a.m. Judy died. Two possible witnesses were the victim's small children.

Arranged by child protective services, the children went to stay with neighbors since extended family would not be arriving from out of State until the following day. Rosey was interviewed at a Child Advocacy Center within forty-eight hours of the telephone call to 911. During this initial interview Rosey stated that the police had come to her house and that "some stuff happened." She did not elaborate what she meant by the phrase. Rosey's three year-old brother had delayed language skills so he was not interviewed. As the investigation continued, other pieces of information were discovered.

When checking the home during the initial call out, one detective found a gram of cocaine in a closed drawer. In an attempt to rule out a drug-related death, the detective checked the bathroom area for cocaine residue, and finding none, made a note of the evidence. The medical examiner's report had not yet been completed. The morgue was backlogged and toxicology wouldn't be back for a while. In the mean time, detectives requested a follow-up interview of Rosey for she had been extremely adept at avoiding questions about "stuff that happened."

Rosey's Investigative Interviews

Seven days after Judy's death, Rosey was brought for the follow-up interview. With their father's permission, Rosey and her brother were placed by Child Protective Services with family friends, Mr. and Mrs. Frost, until the investigation could be completed. The Frost's had two children of their own who had often played with Judy's children in the past. Both couples had socialized and Judy's husband stated that they all were close friends. Prior to Rosey's interview, Mrs. Frost tearfully stated that Rosey talked about her mother being in heaven. Rosey would wander out into the garden and put little notes into the birdfeeder so that birds could take the messages up to her mother. Mrs. Frost stated she did not want to cause any undue harm to the children so she had not asked them about Judy's death. In general, she reported Rosey to be boisterous during the day while she played with the other children.

Rosey's Follow-up Interview

Rosey, a perky little girl with long braids, presented with average language skills. She readily entered the interview room and sat on a couch, ready to engage in conversation. Every once and awhile, she bounced up and down on the couch. She was able to state her full name and age. When told that this was a place where girls talk about mommys who died, she immediately stated, "that's my mommy...it's because a long time ago she died because – cause the officers came." She stated that her mom was "in bed when she died." On two occasions, Rosey indicated that she had been frightened from the "noise and stuff" in the house. She was quick to change topics and was easily distracted. In spite of her distractibility, it was important to clarify some information about Rosey's household.

Questions Related To Household Members

Since this was a homicide investigation, one would be most concerned about anger and physical acts that may have resulted in violence. Given the sensitive nature of violence in the home, correctly wording questions about household residents is important. When inquiring about individuals in the home, be certain to ask the child how everyone is treated, not just the victim. The reasons for this are twofold. First, one doesn't want to intimidate a child by immediately asking about how authority figures treat each other in the home. Second, one would not want to suggest that someone in the home may have harmed the victim.

Start by telling the child that trouble or arguing happens sometimes in every home. Then, obtain information about what happens when an adult in their house becomes angry. When you ask about how anger is directed at various people in the house, start with someone other than the victim. In this case, the topic was introduced during a portion of the interview as follows:

Interviewer:	You know what else I talk about with girls...in everybody's house sometimes mommy's and daddy's get mad – when daddy gets mad what does he do?
Rosey:	He puts me in time out.
Interviewer:	How about when he gets mad at the Nanny?

Rosey:	No he doesn't get mad at the Nanny.
Interviewer:	How about when he gets mad at your mommy?
Rosey:	He – that bad word...sh sh sh...well he just like – well he has handcuffs that are just pretend.
Interviewer:	Well what does he do with them?
Rosey:	Well he's not really an officer...she's just in the kitchen and sometimes they – she – they just kinda – like you know like dinosaurs fight....
Interviewer:	Tell me more about how they fight.
Rosey:	They kick and punch.
Interviewer:	Who does the kicking and punching?
Interviewer:	My mom does the kicking and my dad does the punching. My mom does both and my dad does both...my dad punches...

At this point Rosey lay down on the couch and began fidgeting. It was only eight minutes into the interview. Rather than end the interview, a change of tasks was warranted. Rosey was asked to draw a picture of her mother.

Drawing As An Aid For The Young Child

Some experts argue that the use of drawings during an investigative interview is not proper. Their argument revolves around the use of projective drawings, or those in which an individual interprets what the child has drawn. The drawings advocated during the use of child interviews are not intended to be projective drawings. Rather, these drawings are offered as a developmentally appropriate tool for children to fully explain their experience. The picture, drawn by the child, serves as an anchor for the child to retrieve memory about the event. Remember, there are many retrieval paths to memory.

It is recommended, therefore, that the task provided to the child is one that involves the child drawing something relevant to the investigation. Children can be requested to draw the victim, the location of the crime or how the crime occurred. The intent is to allow the child to draw a picture that provides an image that assists him or her with recall. If the picture is an illustration of the crime victim, it can also be used to document injuries that were visible to the child. This technique was used with Rosey.

Rosey's Picture

When Rosey finished drawing the picture of her mother, she was provided with a colored marker and given the following directive, "take this blue marker and color in the places where your mother got hurt." Rosey immediately started coloring and declared, "I don't know...that's blood she got it on her eye...I'll make it this little circle." She continued drawing, stating, "on her leg – and these are her knees – there she got punched that's why I'm coloring this blue right over here." The completed picture is illustrated below.

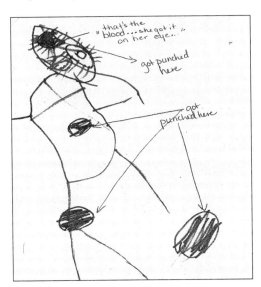

Figure 10.
Rosey's
Drawing

When Rosey completed her picture, she immediately became distracted. She talked about a bunny rabbit she saw at the neighbor's home and started hopping around the room like a rabbit. When attempts were made to redirect Rosey back to the picture her attention remained poor. Given her level of activity, only a few follow-up questions were asked. A question about what happened to the blood from her mother's eye resulted in Rosey pointing down to the floor. The question, "did somebody clean up the blood" produced, "well my dad cleaned everything...the mop with a wet mop." She stated the wet mop was hanging in the closet.

Rosey once again began hopping around stating, "I don't know. It's just a story...it's not really adventure...well it really does happen to mommy – I get time out." She continued hopping, making it apparent that the interview was over.

Back in the interview monitor room, everyone appeared confused. The CPS Specialist exclaimed, "what handcuffs, I didn't know anything about any handcuffs?" The detective wondered when the hitting and punching occurred. Was this a prior incident or one that contributed to Judy's death? Given Rosey's limited attention span, the interview could not be continued at this time. Rosey was scheduled to come back in two days.

In the mean time, Rosey's dad had agreed with Child Protective Service's recommendation that the children remain with family friends. He stated that he needed time to grieve. He was also busy granting TV interviews to most of the local stations and offering reporters a full account of the story. His house was in total disarray as he sorted out his wife's things, packing items and gifting friends with a variety of Judy's keepsakes. He was interviewed prior to Rosey's next interview. It was important to have some information from the only living parent of this child.

Information From Rosey's Dad

When Rosey's dad arrived, he alarmed the receptionist with his constant pacing around the waiting room. He carried a backpack with a hand made sign, "mom's eternal picnic basket." During the course of his two-hour interview, he rambled on about his life, unable to sustain a substantive conversation about his children. He indicated their "regimens" were in his computer. With pressured speech, he expounded on his sexual escapades and sexual prowess. He swore that his children had never seen any violence in the home. The only violence they may have witnessed was the family dogs fighting. In particular, he was asked about any arguments with Judy.

He stated that the night he left for the casino, he and Judy had fought about money. In the kitchen, he asked her where all of her money was going. In particular, he wanted some cash to go to the casino since he recalled giving her $300 earlier in the week. He indicated that Judy stated she had spent it on their son's shoes which he "knew was a lie" because he had seen the item on his credit card statement. He stated the argument ended amicably at which point he kissed his wife goodbye, took the ATM card and got cash prior to going to the casino. Unsolicited, he continued talking about Judy and her family.

At length he berated Judy's family, elaborating on their "selfishness" during the services including their need to "grieve" over their daughter. He stated that during their marriage, Judy always wanted to "be the boss" and that "even in death she was finally the boss." He was asked to explain this confusing statement. He indicated, "I went to see her at the grave and she would only give me ten minutes at her gravesite." When asked what he meant, he replied, "I couldn't stay there – I was late for dinner."

With some difficulty, the interview was finally terminated. Judy's husband had an attorney who was notified that his client could benefit from an immediate mental health evaluation. While the interview provided some insight into Rosey's father, it didn't offer much understanding of Rosey's daily life, although one could speculate about the environment to which she was exposed. The interview questions in Rosey's next interview would need to be designed based upon the information she had already provided.

Conducting Sequential Interviews

When conducting sequential interviews with children about a complex event, pick up from the last interview instead of starting from scratch. Briefly summarize the previous content or introduce a particular aspect of the previous interview that needs clarification. If you choose to summarize the original content, be sure to ask the child if you got it right before continuing with questions.

With Rosey, the decision was made to select one particular aspect that she had already disclosed and ask for clarification. Any number of words that Rosey previously used could be selected to design a question to cue recall. The word that is chosen should be an item of importance that requires clarification. In Rosey's case, the word handcuffs could be inserted into a statement such as "last time we talked you said something about handcuffs. Tell me more about that." The handcuffs were important because Rosey originally offered them in response to a question about her father being angry. It was Rosey's perception that the handcuffs were associated with what her father did to her mother "when he was mad."

Although any number of words could have been selected to design a question to cue her recall, it was determined that the picture she drew would be used to elicit more information about the event. The picture was selected since additional clarification was required regarding Rosey's earlier statements about "kicking and punching." She had ended the last interview with, "it's just a story…it happens to mommy and I get time out." It was critical to obtain information about whether or not this was a story or an event that really happened.

Rosey was shown the picture she drew during her first interview and asked to explain what she had drawn previously. Rosey pointed to the areas colored in blue and indicated, "the punching was right here and here…" Since Rosey was only five years old, further clarification using direct questions was necessary. In addition to the typical "who, what, where when and how" questions, a multiple-choice format offered some startling and informative results.

The Use Of Multiple Choice Questions

Multiple-choice questions can be highly effective if designed well. In contrast, if developed poorly, they can readily confuse a child. Keep multiple-choice questions short. In other words, offer only two options to the child as opposed to three or four. For example, "was John running or something else" is better than "was John running or walking or jumping or something else?" Too many choices will result in young children losing their train of thought half way through the question.

In addition to the design, give careful thought to the content of the question. I recommend picking one choice that is slightly implausible. This allows a young child to correct you. The child's response, therefore, is more likely to be in his or her own words. In addition, when children correct adults, they tend to elaborate upon their response. There are circumstances, however, when the child will respond with the choice you offered in the question.

If a child selects your choice, it is important to follow up with questions that require the child to elaborate. Asking a question that begins with the word "how" easily accomplishes this task. The word, "how" requires children to provide explanations as opposed to a one word response. For example, with "was John running or something else" the child might respond "running." An explanation can be obtained from the child by stating, "I'm confused, how could John get hit if he was running." The interviewer may have inadvertently offered the correct choice and the child may have a perfectly good explanation. Alternatively, the child might be suggestible and engage in an illogical response that will easily be spotted. The multiple-choice format proved effective during Rosey's interview. Note the following exchange:

Interviewer: When your daddy was punching your mommy, was she standing or something else?

Rosey: She was bending on the kitchen (bends self backwards) when my daddy just punched her – like this (punches self in eye) and then ouch – and she just kicked him..."

This question and response were particularly important for a number of reasons. While the question was suggestive to the child with regard to her mother standing, it also offered her an open-ended option. Had Rosey answered, "she was standing" there would be little confidence in her response since the interviewer suggested the word, "standing". Rather, her explanation, "bending over the kitchen (counter)..." plus her demonstration was compelling. Rosey's response indicated that she was not a suggestible child. She did not incorporate any words from the question into her answer. Her response to this multiple-choice question provided one violent act and the location of the incident. What was missing now was the time frame.

Although Rosey had not provided a time frame, the scenario in the kitchen made sense, given her father's description of the argument that occurred in the kitchen on the night of Judy's death. The question became whether or not the physical altercation caused her death. The medical examiner's report was still not complete. Although many investigative questions were not answered during this interview of Rosey, it was equally important to provide her with support services or counseling. Concerned about Rosey's mental health, a juvenile court judge ordered a psychological evaluation of Rosey so the court could consider a professional's recommendations about her mental health needs.

Rosey's Mental Health

Six weeks following the death of her mother, a psychologist

evaluated Rosey. He documented that her composite score on the Kaufman Brief Intelligence Test placed her in the sixty-first percentile, or average range of general mental ability. Little difference was seen between her verbal and nonverbal scores. The psychologist wrote that there appeared to be "some areas of conflict with regard to the parental figures...she is clearly uncomfortable and anxious talking about parental violence." He recommended that Rosey continue to see the forensic interviewer since she had established some rapport. The evaluator advised the court that it would not be in the child's best interest to introduce Rosey to another new person. The court issued an order directing child protective services to comply with the counseling mandate.

Since clinical and forensic services are ideally kept separate, audio-taping all of the clinical sessions would protect any disclosures that Rosey might make to the provider of services. The bereavement therapy that began was designed to be supportive in nature and address issues of sudden and multiple losses. Themes of family violence, however, emerged in almost every session. It became difficult to separate forensically relevant material from the clinical content. Throughout her weekly thirty-minute sessions, Rosey drew several different incidents of her father hitting her mother. One picture was particularly compelling. The pencil drawing of two figures was completed with a heart drawn in red crayon. The penciled figures were of her mother and father. Rosey explained, "he broke my mother's heart when he punched her."

During other sessions, Rosey drew her mother in a big house up in heaven. At the neighbor's residence, she would leave coins at the bedside table so that her mom could "come down and get the money in case she needed to go shopping." Amidst these bereavement issues, Rosey interspersed descriptions of family violence along with statements such as, "it's really just a story...but it does happen sometimes."

It's Really Just A Story – Distinctions Between Fact and Fantasy

It was towards the end of the second month that Rosey started out a counseling session with, "you know I don't say the truth sometimes." At this point she was asked to "tell the truth" whatever it might be. Rosey responded, "well he really does hit her and I say it's a story because it only happens some times.

Phrases such as "it's just a story" allude to the possibility of fantasy and can be misconstrued as whims of the imagination. In most investigations involving preschool children, it is not uncommon to hear professionals focus on the child's ability to distinguish fact from fantasy. The immediate question relevant to criminal investigations is, "do preschool children have the capacity to tell about real versus imagined events?"

Most authors indicate that as children get older their capacity to identify facts versus fantasy increases with age.[19] One of the first studies of fantasy/reality classification was conducted in 1978 by Morison and Gardner. In this study, preschool children were asked to sort out cards based on a reality or fantasy classification scheme. Some of the cards depicted elements found in fantasy, such as dragons and others depicted actual persons. Children were asked to make pairs of the cards and explain their selection indicating which cards were "pretend" and which cards were "real" individuals. Overall, preschool children made few classification errors with older children making fewer errors than younger children. The researchers indicated that development of an awareness of the fact/fantasy distinction develops at least by age five.

Other authors indicate that the distinction actually develops by the age of three.[20] Those that believe in the three-year range suggest that the difficulty lies in children's inability to explain the fact/fantasy distinction given their limited language skills.[21] The biggest problem with studies of real and imagined events is that they rarely apply directly to situations involving children who witness violence. The activities in laboratory studies are necessarily artificial versus those that are perceived and stored during the context of an emotional, violent event.

Rosey was eventually able to explain her use of the words, "it's just a story." The statement referred to her concrete thinking and difficulty with understanding multiple violent events perpetrated over a period of time. To Rosey, the violence was just a story because "it only happens some of the time…not all of the time." In an effort to assist Rosey in describing specific incidents of violence, another task was designed to cue her recall.

Cued Recall Using Photographs

Cued recall is based upon the principle that specific cues will assist children to retrieve information from memory. It is generally undisputed in the literature that cued recall, while not completely error-free, results in more information from young children than responses to open ended questions.[22] In addition, cued recall appears to be most helpful in eliciting information about central features of the event such as actions versus peripheral details. Using cued recall, children as young as three years old can provide accurate information about a witnessed event.

In designing tasks to cue recall, the cue about a violent event must be related to the crime but only be peripheral in nature so that the child is not mislead. In order to cue Rosey's recall, it was determined that location would be a salient cue. Neutral photographs of rooms in her house were used to cue images of events that occurred. The photographs selected were of her bedroom, her parent's bedroom, the kitchen, living room and bathroom. Rosey was asked to identify the rooms. She correctly identified the rooms and readily talked about each photograph. Rosey was then asked to mark an "X" on the picture where her mother was located when dad punched mom in the eye.

Rosey put an "X" on the upper kitchen cupboard, pointing out a counter where dad had bent her mom backwards when he hit her. Once the photographs cued Rosey's recall, she further elaborated about the context of the violence. Rosey indicated that the back of her mother's head hit the kitchen cupboard. Rosey and her brother were in the bedroom watching videos and coloring when Rosey heard the noise from the kitchen. She went down the hallway and saw what happened to her mother. During other sessions, Rosey elaborated about events using the pictures as a cue.

Other Follow-Up Sessions

In follow-up sessions, while looking at photographs of her residence, Rosey stated that her mom "died in the bed." She pointed out that dad "carried mom by the toilet." The words that her dad was saying at the time were "she's the boss...she's the boss." She also added an explanation about the handcuffs mentioned earlier in the interviews. Rosey said her father would put the handcuffs on her mother in the kitchen. She could hear her mother saying, "stop it... stop it... stop it" so Rosey would hide in her room and cry. Rosey never spoke about the handcuffs again. But resolution of the case did not rest solely on Rosey's statements.

Other Pieces Of Evidence

During the course of the investigation, Judy's parents, who

resided in another state, notified the lead detective that they received a federal express package from their son-in-law. The box contained some of their daughter's clothes and other personal items. Between her clothing, the elderly couple found some drug paraphernalia and what appeared to be cocaine. A law enforcement agent from this jurisdiction assisted in packaging the evidence and submitting it for analysis. It was also during this period of time that Judy's husband engaged in several conversations with other adults during which time he referred to his wife as a "coke whore." He indicated to one individual that she had a "substantial amount of cocaine in her" and probably died of suicide. Not long after these conversations, the medical examiner released his report.

Cause of Death

The original report from the medical examiner read as follows:

Cause of Death: Intracerebral hemorrhage due to cocaine intoxication
Other: Blunt force head injury
Manner: Undetermined

Under the pathological diagnoses, the medical examiner wrote the following: 1) intracerebral hemorrhage, 2) cocaine intoxication, 3) cutaneous abrasions and contusions of head and extremities, 4) paraspinal soft tissue hemorrhage of the neck, 5) contusion left parietal scalp, and, 6) epistaxis.

Although all of Judy's specific injuries were too numerous to mention, documentation of her head and neck included multiple contusions and abrasions. Her scalp revealed a deep one and one-half inch contusion. Judy also had bruises to the right forearm and lateral aspect of the right hand, which is a common site for injuries referred to as defense wounds. Bruises were evident on her knee and left thigh. Dissection of the neck revealed hemorrhage in the soft tissue on the right and left sides of the neck as though some one had grabbed her there with force. The medical examiner's report was not released until two months after Judy's death.

The toxicology report was also too lengthy for a full description of the findings here. Importantly, femoral blood and gastric contents were positive for cocaine. Jurors eventually heard various experts from major metropolitan areas debate the autopsy findings, injuries and ultimately the cause of death. The majority of experts agreed, however, that there was no evidence of chronic cocaine use days before Judy's death.

A Summary Of The Trial

It was more than a year after Judy's death that her husband was indicted with two felony counts. The first count, murder in the second degree and the second, transfer of narcotic drugs. Upon his arrest, the children went to live with the defendant's sister in another state. The victim's family also wanted to care for the children, however, the defendant, having custody of his children prior to his arrest sent them to live with his sister. The case was going to trial largely because of the dogged efforts of a veteran detective and the resolve of a young prosecutor and co-counsel. The highly publicized trial lasted several weeks.

Trials seem to take on a different dynamic when filmed by national television. Attorneys and witnesses alike, even subconsciously, posture for the cameras. The press sensationalizes testimony that might ordinarily be considered innocuous. Such was the case with this trial. The family of the victim and jurors endured it all.

The jury heard lengthy descriptions from both prosecution and defense experts on cocaine metabolites and their levels in blood and urine. At the risk of being overly simplistic, prosecution experts argued that one-gram of cocaine was the approximate dose found in the victim. Comparing the metabolites in the blood and urine, testimony was given that the cocaine was likely ingested one to two hours prior to death. It was not possible to snort this amount through the nose during the specific time frame in question. The gram of cocaine in the victim's system was introduced in one large amount.

The prosecution argued that it was unlikely that the victim ate one gram of cocaine. It was their theory that Judy's husband forced the cocaine down her throat. Even in the remote but unlikely possibility that she had taken the cocaine, her husband had intentionally, knowingly and with extreme indifference left her there to die with two small children in the home. In addition to the toxicology reports about cocaine, there also existed the blunt force trauma to the back of Judy's head.

The Chief Medical examiner testified that the victim suffered a severe injury to her head that would have made it difficult for her to walk after such a blow. Rosey's statement corroborated the information when she described the punching and the fight that resulted in the victim striking her head against a kitchen cabinet. It was not only the content but also the timing of Rosey's drawing that seemed most remarkable. Rosey drew her picture one month before the medical examiner released his report. The similarities are striking:

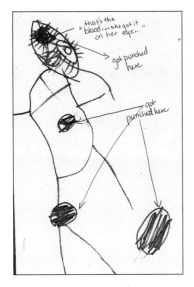

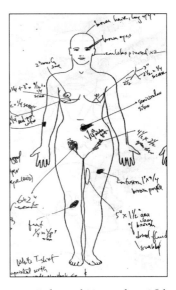

Picture Drawn October 1st   *Document Released November 16th*

Rosey's drawing, while crude, matched several of the injuries on Judy's body. The picture was a 5 year-old child's perspective of what happened. Rosey was called to testify.

Prior to the trial, Rosey's Aunt allowed her continuous and frequent telephone contact with her father in jail. During her testimony, Rosey answered most questions with "I don't remember" or "I don't know." She did indicate that she drew the picture and in fact let slip, "it wasn't punching – just hitting." She also admitted that her father would "put those things (handcuffs) on her mother's hands." Following Rosey's testimony the videotaped interviews were introduced into evidence. As predicted, the defense argued that Rosey was an unreliable witness.

Defense Criticisms Of The Interviews

The defense attorney argued that questions in the child interviews

67

were suggestive. Careful scrutiny and systematic analysis of the interview transcripts countered his claim. The few suggestive questions that were asked of Rosey towards the end of the interview demonstrated her resistance to suggestion. Suggestibility, however, is a common criticism leveled at young child witnesses.

Dating back to the Salem Witch trials, skepticism about child witnesses has prevailed. Most of the research on children's memory and suggestibility, however, appeared in the last twenty years. Suggestibility refers to the extent to which reports about an event differ from their original form due to a variety of influencing factors. Cognitive, social factors or an interaction of the two can create a "misinformation effect." Pioneer researchers in the area of suggestibility, Loftus and Davies, support the premise that while adults spontaneously recall more about witnessed events than children, most children by the age of eight years resist suggestion as well as adults. Not all younger children are necessarily more suggestible.

Most researchers agree that preschool children give less spontaneous information in free recall portions of speech requiring that direct or suggestive questions be used to obtain complete accounts of an event. The concern is that direct or suggestive questions may increase error rates in children's responses. The degree to which errors are made relates to a number of issues including the age of the child, the nature of the witnessed event and the strength of the suggestion. Age in of itself is an overly simplistic determination of suggestibility.

Repetition of the suggestion may also lead to distortion of information by some children. Repetitive suggestions to young children have been a major focus of studies regarding suggestibility of children in the past decade. Overall, however, caution is warranted in interpreting current studies related to suggestibility of young children's memories.

In the real world of violence, suggestions made to child witnesses may be weak or strong, depending upon the circumstance in question. For example, "the bad man killed your mommy" stated several times over to a child is qualitatively different than the question, "who killed your mommy?" While suggestibility is a complex phenomenon, trends in courtrooms across the country indicate an attempt to focus strictly on age and suggestibility. Perhaps the most common reference for this type of testimony is the book written by

Ceci and Bruck, "Jeopardy In The Courtroom."[23]

Three specific studies described in "Jeopardy In The Courtroom" have fueled views of children being unreliable. Commonly referred to as the Sam Stone Study and the two Mousetrap Studies, researchers in these studies provided incorrect information to preschool children and interviewed them over the course of several weeks. While the studies are comprehensive in nature, many professionals simply quote the percentage of children determined to have incorporated suggestions into their answers by the end of the study. The problem with applying this research to preschool children who witness violence is that the study design does not adequately reflect the experiences of child witnesses or investigative interviews in general.

Researchers in the study went beyond suggestion in their questions by telling the children rather than asking them what occurred. In short, while some professionals cite these studies as confirmation that all preschool children are unreliable, careful examination of the methods and findings of the studies indicate otherwise.

One of the study's authors indicated that about two thirds of the interview transcripts that he reviews in actual cases do not contain inappropriate suggestive questions.[24] What these studies do tell us is that it is imperative to avoid coercive and repetitive practices (e.g. telling the child what happened) during interviews of child witnesses. Many of Ceci and Bruck's comments are also directed at counselors versus those conducting investigative interviews. In Rosey's case, however, having the same professional assume both clinical and forensic roles created another obstacle.

Clinical versus Forensic Roles: Dual Relationships

As mentioned, it is best to keep forensic and clinical roles separate. Clearly, treating therapists or counselors engage in different methods and procedures than those used in forensic information gathering. Reaching a certain level of clinical certainly about children's diagnoses and then providing treatment requires a different professional stance than conducting investigative interviews. While most ethical guidelines for mental health providers recognize potential conflicts of interest in dual relationships, it must be acknowledged that it will be necessary to provide both evaluation and treatment services in some cases. There are many instances across the country where the same individual interviews a child and then provides crisis intervention, supportive or counseling services. If you find yourself in this potentially problematic position, take reasonable steps to be clear about the differing purposes and responsibilities of each role. Explain to the client how each role is different. Audiotaping also preserves your practices both in a forensic and clinical context.

Forensically relevant material sometimes does get disclosed in a clinical setting and an audiotape will indicate the manner in which this information was elicited. In Rosey's case, audiotapes clearly documented Rosey's descriptions of chronic family violence. Although there was a criticism that forensic information came out in a clinical context, it was apparent that if Rosey had not witnessed anything relevant to the criminal matter this would not have been an issue. Even though Rosey related many instances of family violence, given her young age, she had difficulty placing the events in a time frame. This was another issue raised by the defense attorney during the trial.

Establishing Time Frames For Events

Because of her age and the fragmented nature of her disclosures, time frames of various violent incidents could not be established with any certainty through Rosey's testimony. Given the defendant's description of an argument in the kitchen, it is likely that the altercation resulted in Judy hitting her head on the kitchen cupboard the night that she died. Although Rosey was not able to tell us about time in days or hours, jurors were provided with other evidence obtained by the police that might help to establish a time frame for the domestic violence incidents. The clothing that the victim was found in by police matched those described by Rosey when she saw her mother injured.

Corroborating information or data that comes from sources other than the child takes the burden off of a child when trying to establish when a violent event occurred. Many times children's descriptions of the context of an event can assist investigators with establishing time. For example, what television show was playing during a violent incident or the particular season of the year can provide a window of time for investigators. One incorrect assumption is that if children can count, they are able to respond to how many times an event happened as well as have the capacity to place those events in a time frame.

Even though children can count, they are not necessarily able to know exactly how many times chronic violent acts occurred. In fact, many adults who are victims of chronic violence are unable to identify the exact number of violent incidents that occurred. Asking children how many times an event happened can lead to a response that will later be used to impeach a child. Most children, however, are able to indicate how old they were when a particular act occurred.

Rosey was able to indicate her age during different incidents of violence. She was not able to specify when the violent incident occurred in the family kitchen. In fact, it would have been inappropriate to ask her a specific question in this regard. The jurors in this matter eventually made an assessment about when and how Rosey's mother died.

The jurors, an extremely attentive group of people eventually heard from the defendant himself. There are those who believe that the defendant was his own worst enemy. Jurors deliberated for eight hours and eventually returned a guilty verdict on both counts. The following headlines indicated the media's take on the events.

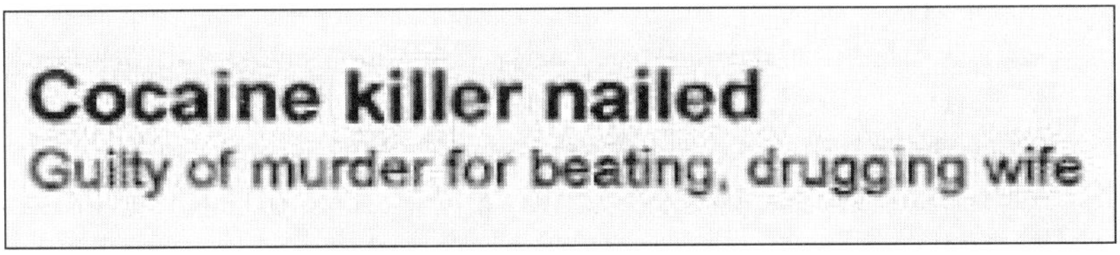

Cocaine killer nailed
Guilty of murder for beating, drugging wife

Figure 12. Newspaper Article of Verdict

The children remained in the custody of the defendant's sister. Liberal contact with their mother's family was ordered through the courts. According to a treating psychologist, the youngest child was diagnosed with autism. What the little boy saw on that fateful night is uncertain, however, his toy animal was noticed on the bed close to his mother's body in a crime scene photograph. Perhaps some recollection of those events is locked in the recesses of his three year-old mind. Time will tell, for he too was a preschool child when his mother suddenly died.

Conclusion

These two compelling cases reflect the multitude of problems associated with interviewing preschool children. Individual differences were evident in the children's capacities to recall and describe the crimes. Billy was delayed in speech and social skills. Rosey was more expressive and clearly resistant to suggestion. Both were capable as preschool witnesses to describe violent acts that were directed at their mothers. Both were able to identify who perpetrated the violent acts. While researchers to date have focused on group differences among preschool child witnesses, these two cases indicate that in real life situations, emphasis should be placed on individual capacities versus generalized age effects on children's memory. It is imperative, therefore that all children be included in criminal investigations where they may be able to contribute vital investigative information. When interviewing preschool children, the following suggestions are offered.

1. Preschool children have short attention spans. Keep your interviews short, lasting about fifteen to thirty minutes. If needed, conduct sequential, follow-up interviews.

2. Remember that young children perform inconsistently in unfamiliar settings. In sequential interviews, try to keep the same interview location, preferably in a child-friendly environment.

3. While you may begin interviews of preschool children with open-ended questions, some will not understand such a broad request for information. Your interview will be incomplete without direct questions. Design cue questions, which are highly effective in assisting preschool children with retrieving memory about an event.

4. Preschool children are less able to organize their memories. You may need to ask about a particular aspect of the crime in several different ways. Multiple choice questions may be helpful in this regard.

5. Keep your questions short. About six to eight words per sentence would be ideal.

6. Avoid compound questions such as "who was it that hurt your mom and where did this happen?"

7. Question the child about substantive material fairly quickly. If you spend fifteen minutes playing with the child, you'll have about five minutes left to ask questions relevant to the investigation.

8. Manage the interview so preschool children are not exposed to lots of toys or distractions, creating a situation in which they would rather play than answer questions. Play therapy has its merits in counseling. It lacks suitability in an investigative interview.

9. Do not use techniques that encourage play during an interview. Making statements such as, "let's pretend" or "picture a story in your head" are similar techniques to those used by researchers in the Mousetrap Study. If you are using a doll or other object such as a teddy bear to allow young children to demonstrate something, tell the child that the object is not for playing but for showing what happened.

10. Avoid asking preschool children "when" something happened. They are typically unable to place complex events in time. Instead, try to establish the context of the event and place the burden for establishing time frames on older individuals or those who have examined all of the evidence.

11. If the child's attention span is dwindling, switch to a task other than talking. Preschool and Day Care centers use this concept routinely when they schedule different activities for children every thirty minutes.

12. Interview young children when they are not tired, hungry or feeling ill. If these conditions exist, reschedule the interview if possible.

13. Tape your investigative interviews. Videotapes are the most accurate representation of both verbal and nonverbal responses of children. Young children often demonstrate actions that are captured on videotape. The tape also preserves the nature of your questions.

14. Carefully examine the questions and responses documented in the interview. Many criticisms about suggestibility and unreliability of young children are unwarranted.

15. Acknowledge the strengths and limitations of the preschool child you have interviewed. A fair and balanced account of the child's capacity is important in order to understand the testimony.

Remember that in spite of their weaknesses and strengths, interviews of preschool children are one small but important piece of an overall puzzle.[25] All by itself, an interview might not have the weight it would when all of the pieces of evidence are put together. That insight is comforting. For what would it be like for children to feel like they stand alone? The foster children in the next chapter were unfortunately in such a position.

73

CHAPTER FOUR

Investigating Child Deaths In Foster Care

"Home no more to me
Whither must I wander?
Hunger my driver
I go where I must..."
                    Robert Louis Stevenson

Foster parents and state funded residences for children generally provide care for more than one child at a time. Criminal investigations in these settings, therefore, will likely involve interviews of child witnesses. In addition to the complexities associated with all investigations, foster care settings have a host of unique dynamics that require careful consideration by investigators.

First, officials from the State are often conducting their own investigation concurrently with the criminal investigation. Second, finding placements for children these days is difficult at best. Unexpected deaths in residences with a number of children place a strain on child protection workers expected to quickly find homes for the remaining children. Very few places have room for large numbers of children in the event of an emergency. And third, most children who are placed in care bring with them a history of abuse or neglect that led to foster care in the first place.

The latter consideration requires a great deal of data collection and review during the course of a criminal investigation into a child's death in foster care. Determining what injuries, if any, were inflicted on the child prior to placement in contrast to the cause of death is an important part of the investigation. Obtaining child witness statements about the event under investigation versus acts that led to the witnesses' own placement is critical. Finally, if someone in authority has killed a child, it is likely that children in the individual's care will fear reprisal if they disclose the circumstances of the death. Foster children, whose lives are spent moving from one home to the next, have a very real fear of where they might eventually have to live. Several of these dynamics are present in the following case.

In Memory of China Davis

On early October 20, 1993 a young child named China was admitted to Good Samaritan Hospital and pronounced dead on arrival. Her injuries included a perforated bowel, and fractures of the left arm, clavicles and ribs. She also suffered a T-6 compression fracture. Both arms had calcification spots, often seen as a result of old injuries. There were numerous bruises on the tops of the child's feet. The child was two years old.

At the time of her death, China was in the care of a thirty seven year-old foster mother, Dorothy. China had lived with Dorothy for the past eleven months. Dorothy also cared for two other children. Six year-old Sandy lived with Dorothy for about five months. Eleven year-old Katie, a mentally challenged child, had been adopted by Dorothy several years ago. All of the children in Dorothy's care had been placed with her by social workers for the State.

Typical of reviews in many child fatality cases, China had a lengthy history of injuries since her placement with Dorothy Livingston. China's medical records reflected the following injuries and explanations by her caretaker between 1992 and 1993.

Date	Injuries	Dorothy's Explanation
December 1992	Fractured Clavicle	Child fell down stairs
January, 1993	Tooth Knocked Out	Child fell out of chair
March 1993	Fractured Left Arm	Child fell down stairs
September 1993	Sutures	Child ran into gate
October, 1993	Multiple Fractures, Contusions & Perforated Bowel DEAD ON ARRIVAL	Child hit her head at the babysitter's home the previous day

The pattern of injuries was fully documented by the child's pediatrician. In retrospect, the series of fractures documented in this young child's medical records should have raised concern about the child's welfare as well as the safety of the other two children in Dorothy's home.

Both Sandy and Katie remained in Dorothy's home even though there had been a child's death. Child welfare policies were much different nine years ago. Children were typically left in foster homes pending completion of the criminal investigation. Today, it is standard procedure to remove foster children from a residence during the investigation of an unexpected death. Sandy remained in Dorothy's home for five days after the death of China. Katie stayed a considerably longer amount of time. During this time, Mrs. Livingston had the opportunity to influence the statements of the only two witnesses to the crime.

The first witness, Sandy, had her own history of abuse. During the first six years of her young life, she had already lived in three placements. The first was emergency shelter care. Next she was placed with Dorothy Livingston. Her placement during the latter part of this investigation was at a crisis nursery.

Detectives brought Sandy for an interview approximately two weeks after China's death. She had been briefly interviewed by a police officer who felt that Sandy might know more about the death than had originally been disclosed. Sandy's psychologist had also documented depressive features and increasingly withdrawn behavior. Sandy was tearful when she arrived for the interview. The detective who transported her stated that she was quiet during the drive and provided only limited responses to neutral conversation. She had been told that she was not in trouble. The detective further informed her that she was being taken to visit with a doctor who would visit with her about how things were going.

The interview with China began with a discussion about how nice she looked. In response to the question, "who did your hair so nicely?" she replied, "Rose...she works at the place I live now." The interview continued as follows:

Interviewer: Where did you live before you went to the place where Rose works?

Sandy: A foster home.

Interviewer: Who all lived in that foster home?

Sandy: Dorothy, Katie and China...but China died.

Interviewer: Well I need to understand as best I can what happened to China. So maybe you could tell me as best you can what might have happened to her.

Sandy: (shakes head negatively)

Interviewer: Cause you said she died and I was kind of trying to figure out...how did she die?

Sandy: My mommy told her to clap her hands and she didn't so she kicked her down the stairs.

Interviewer: What is your mommy's name?

Sandy: Dorothy.

In any investigative interview obtain names of parents when children refer to "mommy" or "daddy." Especially in this age of blended families, references to a parent can mean any number of people. With foster children who have been in multiple residences, this clarification is critical to the integrity of the investigation. In addition, more than one defense attorney has used the tactic of, "this child has been in so many homes, she goes around calling everyone mommy or daddy...even the babysitter."

In this interview, once Dorothy was identified as the individual that Sandy called mommy, other direct questions were asked to clarify what happened to China. The interview continued as follows:

Interviewer: Dorothy kicked her down the stairs...and where were you when Dorothy kicked China down the stairs?

Sandy: She was doing my hair and...I was eating the first time she kicked her down the stairs...one time and when she was doing my hair she kicked her down the stairs a lot of times...I was sitting on the toilet when she was doing my hair.

78

Interviewer: In which room?

Sandy: The bathroom...and China was by the door...

Sandy continued to give her account of Dorothy kicking China, indicating that the incident first started when Sandy was eating breakfast, followed by kicking when Dorothy was fixing Sandy's hair in preparation for church. Dorothy and the three children then proceeded to attend church. Sandy described the following events at church:

> "we prayed and read the Bible study – mommy was singing in the choir and we had to watch China cause she fell asleep on the blanket and was throwing up. And she couldn't walk anymore so mommy said let's go so we could get home and get the hospital card...we were in the car and I told mommy that stuff was coming out of her mouth and...then her stomach wasn't moving...she just died with her eyes open there..."

Sandy's description of attempting to resuscitate China in the back seat of the car was heart-wrenching. Unable to help China, she cried until Dorothy, stuck in traffic, flagged a patrol unit down. Police radioed for an ambulance whose personnel immediately transported China to the hospital. Sandy stated the last time that she saw China, "the ambulance man put her on this little bed and then she was gone..."

During the course of the interview, Sandy stated that Katie, the mentally challenged foster child, had also witnessed Dorothy kicking China down the stairs. According to records, Katie was functioning at a developmental age of approximately three years. She was not interviewed. According to Sandy, Katie was seated in a living room chair when Dorothy kicked China and repeatedly told her to get up. The stairwell was next to the living room where Katie sat.

Sandy eventually began to repeat her statements about China being kicked down the stairs. She stated:

> "China cried and my mom told her to get up the stairs...she got up the stairs and she didn't clap her hands to music so my mom kicked her down

the stairs and then she told her to climb up, kicked her down the stairs and she told her to climb up, kicked her down the stairs, she told her to climb up...and then I don't know very much..."

After the repetitive speech, Sandy appeared tired and taxed by the interview. Rather than continue with verbal tasks, she was asked to draw a picture of what happened. The picture is found below.

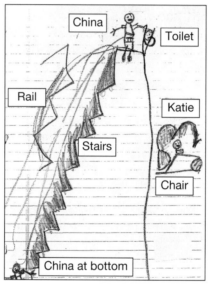

Figure 13. Sandy's Drawing

Once the picture was complete, Sandy explained each item in the drawing, demonstrating how China fell to the bottom of the stairs. She also drew Katie seated in a chair next to the staircase. Interestingly enough, when the case eventually went to trial, one criticism from the defense attorney was that the picture was inaccurate because "clearly, there isn't enough distance from the stairs to the chair." Most jurors fortunately understand that six year-old children don't draw pictures to scale.

Irrespective of whether the drawing was spatially correct, Sandy was able to respond to direct questions about her picture. Perhaps the most critical follow-up question that Sandy answered was, "where on China did Dorothy kick?" Sandy replied, "in the stomach." One of

China's injuries had been a perforated bowel. It is unlikely that a six year-old child would know that a kick to the stomach could cause a perforated bowel. Sandy's account was consistent with the medical examiner's findings.

Questions regarding where injuries were inflicted on the victim are imperative during an investigative interview. Unfortunately, such questions are often inadvertently omitted, even though children's responses often contribute corroborating information regarding injuries to the victim. Children do not have sophisticated medical knowledge that would lead them to correctly match violent acts with injuries documented by a medical examiner.

In this instance, Dorothy kicked China with her foot. With an act of kicking, one might naturally think that the act occurred with a foot. Such assumptions, however, can often get us in trouble. In one homicide investigation, the child stated, "daddy stabbed mommy." While a knife seems the most reasonable weapon of choice, when asked what daddy stabbed mommy with, the child replied, "a fork."

In another case, during a sexual abuse investigation, a young child stated, "daddy kissed my pee pee." When asked what daddy kissed her pee pee with, the child replied, "with his pee pee." If the follow-up question had not been asked, the sexual act may have been interpreted to be oral/genital instead of penile/vaginal contact. The same concept applies to homicide investigations.

Even when children describe acts such as shootings, the injury can be made with a number of weapons such as guns, arrows, and even, in one instance, a spear. In China's case, the injuries occurred with a foot, belt and shoe. Injuries were also inflicted on Sandy and Katie when they misbehaved. Sandy's interview enlightened the investigator to the abuse suffered by all three children in the home. The girls' foster mother would later describe the abuse as acts that constituted "normal punishment" of children.

The Trial

Dorothy was eventually arrested for the murder of China Davis. During the trial, Dorothy testified, "I spanked them because I wasn't acting as a foster parent. I was being a mom." She also stated that other witnesses were lying when they described Livingston using her fists and feet on China, throwing her into a bath for not cooperating and slamming her down into the toilet because she was not potty training quickly enough. She did admit to leaving China and Katie alone, locked in the apartment for at least two hours. An apartment worker unlocked the door and let them out when he heard the girls crying for help from an open window.

In spite of this testimony and the plethora of injuries that China had endured in the eleven months that she lived with Dorothy, a physician called by the defense testified that China's injuries could have been caused from congenital syphilis, causing her bones to weaken and break easily. There was never any indication that China ever had congenital syphilis. Eventually, the jurors heard from Sandy. But Sandy was no longer six years of age.

Sandy was ten years old when she finally testified in the criminal matter. The trial had been continued for four years. At age ten, her language skills were much better than at six. The prosecutor, extremely knowledgeable and effective with child witnesses, did an exceptional job eliciting China's testimony on the stand. Challenges, however, arose because so much time had passed since Sandy had first described the crime. The defense argued that the passage of four years had affected Sandy's memory of the events.

Sandy Testifies

At 4 foot 2 inches, Sandy's face barely peeked over the microphone where she sat in the witness chair, hands carefully folded in her lap. For three hours she spoke in a matter of fact style, with tears streaming down her face. Newspaper articles, such as the one found below reflected controversies about the reliability of children's testimony four years after an event.

Girl kicked 3 times down steps in day

10-year-old tells court of last attack on China

By Karina Bland
The Arizona Republic

time.
Livingston, 50, is charged with first-degree murder and 10 counts of child abuse. This is the start of the second week of testimony in her Maricopa County Superior Court trial.

The girl who testified Monday said she was in the upstairs bathroom of Livingston's

Figure 14. Newspaper Article

In the end, the jury not only believed Sandy, but also stated that she was one of the most compelling witnesses during the trial. Dorothy Livingston was found guilty and sentenced to life in prison. But not thirty miles from this residence, in a neighboring county, yet another child suffered a similar fate.

In Memory of T.J.

Tina was born in 1990 to a mother who self-reported snorting cocaine throughout her pregnancy. She admitted to using the drug two days prior to the child's premature delivery. From birth Tina spent one month in the hospital during which time her mother never visited. Repeated attempts to locate Tina's mother were futile and the father had been listed as unknown. As an infant, Tina became a ward of the court.

Tina spent the first three years of her life in a series of shelters and foster home placements. Eventually she was to live in a foster home for special needs children. Given her exposure to cocaine, Tina was an extremely active child who was delayed in her development. After a brief stay at the special needs home, the foster parents indicated that they could not meet all of Tina's needs. At the age of three years and two months, she was placed in yet another foster home identified as her pre-adoptive placement. The home, in a remote area of a rural community, belonged to Jacqueline and Tom Potter. Within four months of residing with the Potters, Tina was dead.

The Crime Scene

When paramedics arrived at the Potter's home, they were responding to a call of a child not breathing. They found Tina lying in a bed. One medic stated "she was in the bed with her head on a pillow and the covers were pulled up and folded back...just like you would put a little kid to bed...except that she was all dressed up and she was dead." The visibly shaken paramedics transported Tina to a nearby hospital.

Tina was pronounced dead on arrival and her autopsy revealed a number of injuries to her body. There was evidence of injury to the abdomen, chest, abrasions on her back, contusions to the lower buttocks, right thigh, knee and legs. The bruises and abrasions ranged from days to hours old. She also had a black eye. A fracture of the right scapula with surrounding hemorrhage appeared to be at least seventy-two hours old. There were hemorrhages and multiple contusions of the brain. The cause of death was listed as blunt force trauma to the head. The manner of death was homicide. While the medical examiner was completing his report, interviews of household members had already begun.

Members of the Household

The individuals that resided in the Potter home included Mr. and Mrs. Potter, and their 9 year-old, Ben. Mr. Potter also had an adolescent female daughter from a prior marriage. She lived with the Potter's for approximately two years and left to live with her mother in California at the age of fourteen.

When paramedics arrived, Mrs. Potter accompanied them to the hospital. The statement given by Mrs. Potter to the emergency room nurse was:

> "...she was on the potty and called for help to get off the toilet and then she had a seizure like and her eyes rolled back and she fell off the toilet seat...I did CPR for about 20 minutes and then called 911..."

In response to a physician, Mrs. Potter stated,

> "...I found her laying next to the toilet and blood was coming out of her mouth...I went to check on her because she was in there too long...I cleared the blood from her mouth and started doing CPR..."

The physician also questioned Mrs. Potter about the multiple bruises on Tina's body. Mrs. Potter replied that the black eye was from Tina "running into the sink yesterday." The other bruises were from "children kicking her at the Day Care."

While Mrs. Potter was at the emergency room, Mr. Potter gave the following statement to a detective at the scene:

> "...my wife was combing Tina's hair in the bathroom and she was going potty and...and then she were talking to her and then all of a sudden she just went – ah, she just went limp you know. And ah, she just laid her down...so after about 20 minutes you know, my wife started

84

doing CPR and then she carried her out and said...nah, something else is wrong and she says why don't you call 911..."

Mr. Potter acknowledged that Tina probably got a whipping or a spanking the day before, indicating that both he and his wife punished Tina with a belt because "she usually is doing something to get in trouble." The detective who noticed a tree branch during his search of the home followed up with:

Detective: I noticed there was some switches in the house. Was she punished with those?

Mr. Potter: No, we keep a switch in the house for our son...he's so a belt don't bother him no more so we use a switch.

A report about the Potter's nine year-old son, Ben, had previously been made to Child Protective Services. During this earlier investigation, Ben denied any type of abuse. Others, however, now came forward to talk about the abuse to the two children. Mr. Potter's brother told police:

"...one day I was there fixing some breakfast and I told Ben no he couldn't have more food cause he just ate and so he called his mom on the job and his mom got mad cause he called her at work. Just for that when she got home she, man she let him have it with that board...and she also whipped Tina that same day cause she had peed on herself at school. So she hit her with the board on the butt..."

An Aunt from another State reported,

"...one time Tina didn't know the color or something and they didn't want her to be stupid so she struck her all over and then pulled her out of the stopped vehicle just by grabbing her wrists. I said you shouldn't hit her that hard and she said, if Ben can survive, so can she..."

Based on statements from relatives, it was apparent that Ben was also the victim of abuse. Given the severity of the beatings, and the possibility that he experienced abuse for the past nine years of his life, it would be unlikely that Ben would immediately be forthcoming about what happened to Tina. Particularly if he felt that he was still in danger, information from Ben would be limited. In fact, Ben was still in the care of his parents. He was transported to the police department by his mother. During the initial interview with the detective, Ben stated:

> "...she was on the toilet...they both carried her and set her on the living room and tried to make her come back but she just fell out kind of and they put ice on her tongue and they started to just shake her and stuff and say stop it and she wouldn't stop it...then she just fell out...and then my mom gave her a bath and we took her and dried her hair and put clothes on her and laid her on the bed...and we took the bible and we pray for her but it didn't work...when I went to sleep they was still doing the Bible stuff and then they gave up and called 911..."

Since Ben was still in the care of his mother when police interviewed him at the station, detectives tried to ascertain if Mrs. Potter was coercing Ben. Unknown to Mrs. Potter, a detective placed her in a room with a tape recorder running. When Ben's interview was over, he was accompanied to the room where his mother waited. Mrs. Potter could be heard asking the following questions:

Mrs. Potter: What did they ask you?

Ben: They asked me if I get whoopings and I said no. I said sometimes cause I do bad things and they just wrote it down and I said sometimes they just talk to us...

Mrs. Potter: You have to stay someplace else they said until we're done with all this shit. We're just praying...what time is it god damn it?

In addition to the interview by detectives, a Child Protective Services Specialist also interviewed Ben. Ben told the social worker that he had a pact with the Holy Ghost. The pact was about a secret he had. If he didn't tell the secret, Tina could be brought back to life. If he told about his secret then she would remain dead. In an effort to assist the child, the social worker asked Ben's mother to inform Ben that it was okay to talk about his pact with the Holy Ghost. Her response was, "whatever he has with the Holy Ghost is between him and the Holy Ghost." Social services personnel decided to place Ben in foster care.

Although Ben was removed from his parents, he continued to see them when the juvenile court ordered supervised visitation. Desperate to try and get Ben some peace of mind, the Detective sought out yet another interview with a mental health counselor. During this interview, Ben denied witnessing anything happen to Tina. It was five months after the death of Tina that yet another interview was attempted with Ben. This final attempt was made in order to determine what had happened to Tina.

Ben's Mental Health

Prior to meeting with Ben, over one hundred documents were reviewed pertaining to the case. Among the reports reviewed was a statement by Mr. Potter's stepdaughter who resided in another state. Needless to say, she reported chronic physical abuse from both parents, stating that most often Mrs. Potter would beat her with a board. She also reported chronic sexual abuse by Mr. Potter, which prompted her to run away. Following her relocation, she sought counseling where her therapist documented and reported the sexual abuse to child protective services in the jurisdiction where the Potter's lived. The counselor's notes corroborated the girl's report along with reports that Ben was also the victim of chronic physical abuse.

During this last interview of Ben, by all accounts he was doing poorly. His school performance had declined and his psychologist wrote, "his degree of anxiety is such that I would recommend referral to a pediatric psychiatrist to asses whether or not he needs medical intervention to manage the anxiety." Based on this information, the interview with Ben was extremely limited. He was fearful and anxious, offering only a few bits of information that were similar to his original account. In retrospect, it may have been wiser to refrain from re-interviewing Ben. Instead, emphasis needed to be placed on collecting, organizing and summarizing the mounds of historical data about the Potter family.

After reviewing the documents, it was evident that at least thirteen adults, independently of each other, gave statements to the police or Child Protective Services indicating that they witnessed the infliction of injuries to Tina and Ben by both Mr. and Mrs. Potter. Further review indicated that Child Protective Services had "revoked the day care certification" of the Potters in 1989, four years prior to the placement of Tina in the Potter home. The revocation was due to "substantiation of sexual abuse allegations of Mr. Potter's daughter with the perpetrator identified as Mr. Potter." No police report had been made at the time. Somehow, this piece of paper had gone unnoticed. Although this information was too late for Tina, perhaps it could salvage Ben. As fate had it, the detective's tenacity came through once again.

Persistence and Patience Pay Off

The detective in this case hounded prosecutors, Child Protective Services specialists and professionals throughout the state to assist with this matter. It was fitting that his work would lead to the most incriminating piece of evidence against the Potter's. After interviewing the Potters separately, the detective intentionally placed them in the same room and instructed them to remain there until further information was available. The following statements were recorded in that room:

Mr. Potter:	Ah...they didn't break you did they?
Mrs. Potter:	The cop said he's gonna take however long it takes to solve this one. That if the Medical Examiner says she died of physical abuse or something...he didn't say that but I know she died from that...then we probably be arrested or something...

In this case, it was the Potters who eventually implicated themselves. Ben was not able to give a full and complete account of what happened to Tina. Given his extensive abuse, one could only imagine the fear and anxiety he must have experienced when questioned about his parents. Ben's most complete and detailed statement had been the original one given to the detective.

Sometimes, in circumstances such as this, less is actually more. The more Ben was asked about the crime, the more anxious he became until he eventually denied witnessing anything. While a child may be the only witness to a crime, some children are not ready or able to talk about the events in an investigative interview. Even counseling did not allow a safe enough place for Ben to reveal the trauma of his life. But we can all learn from mistakes made in this complex situation as well as in the investigation regarding the death of China Davis.

These two case summaries teach us some basic principles for investigating deaths in foster care settings, residential facilities or other places such as boot camps where children are at the mercy of the adults who may have perpetrated the abuse. Most of these children don't have families to look out for their welfare. They know that if they tell, they may well end up in danger. The investigation must include alternate sources of data that generally exist in matters related to placement of children in care. Consider the following suggestions when interviewing children in foster care.

1.   Upon notification of an investigation, immediately separate the children in the home and schedule their interviews at a location other than the foster placement.

2.   Obtain medical examinations of the surviving children.

3.   Interview the children as quickly as possible since this will diminish the opportunity for influence by adults or other children in the home.

4.   Use several different interviewers if there are many children in a facility such as a residential home. This reduces the risk of one interviewer inadvertently influencing a child based upon what another child witness may have said. This does not mean that you should not be familiar with the case facts. Rather, the exact words that children use will not be unintentionally repeated from one interview to the next.

5.   Do not tell one child what another has told you. No matter how nicely you say it, this strategy can be coercive and may in fact produce information that is incorrect, particularly with very young children.

6.   Remember that many foster children may also be victims of prior abuse since there is a reason that they are in care. Reassure them that they are not in trouble.

7.   Do everything in your power to place children elsewhere during an investigation of this nature. The level of anxiety that can manifest from fear of reprisal from the perpetrator

can be debilitating. Older children in this situation have also been known to attempt suicide or run away rather than face the perpetrator of the homicide.

8.   Lastly, investigations conducted in residential settings and foster homes tend to be cases that generate mounds of paperwork. Typically there are "years" of case files on the children in these situations. Familiarize yourself with the child's history and past problems. Know what mental health diagnoses the child has. Document what medications the child is taking. Look through every piece of paper carefully. Get someone to help you if necessary. There may be that one piece of paper stuck somewhere in a file that ties all of the pieces together.

Boxes of paper and evidence are the foundations of particular units of law enforcement known as cold case squads. Investigations of old homicide cases, set aside when leads dry out, are difficult and problematic given the passage of time since the crime occurred. There are those, however, who pursue these cases, knowing that another family out there might eventually get closure on the death of a loved one. Chapter five outlines the challenges of investigating cold case homicides involving young child witnesses.

CHAPTER FIVE

Child Witnesses In Cold Case Homicides

Cold case homicides present unique challenges for police investigators. Ascertaining who has committed a crime years after the offense requires thorough and thoughtful analysis. Attention to detail is critical. For the cold case investigator, no piece of evidence is too small. Similarly, no witness is to be overlooked.

Conducting investigative interviews of children listed as witnesses in cold cases is a relatively new consideration and many questions arise in such circumstances. First, one is uncertain where the children are living now. Locating children subsequent to the commission of a crime is often difficult. Many children have been placed with relatives out of state and others are placed in foster care. Second, when the children are located, will the family or guardians be cooperative in allowing them to be interviewed? Third, will the passage of time have affected the child's memory? Fourth, will an interview at this late date cause undue distress for a child who may "relive" the situation during the telling of the event? And lastly, what post-event influences if any have affected the child's memory?

Post-event Influences

Post event influences refer to any information a child was exposed to after the homicide that caused distortion or error of the child's memory.[26] For example, a person questioning or providing information to a child over the years is one source of possible contamination. Events, such as media reports may have also influenced a child between commission of the crime and the current interview. An assessment of possible sources of influence is important prior to interviewing child witnesses in cold cases.

In determining sources that may have affected a child's memory of events, one needs to carefully examine the entire case file. Speak with old case agents if possible. In addition, interview the child's current caretakers or guardians. Inquire about all persons who may have formally or informally spoken with the child. Document these in chronological order along with the nature of the interview or conversation. Clearly not all conversations between children and others will be determined, however, document both brief and lengthy interactions you are aware of. If a child has been interviewed previously, this alone does not mean that the child has been unduly influenced. Similarly, factors such as a young age at the time the homicide was witnessed are not reason enough to reject interviewing a child.

Children who are as young as three years of age can store salient aspects of a crime in memory. In contrast to when the crime was committed, a child who is now older is likely to have enhanced memory performance in part due to more sophisticated cognitive skills and better strategies for memory retrieval.

Memory Strategies and Metamemory

In contrast to preschoolers, older children can spontaneously use strategies to improve their memories. They have better knowledge of their memories, known as the concept of metamemory. A basic definition of metamemory is important to help one understand why children who see violent acts at a very young age may be able to retrieve the memories in a more sophisticated manner when they are older. John Flavell, who identified the concept of metamemory in 1971 describes it as, knowledge of memory, which includes things such as organization of information in memory, an awareness of which items are easier to remember than others as well as activities aimed at retrieving information.[27] By the age of ten years, children are likely to have more knowledge of their memory organization. They also have had more practice at memory retrieval than preschool children.

Most research related to memory strategies focuses on purposeful memory or that which is related to information that children will be tested on.[28] School age children retrieve information in a more complex manner since they are more sophisticated at organizing an event and at monitoring their own responses if they are incorrect. For example, it is not uncommon to hear a school age child spontaneously correct him or herself during disclosure about a witnessed event. Preschool children are less apt to correct themselves spontaneously. While the older child may be better at memory strategies and language skills to articulate memory, other considerations such as how the memory was encoded at an earlier age are important with regard to the memory itself.

Attention and Encoding of Violent Events

Perception of and encoding of violent events depends in large part upon the child's attention capacity. Both the type and quantity of information attended to will affect what children encode in memory. Preschool children typically attend to a great deal of stimuli in their environments and often are distracted by things investigators may consider irrelevant. Their recollections of the event, therefore, may include various features of the crime scene, particularly if some aspect of the crime has captured their attention. How interesting an event is to a young child will therefore affect attention and eventually recall of the event. Similarly, how stressful an event is to a child may affect perception of and encoding of the event.

Homicide, by its very nature, is typically a distressing event to children. In many instances even when the results of violence are not visually horrific, sounds or other auditory cues can cause high levels of distress for children. For example, the conversation between a victim and offender may be volatile. Victims may call out for help to their children. In addition, the complexity of the event itself can be disturbing to a child. Some children are left with the victim's body for a period of time before police are called. Any one or a combination of these situations is traumatic for children.

Traumatic Memories

Historically it was thought that traumatic memory is perceived and stored differently than memory of normal events. This premise dates back to the foundations of psychoanalysis when scholars such as Janet, Charcot, and Freud noted that memories of terrifying events do not appear to be encoded or retrieved in the same manner as everyday events. When a child witnesses an event that involves a state of shock, typically a fight/flight response occurs, during which there is an extreme activation of the nervous system and intense emotional arousal.[29] Therefore, one's entire system of perceiving may change. Throughout history, controversy has existed among psychiatrists regarding the reliability of traumatic memories.

Research findings, however, about the effects of stress on memory are conflicted. Researchers, Peterson and Bell as well as

Goodman and her colleagues examined the effects of stressful events on children's memories.[30] Their studies, examining children's recollections of traumatic injuries, revealed that central features of the event can be retained well in memory but peripheral details may not be remembered well or may fade over time. Suggestibility of children about stressful events is less likely since the memory accessed is personally meaningful. Young children may acquiesce to the meaning of ambiguous events but they are less likely to be inaccurate about what was observed. In other words, a young child may be able to tell you, "Daddy punched mommy." He or she would be less able to describe the meaning of this event or that the injury resulted in mommy's death. Just as there is no simple relationship between memory and factors such as a child's age or situational stress, similarly the passage of time between storage of the memory and its retrieval is equally complex.

Passage of Time

Few studies have examined the effects of long-term delays between witnessing a violent event, recalling it, and talking about the event. Studies that do exist provide mixed results. In one study, preschool children interviewed about a trip to Disneyland six months and eighteen months after the trip remembered information about the trip. As expected, the younger children remembered less detail than the older children but age did not significantly affect retention.[31]

In contrast, researcher Helen Dent, found that a two-month delay in interviewing ten and eleven year-old children about an event did affect their recall.[32] The importance of the event to the child, however, may explain the differences. The preschool children were remembering a fun event while the school age children were being interviewed about a film they watched. Given that witnessing a homicide is a highly personal event, it is likely children would recall central features of the event even though lengthy periods of time had passed between the homicide and the cold case interview.

As with all children there would be both accuracies and inaccuracies in accounts of memory by children reporting horrific events. Each child's capacity in this regard must be considered individually. Where children's eyes are fixed during a violent event as well as what they heard, touched or smelled will all differ depending upon the child and the unique circumstances of the crime. Here are two different examples of children interviewed about homicides that occurred four years prior to the interviews. Each child remembered events in varying degrees of cohesiveness and accuracy.

Andrea's Story

The weather was clear, daylight and humid when the police chief in a small town approached the stucco white home. The residence consisted of one large living area, a bathroom and kitchen. At 6:40 in the morning, officers had been called to the residence by Mrs. Castle, a terrified and distraught elderly woman. Mrs. Castle stated that four year-old Andrea lived across the street with her mother and one year-old sister. Andrea, naked, with ropes binding her wrists, had wandered across the street and knocked on Mrs. Castle's door. With a blank expression Andrea told Mrs. Castle, "mommy is dead." Mrs. Castle ran across the roadway to Andrea's home and entered through the front door. There on the floor she saw Andrea's mother, unclothed and bleeding profusely from the head. Frantic, Mrs. Castle called 911.

The Crime Scene

When police arrived at the scene, the area was sealed off and State police officials were requested to assist with crime scene processing. Such a grizzly site had never before been discovered in this small town. The police chief noted that the victim's blue Ford was parked outside the home with the keys still in the ignition. There did not appear to be forced entry to either the front or back doors of the home. There was a distinct shoeprint that appeared along the fence by the house and similar footprints headed toward the street and out to the local college where no further evidence was found.

In the small living area of the home was a bed in which the victim, four year-old Andrea, and her infant sister slept. Clothes and boxes were strewn about the floor. According to Mrs. Castle, Andrea's mother had a yard sale the morning prior to her death. The house was in disarray, although no drawers or cupboards appeared to be ransacked. A portable stereo remained against one living room wall. A 35 mm. camera was in full view on a table top. The victim's purse was not disturbed. This did not appear to be a burglary.

Andrea's mother, a twenty nine year-old female, had been an art teacher at the local college. Her naked body was laying in a fetal position on the floor of the main living area. Next to the body were the victim's clothes, which appeared to be cut. Her head was bloodied and there appeared to be cuts to her forehead and underneath the chin. Her hands, folded in toward her chest, were handcuffed. There was fecal matter and blood on the floor. Bloodstains were on the sofa and a red blood smear was found on the wall above the couch. When the body was lifted, a bloodied white rope with knots was found underneath the victim's neck. A small child's blanket with bloods stains was found beside the body.

Andrea's Initial Statements

Four year-old Andrea was immediately transported to an emergency room where a physician who examined her indicated that he detected no apparent genital or other type of physical trauma. Andrea's spontaneous utterance to the physician was, "a big mean old guy" had killed her mom and "tried to put handcuffs on me too." She then stated that a "lion killed mommy." Following the physical examination, a clinical psychologist interviewed Andrea. The interview was not preserved on audiotape or videotape. The psychologist stated the following in a written summary:

> "Andrea stated that she had been asleep all night and had seen and heard nothing. She indicated that she read a book with her mother before going to sleep...awakened to find her mother and went to get help. During the evaluation she stated that maybe a mean big boy had come in through their back door with a big knife. She stated that he could have cut her clothes off too. During the evaluation she startled at the slightest noises and did not want to be left alone. She stated that she wants to have a party for her mom when she comes back."

Two more interviews of Andrea in a counseling setting were documented during the week following the homicide. Andrea did not reveal any further information about the crime. The counseling activities, as documented in the records, addressed bereavement and Andrea's understanding about the upcoming funeral. No information was documented about the crime itself. According to all reports, Andrea had not identified the suspect.

Like most other homicides, there seemed an endless number of suspects, including the father of Andrea, father of Andrea's sister, current and previous boyfriends, college students and colleagues, acquaintances, people at the yard sale, as well as the possibility of a total stranger. Neighbors indicated that they had been up until two o'clock in the morning and had not noticed anything unusual. No neighborhood dogs had barked alerting the community to unwelcome guests. After extensive investigation, the leads seemed to dry up. A $15,000 reward produced no new leads. Eventually, the case files were boxed up, remaining a silent reminder of what might lurk in the dark.

The Decision To Re-interview Andrea

Four years after this crime, the police chief of this town wondered if it was possible to re-interview Andrea who was now eight years of age. Haunted by the brutality of this sexual homicide, the chief wanted some type of closure for the children, their grandparents, and the small community that still mourned the death of this young and vibrant woman. The victim's elderly parents, now caring for the children in another jurisdiction, wanted justice for their daughter. They telephoned the police chief on a monthly basis inquiring about the case and keeping law enforcement informed of Andrea's whereabouts.

Andrea's grandparents indicated that she routinely cried out in the middle of the night and would crumble to the floor, gasping for breath in the middle of activities or conversations. Counseling had been attempted with Andrea several years prior, however, her grandparents stated that Andrea cried when her sessions were scheduled, refusing to attend. Currently retired, Andrea's grandparents were exhausted with the daily care of two young children. Like many caretakers in similar situations, the grandparents decided that they would "go it alone" and try to be supportive of the children as best they could. According to the grandparents, both Andrea and her sister were honor students at school.

When the children first came to live with their grandparents, they were transported to and from school as the grandparents feared that the killer would decide to find and harm the children. Four years after the crime, they still transported both girls to and from all activities. Under no circumstances was Andrea allowed to walk alone down her street. As one could imagine, with this level of hypervigilance, Andrea's grandparents were reluctant to allow an interview without either one of them present. Andrea's grandmother strongly believed that the father of Andrea's sister had committed the murder. It was "a

97

feeling" that she had for a long time. Law enforcement, however, had clearly documented that this suspect had a solid alibi. Andrea's grandparents did not want the investigation to remain at a standstill. They agreed to have her re-interviewed.

The grandparents stated that they would support interviews of Andrea as long as the interview methods did not re-traumatize her. A great deal of time was spent explaining the process to the grandparents along with the reminder that Andrea's well-being was the primary concern even during an investigative interview. The grandparents consented to a weekend visit with Andrea and arrangements were made to conduct the interviews in the state where Andrea now resided.

Planning Interviews In Cold Cases

Prior to interviewing Andrea, all case material was reviewed. When reviewing documents in cold cases, plan to examine as many independent sources of data as possible. At a minimum, review all investigative reports, psychological evaluations, counseling notes, medical findings, medical examiner's findings, crime scene photos, lab results, and any other evidence or investigative material that is still available for review. In cold cases, this usually means boxes of information. Even though some documents may appear to be useless for your specific purpose, examine everything. As you review documents, it is helpful to list them in chronological order. Include the type of report, who wrote the report and the number of pages reviewed. For example, your list can be developed as follows:

A. Review of Documents

Santiago Police Report by Detective Eliot, DR# 9567333 dated 05-05-95 26 pages
Diagram of Residence by Detective Johnson DR#9567333 dated 05-06-95 2 pages

Transcript of Counseling Notes Regarding Andrea J. prepared by J. Martin, Ph.D. (clinical psychologist) dated 05-07-95 to 06-12-95. 58 pages

Be sure and list every single document, photograph, videotape, or piece of evidence that has been reviewed. While this is time consuming, it helps in the development of timelines and generates questions to be considered prior to the child's interview. While reviewing the documents in Andrea's case, the following questions were kept in mind:

1. What was the crime scene like, particularly if seen through the eyes of a child?
2. Where was Andrea found when police arrived?
3. Who conducted the initial interview of Andrea and was it video or audio-taped?
4. What were the spontaneous utterances, if any that Andrea made at the time?
5. Who provided counseling to Andrea and were the notes available?
6. What questions had Andrea's grandparents asked her?
7. What media coverage had Andrea seen?
8. What evidence, if any, had Andrea been shown?
9. What evidence, if any, had the grandparents been shown?
10. What other family members spoke with Andrea about the crime?
11. When was the last time that Andrea was interviewed about the crime?
12. What is Andrea's understanding about what happened to her mother and who informed her of the explanation?

Once the material was reviewed, several hypotheses were developed based on the evidence in several documents. For example, examination of crime scene photos revealed that the floor plan of Andrea's home consisted of one large room where the children and their mother slept. This room also served as the general living area. It was here that police found the victim's body. If Andrea were awake, the attack on her mother was likely in her direct line of vision. Since reports indicated that Andrea's hands had been bound, it was likely that Andrea awoke during at least part of the incident. Since her hands were bound in front of her, it was reasonable to believe that she would have seen the suspect's face if he or she was not wearing a mask. The following possibilities therefore, were generated about the night of the crime:

1. Andrea was asleep and did not see, hear, smell or touch anything relevant to the homicide
2. Andrea was asleep, awoke to noise and could offer partial information

3. Andrea was awake and could relate all of the events that she remembered prior to, during and following the homicide.

It was now time to proceed with Andrea's interviews.

Since Andrea resided in another State, the plan involved conducting taped interviews over the course of two days. The grandparents were informed that the audiotapes were considered as evidence such as DNA or bed sheets and therefore their knowledge of the content or possession of them would jeopardize the case. However, they would be informed briefly about her statements along with how she did emotionally during the interview.

This type of reassurance is important for any caretaker who has agreed to the interview of a child many years after a crime has occurred. Like most other guardians, Andrea's grandparents didn't want to open up old wounds and cause their granddaughter duress. On the other hand, they did feel that perhaps she had some relevant information to share. If the homicide could be solved, they might eventually have closure in the death of their daughter. Andrea's grandmother indicated that the capture of her daughter's killer would be a blessing. Her tearful admission, "after four years, I still haven't been able to bury my daughter" spoke volumes. In addition, Andrea's grandfather suffered from a rare disease. In spite of aggressive medical treatment, it was unlikely that he would survive long enough to see the results of this investigation. Both he and his wife agreed to the interview plan.

It was decided that if Andrea stated that she didn't know or could not relate information about her mother's death during the first interview, the second day of interviews would be canceled. Likewise, if the first interview resulted in distress, the second interview would be canceled and referrals would be made to local support or counseling services.

Preliminary information about Andrea looked promising. Since Andrea was almost four years of age when the homicide was committed, it was likely that central features of the event would be stored in memory. Andrea, now eight, had more sophisticated memory retrieval strategies and language skills. Assuming that Andrea was not a reluctant witness, the interview might yield new information about the old crime. Her mental health status, as reflected by the grandparent's observations, however, was of concern.

Andrea was not currently seeing a counselor but even four years after the crime she continued to have nightmares every two to three weeks. At times, she would break down and sob without any apparent provocation. Erring on the side of caution, this limited information would indicate that her mental health status was fragile. In addition to concerns about her mental health, there also existed the possibility that Andrea's grandmother had suggested to Andrea that the suspect was Ross, Andrea's step-father.

Prior to interviewing Andrea, both grandparents were individually interviewed. The grandparents stated that immediately following the homicide, they had asked Andrea what happened to her mother. She did not offer any information in response to their inquiry. It is important to note that many families will talk with children about crimes they have witnessed. It would be unnatural for adults to refrain from asking any questions about the child's experience and neglectful to totally avoid a child's needs following a horrific event such as a mother's homicide. Rather, the concern lies with those adults who repetitively provide information to young children about a complex event.

In this instance, Andrea had not been questioned about the homicide during the past year. Her grandparents did admit that it was possible Andrea may have overheard the adults talking about Ross being a suspect in the case. Andrea's grandmother also acknowledged that she had specifically asked Andrea on a number of occasions if Ross killed her mom. Andrea consistently rejected this suggestion. While these post-event influences were noted, there did not appear to be any other sources of suggestion to which Andrea was exposed. Although she attended her mother's funeral, the family made a conscious effort to keep television and print media away from Andrea. None of the crime scene material or evidence had been shared with the grandparents or other family members. Given all of this information, post-event influences seemed to be minimal. It was possible to proceed with Andrea's interview.

Andrea's Statement Years After The Crime

Andrea, a neatly dressed, dark-haired child with somber eyes immediately greeted the police chief whom she recalled from the small town where she had lived with her mother. In the initial phase of the interview, rapport was developed with Andrea by conversing about the ducks swimming in the pool behind her grandparent's home. Andrea's grandparents suggested that the interview be conducted in one of two locations, Andrea's room or out in a park down the street. Andrea, exerting some control, chose neither of the options but did agree to visit in the basement "cause it was the biggest room in the house and we'd have lots of room."

Andrea did not appear reluctant to talk nor did she appear anxious in any regard. Like most children, Andrea readily agreed to the audiotape when given the explanation that it was easier to pay attention to her instead of writing things down. Andrea was easily engaged in conversation and provided a rich narrative language sample when she was asked to relate information about her friends and school. She provided eight sentences of uninterrupted speech in response to these neutral topics. There was optimism that the narrative about the homicide would be equally rich. Unfortunately, this was not the case.

In response to, "I talk with lots of girls who have a mother that died and I understand that your mom died." Andrea stated, "yeh it was when we lived in the town of Thompson." The next question was not even completed before Andrea huddled down in a fetal position and began trembling. Andrea was reassured that she was safe here and instead of talking she could draw. She slowly sat up and agreed to the change in task.

Rather than have Andrea free draw, a picture that was relevant to the investigation was requested. Andrea was asked to draw where she was when something happened to her mother. Without hesitation, Andrea began to draw. Once the task was switched from speaking to drawing, Andrea's anxiety was noticeably reduced. Using the picture, she was able to describe the events that occurred the night her mother died. Andrea explained that she was asleep when she heard a "crash," which she wrote across the topic of her drawing. She awoke to see a man hitting her mom over the head with an axe. It was the axe that hung on the front porch of the family home. Her mom used it to kill rabbits. Andrea heard her mom fall to the floor around boxes and clothes. It was at this time that Andrea fixed her gaze on the suspect who was now approaching her. Andrea drew his footsteps on the picture as the male walked towards her on the bed.

Andrea explained that the suspect was a man who wore "black shiny things on his pants with holes on the sides" that covered pants underneath. She said that he had "red like blood" on his chest that she saw as his black leather jacket was open. The man had yellowish hair that was in a ponytail. She also described facial hair on his upper lip that could have been mustache. Andrea did not know the man's name but she could reproduce conversation from the scene.

The man came up to Andrea and threatened, "if you tell anyone about your mom I will kill you and dig a hole by the lake and bury you in it." The suspect then left through the side door and Andrea went and sat by her mom on the floor. In compelling fashion, Andrea described her mom's eyes, "black like...I thought the man poked my mom's eyes out." Andrea reverted back to the threat about being killed and began to shake, once again, visibly upset.

Given Andrea's distress, she was directed to a neutral topic and asked to complete a fun drawing of her choice. She drew a rainbow and flowers during which time she calmed easily. Given that the interview appeared to tax Andrea immensely, it appeared that short, sequential interviews would be most productive and do the least amount of harm. With Andrea's consent, an interview was scheduled for the following morning.

When the second interview began, Andrea appeared bright-eyed and willing to proceed. She agreed to walk together to a local park and converse along the way. As we were ambling towards the picnic area, a motorcycle went by. Andrea immediately started shaking and dropped to the sidewalk. When asked what was wrong, Andrea replied that she did not know. She reported that as long as she could remember, she had a terrible fear of motorcycles. I couldn't help but wonder if the sound of the motorcycle was a triggor stressor, causing hyperarousal, anxiety and other post trauma stress symptoms. Her description of the suspect the prior day included a man who may have been wearing a black leather jacket and what appeared to be motorcycle chaps. Andrea was instructed in some deep breathing exercises and was able to continue on our walk to the park.

Once at the park, information provided by Andrea during the first interview was summarized. She was asked if any of the information was incorrect or if anything had been misunderstood. Andrea replied, "no, that's what happened but I forgot to tell you about when he left. I heard a loud noise like a truck starting or something." Aside from this addition, Andrea indicated that she could not remember anything else. In an effort to contextualize the events of the homicide, Andrea was asked to describe what happened earlier during the day that her mother died.

Andrea stated that the last day she remembered with her mom, she and her sister were napping while her mom had a yard sale.

Awoken by people yelling in the yard, Andrea jumped out of bed and proceeded to open the screen door leading to the front yard. From her view on the porch, Andrea reported seeing a "tall girl" raising her arm as though to hit her mom. When the girl lifted her arm, she saw "string things hanging down from her jacket." The jacket was black and the woman was wearing blue jeans. After the woman left, her mom said that the woman was angry over the dresser that was for sale. Andrea did not remember how the woman left – whether on foot, in a vehicle or otherwise. Andrea stated that once the yard sale was over, her mom put the girls to bed and then went to sit on a couch in the living room.

Andrea was asked to explain what was in the living room and she did not respond. She remained similarly quiet when asked other direct questions such as what she saw in the living room. A cued recall question was designed in an attempt to have Andrea continue. Since Andrea's hands were tied up at the crime scene, and there had been a white rope under her mother's body, Andrea was cued with the word, "rope." The question, "I heard something about some rope" resulted in a blank stare from Andrea. She matter-of-factly replied, "I don't know anything about rope." Andrea was then asked to explain anything else she might remember even if it seemed unimportant.

Once again, Andrea's primary concern was the suspect's threat to kill her. She indicated that when the suspect threatened her, she began to cry and he got angry. Andrea was unable to report what happened next. Leaving out a large piece in the sequence of events, Andrea's next description was of sitting beside her mother's body. Just as Andrea was relaying this information, she paused as though suddenly recollecting more. She turned and asked, "Do you think I can get my "pinky" back. I left it beside my mom." Andrea was asked to talk about the "pinky." She explained that her "pinky" was a white rabbit clothed in a dress sewn by her mom. The police chief was astonished. In fact, he still had the white rabbit packed in evidence. What was also striking about Andrea's spontaneous statement was captured in several crime scene photos. Photos taken by police on the morning of the homicide reveal a white cloth rabbit lying in a pool of blood next to the victim's body.

Photos also depict boxes and clothes strewn on the floor. Similarly, Andrea's drawing also portrayed the same items on the floor. She had also drawn the bed in the exact corner where police had photographed it during the investigation. A wall heater and window were also drawn and described accurately by Andrea. When police arrived at the scene, Andrea's sister was sleeping on the end of the bed precisely the way Andrea had drawn the scene four years later. Her picture is found below.

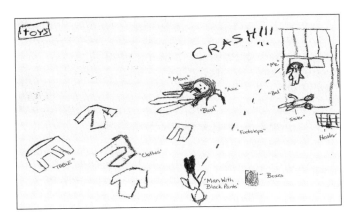

Figure 15. Andrea's Drawing

Andrea's descriptions are compelling because they contain unique details about the crime scene that are corroborated by photographs and police reports. The bed, window, heater, boxes and clutter were all drawn in the same location as photographed in the crime scene. Even the axe, which was possibly the murder weapon, was documented in police records as missing from the residence. Andrea had also encoded, stored and retrieved information about events that occurred earlier in the day.

The suspect description provided by Andrea closely resembled one of the suspects that had been identified by detectives earlier in the investigation. The suspect's girlfriend, a biker, was six feet two inches tall. While caution should be exercised about the reliability of children's descriptions of height, Andrea did describe a female taller than her mother in the argument prior to her mother's death. Andrea had such a visceral response to sounds of a motorcycle, that a biker committing the homicide would not be out of the question. The response may not have been significant in of itself. In conjunction with all of the other data, her extreme reaction was relevant.

In its totality, all of the information provided by Andrea was still fragmented. Pieces of information were missing from the sequence of events. It was still unclear whether Andrea could not remember aspects of the crime or was simply reluctant to report the images given the tremendous anxiety she experienced when recalling the horror.

For a child like Andrea, who provides bits of information in sessions over time, it is important to establish what aspects the child remembers and those she has attempted to "fill in." As Andrea got older, it would be natural for her to try and fill in parts so that the incident would make some sense. Therefore, it is important to instruct child witnesses in cold case homicides to tell you only the information that they remember. Reassure them that it is okay if there is a part they are not sure about. For children who become distressed, proceed slowly, as you don't want to exacerbate any symptoms of stress. Through the course of your contact with the child, identify stress symptoms prior to, during and following the interview.

In Andrea's case, her grandparents were asked to observe any behavioral changes. Andrea herself was also asked about nightmares, night terrors, difficulty breathing and whether or not she could "feel her heart racing." If children or caretakers observing them report signs and symptoms of distress refer the family immediately for support services. Although Andrea's anxiety was readily evident during her interviews, other children may present with more subtle signs of stress.

Children's Emotions When Reporting Stressful Events

A range of emotional responses can be seen during cold case interviews of children who witness homicide. Many children present graphic details in a matter-of-fact way. Others are visibly distraught. Avoid developing opinions about truthfulness or veracity based on the child's emotional presentation. Determining truthfulness of the child's statements belongs to the trier of fact – judge or jury depending upon the proceedings underway. Rather, focus on comparing the information the child has presented with evidence from the crime scene. Some children in cold cases may not remember anything relevant to the criminal investigation. Others will recall the homicide but will be reluctant to discuss their experiences. This too must be respected. Then there will be children like seven year-old Helen.

Helen's Story

Helen was nearly four years old when she went to live with relatives following the death of her brother, Stevie. Stevie died on

December 24th at the age of twenty-three months. An eighteen year-old babysitter had placed a call to 911, stating that the baby wasn't breathing. When emergency personnel responded to the scene, the toddler was in full rigor. Eventually the medical examiner indicated that the death had occurred between four and ten hours earlier. The cause of death was asphyxiation.

Helen and Stevie lived with their mother and her boyfriend. The babysitter who called 911 was Helen's Uncle, Bob. Helen shared a bedroom with Stevie and was in the same room with her brother when he died. Mother, stepfather and Uncle Bob told detectives that it must have been Helen who put a toy into Stevie's crib, leading him to choke to death.

The Crime

Upon entering the residence, investigators located the children's bedroom at the end of the hall. In the bedroom was a crib and a child's bed. A washcloth with red stains thought to be blood was found between the mattress and sidebars of the crib. A plastic egg shaped toy was also in the crib. Another washrag that appeared to have blood on it was observed on the bathroom counter.

The medical examiner's report indicated that Stevie had evidence of recent trauma. Multiple contusions were found throughout his body. Defense wounds were evident on his right hand. There were also abrasions and contusions to the child's lips and old scars were noted on Stevie's scalp. By all accounts, it appeared that Stevie had been a battered child.

Stevie's family resided in this city for only three weeks and a search of local Child Protective Services records revealed no reports about the family. Given the circumstances, however, Helen was taken into the care and custody of the state. Immediately following the discovery of Stevie's body, a counselor at a Child Advocacy Center interviewed Helen. She was difficult to control and ran about the room. She stated that she "couldn't breath in the closet," which did not make much sense at the time of the interview. Additional information was limited. The interviewer did ask Helen a direct and leading question about whether a washrag had been stuffed down Stevie's throat to which she responded "yes." Immediately a list of possible suspects was generated. A second interview with Helen was attempted during the week and she was not able to pay attention to the questions. Due to a number of difficulties, the case was at a standstill.

Who Killed Stevie?

The first difficulty in the case was the presence of several individuals who came in and out of the residence during the window of time that the child was injured. Persons that had access to Stevie included his mother, stepfather, Uncle, and two other adult males who partied at the home. Typical of many child fatality investigations, none of the adults in the home were talking. In fact, they were downright belligerent. After an exhaustive investigation, it was decided that Helen, now four years of age, would testify about the washcloth in front of the grand jury. Detectives felt that her brief statement, along with their evidence implicated mom's boyfriend as the suspect. Reportedly, Helen froze in the grand jury room. When asked questions about the incident, she replied, "I was sleeping." Prosecution of the case was declined and the case file was boxed up for the next several years.

Four years after Stevie's death, a determined and persistent detective decided that it might be worth the effort to re-interview Helen in an effort to bring Stevie's killer to justice. Stevie's memory haunted the detective every Christmas Eve and Helen would now be seven and a half years old. The detective believed that Helen saw what happened on that fateful night but was too young and frightened to provide information to investigators. He wondered if she could remember the information now. Like most other detectives, he was extremely concerned about re-traumatizing the child. He also was uncertain about who had been in contact with Helen over the past several years. The case file was reviewed in order to determine how to proceed.

After reviewing the materials, it appeared that the risk of post-event contamination for Helen would be low. She went to live with her grandparents in another state shortly after the death of Stevie. Helen's grandmother suffered a stroke and now had trouble speaking clearly. It was unlikely that she could influence Helen about events in the past. Helen's grandfather worked two jobs to support his ailing wife and school age granddaughter. He had "disowned" Helen's mother long ago and chose not to discuss any matters related to her. The family resided in a small rural community, which provided no media coverage about child fatality cases that occurred half a continent away. The caretakers had not been privy to crime scene material nor had they questioned Helen about the incident. In fact, they appeared to avoid any discussion of the matter. Even Helen had not discussed the matter with a therapist. Post-event influences were minimal.

Based upon review of the case file, the following hypotheses were generated:

1.   Helen was awake during Stevie's homicide and could describe the entire incident.
2.   Helen was aware of the homicide facts but would be reluctant to relate the information.
3.   Helen was awakened by the incident and could describe part of it.
4.   Helen was not aware of the incident at all.

Arrangements were made to interview Helen. The grandparent's country home appeared cozy with the backyard facing an open school ground where local children were out playing baseball. There was a comfort about the whitewashed picket fence where wild flowers spilled onto the walkway. Rapport building would likely be easy in this setting. As Helen's relatives opened the front screen door, feet scurried and a door slammed as the little girl ran to her bedroom to hide. So much for cozy country homes.

Helen's grandparents indicated that they had not told Helen what the visit was specifically about. They did tell her that some people from Nells were coming to visit. Apparently Helen made the connection that Nells was the city where her brother died. With Helen's approval, a conversation ensued as Helen poked her head out from under the bed. Her gravest concern was whether she was being "taken back to Nells." After Helen was reassured that she was staying with her grandparents she crawled out from her hiding spot, an expansive smile on her face. She was carefully provided an explanation about the purpose of the visit that included the statement, "I talk with girls who have a brother who died." Helen immediately engaged in conversation, replying, "I have a brother and he died." Helen then began to chatter about her home, school, and favorite dolls. She clearly had the capacity to describe events in detail. The question was whether or not she knew what happened to Stevie. There was also one other significant consideration with regard to Helen's interview.

In the state where Stevie's death was investigated, legislation had been enacted that limited the number of contacts with a child victim or witness to three videotaped interviews. The cheery detective had dutifully outlined that there were no exceptions to this regulation.

One patrol officer that inadvertently interviewed a child more than three times spent the night in jail per order of the juvenile court judge. In Helen's case, two interviews were previously attempted. For Helen, this was interview number three.

Since Helen easily developed rapport, inquiry about Stevie's death was introduced quickly. The interview proceeded as follows:

Interviewer: So you said that you had a brother who died...and what was his name?

Helen: Stevie.

Interviewer: I heard that something happened to Stevie and I need you to tell me everything you remember about that so I would know.

Helen: Well, this one night when me and Stevie went to sleep...I wasn't really sleeping. This guy named, Dave, he came into the room and he stuffed a washrag down my brother's throat. After I watched him, he stuck a toy down his throat.

Interviewer: And then what happened?

Helen: He left the room and when he stuck the washrag in Stevie's throat...the washrag he told me to go to sleep ...I tried to tell him to quit but he said if I didn't go back to sleep he would do it to me.

Interviewer: And then what happened?

Helen: He locked the door and he left the room and that's what happened. And one time he locked me and Stevie in the closet and we couldn't breathe.

Interviewer: We'll talk about the closet also. But first, I'm going to ask you some questions to understand better. If I ask you a question you don't understand, tell me or if I say something that isn't correct, please let me know…so what you're saying is this guy named Dave came into the room and stuffed a washrag down Stevie's throat…and a toy…and he thought you were sleeping but you weren't…

Helen: And I was asking him to quit it.

Interviewer: And you were asking him to quit it. You know, I was wondering where you were when Dave stuck the washrag down Stevie's throat?

Helen: I forget the name of the town.

Interviewer: Who were you living with?

Helen: With my mom and Dave, because mom was in love with Dave. And that time when I woke up he had told the babysitter that I did it and I told him "no I didn't."

Interviewer: Who was the babysitter?

Helen: This boy – I don't remember his name…

Interviewer: So you were living with your mom at the time and how old were you when Dave put a washrag in Stevie's throat?

Helen: Three almost four.

Interviewer: Where in the house were you when this happened?

Helen: We were in our room where we slept. We had a bunch of toys.

Helen continued to provide information about the homicide, including the motive for the crime. Stevie wouldn't stop crying so Dave got mad and stuffed the washrag down the child's throat. During Helen's interview she even spontaneously offered information about her grand jury testimony which she described as "trying to talk in front of a bunch of people...but I got scared so I told them I was sleeping." This statement is important because it illustrates a number of points.

First, Helen independently and accurately remembers testifying at the grand jury proceeding, an event equally remote to the homicide. Second, Helen is now old enough to be able to explain earlier inconsistencies, particularly about whether or not she was asleep during the commission of the crime.

During investigations of violent crimes it is not uncommon to have a child witness initially state that they slept through the violence. Children may feel that they will be in trouble if they were supposed to be sleeping but instead were awake during the incident. Some children, curious about the noise, leave their beds to peek only to rush back to the safety of covers. Others, frightened by the sounds and scenes unfolding, pretend to be asleep. And finally, some children in fact are asleep when the violence is unfolding.

Inconsistent statements about sleep can be addressed once a child has the cognitive and language capacity to explain the earlier situation. Sometimes inconsistencies can be addressed by simply asking, "were you asleep the whole time?" Another way of clarifying such information is by feigning confusion and inquiring, "I'm confused, if you were sleeping how did you know what happened to Stevie?" Children often respond with statements such as, "well I heard the noise and then I went to look." This latter method of inquiry also assists in explaining the source of the child's information about the crime.

Source Monitoring

The term "source monitoring" simply refers to whether children can tell you the source of their information. Did the child get the facts about the case from an adult? Is the information from the media? Or is the description based upon actual experience? One way to determine the source of any child's information is to inquire, "how did you know that?" This is particularly important in cold cases where long periods of time can create opportunities for post-event influences. Even young children are able to respond to this inquiry with the typical grammatically poor response, "I know cause I seen it." The following exchange is a good example of source monitoring. During an interview, a seven-year old boy reported the following,

> "My dad shot Phil cause he thought Phil loved my mom...and then he put the gun in the bushes and then he took a taxi to the house...and then my dad shot his self...and I was at Valleyview...Phil was at Albert's...and my dad shot him once in the neck and once in the head...."

It seemed that this child was at one location while the shooting occurred at another. His description of the victim's injuries, however, was accurate. Since English was this child's second language, he could have had difficulty explaining the sequence of events and he may have actually been at the crime scene. The following question, therefore, was asked to determine the source of the child's information:

> "I'm confused, if you were at Valleyview and Phil was at Albert's, how did you know what happened to Phil?" The child replied, "I seen it on the news."

Determining the source of a child's information is important since influences on the child's statement may be inadvertent, as illustrated in the following exchange between a counselor and a child. The counselor stated:

> "Let's play a game where we share secrets. I'll start with mine. When I was a little girl, there was a bad boy who lived down the block. His name was Wayne and he would always want to watch me pee and he would take me out to a field out back by our house. We had a big field behind our house and he would have me take my underpants down and then he would bend over and he would watch me pee. I didn't like it. I felt scared when that person asked me to do that....Okay, your turn...you tell what happened..."

The child responded, "maybe Wayne killed my mother."

This type of technique is most problematic with preschool children and clearly demonstrates the differences between counseling and investigative interview techniques. The exchange is important because if this child witness was interviewed years after the crime and stated, "maybe a man named Wayne killed my mom" the information would probably be inaccurate. Helen, on the other hand was clear about the man who killed her brother. She also placed the suspect in the context of events that routinely occurred during her young life. Her recollection did seem to be a product of witnessing Stevie's death.

The district attorney in this jurisdiction, however, felt that Helen's initial statement about being asleep was too damaging for the case. For now, the story of Stevie's death remains in neatly stacked papers sealed in a box. As you can see, the outcome of a cold case investigation may not be altered simply because a child witness offers new information. In other jurisdictions throughout the country, however, investigators and prosecutors are proceeding to take such cases to trial, relying heavily on the capacity of children to explain to jurors the differences in their recall between "then and now." Whether or not children's statements lead to legal remedies may not be the most important overall consideration for the child witness. There are those who suggest that allowing children the opportunity to provide a clear description of their experiences is itself respectful of their plight. In summary, consider the following suggestions when interviewing children who witnessed violence several years prior.

1.   Review as much material as possible prior interviewing the child witness. Determine if it is likely that the child can contribute new information to the investigation.
2.   Remember that accuracy of memory will not be affected simply by the child's age or the passage of time since the homicide. It is affected by multiple factors such as the situation or type of event, how personally meaningful it was to the child and the degree of influences post-event. A child's memory for remote events will also be affected by how well the event was encoded and stored as well as the manner of memory retrieval.
3.   Determine all possible sources of post-event contamination. Simply because they exist does not mean that an interview should not be conducted. Many children resist suggestion to highly distressing and personally meaningful events.
4.   Extra assurances may be necessary for the child's current caretakers regarding the interview process. Many guardians do not want old wounds opened up for children who witnessed violent crimes years ago. People can confuse interrogation with child interviewing strategies. Take the

time to explain.

5. Since interviews can create symptoms of distress for some children, short sequential interviews may be necessary. Some children may not have received counseling years ago so effective coping strategies might not be developed and healing may not have occurred.

6. Since many child witnesses in cold cases have moved away, plan for adequate time to conduct sequential interviews.

7. When interviewing children who have moved away, identify crisis intervention and support personnel prior to interviewing a child. You don't want to conduct an interview and then leave a child and family without support following your departure.

8. Leave children and families with a way to contact you if the child remembers more information. Sometimes the task of answering questions about the crime triggers a flood of memories that come later.

9. For those children that do not remember the violence, don't push for information.

Sometimes, the shear brutality of a homicide leads interviewers to press a bit harder than normal for the information to solve a crime. This can lead to heightened anxiety and activity by a young child witness during an interview. The most skilled and effective cold case investigators take their time, have patience and recognize that sometimes, the child just isn't going to offer much. Many investigators indicate that the most problematic interviews seem to be with young children who can't seem to sit still. Wandering all over the room, they are distracted and difficult to keep on task. Chapter six offers some suggestions for interviewing young, highly active children.

Managing Active Children During Interviews

The detective present at the autopsy grimaced at the steady voice of the medical examiner speaking into the microphone. "Identification is made by the Medical Examiner's tag on the body bag. The body is clothed only by a disposable diaper – this is the well nourished body of a Caucasian female child appearing the stated age of approximately two years and three months...the scalp hair is dark brown and the eyes show brown irises with pale conjunctivae...the ears are normally formed." For a moment, Detective Olsen closed his eyes.

Any cop will tell you. No matter how many autopsies you've been to, the coroner's examination of a child will always get to you. This one was particularly disturbing. It was close to 1:30 in the afternoon when Detective Olsen finally received the cause of death, formally stated as follows:

Cause of Death: Blunt force injuries of the abdomen
Manner: Homicide
Opinion: Consistent with a homicidal manner of death due to exsanguinations and shock resulting from blunt force injury of the abdomen that has resulted in a laceration of the small bowel and its mesentery with abundant hemorrhage into the abdominal cavity. Evidence of sexual assault.

The ten-page report detailed the injuries further. The body chart indicated that bruises were found on the right abdominal wall. There was a laceration of the bowel that showed extensive hemorrhage of the edges of the laceration. A lot of blood (600 cc.) was found in the abdominal cavity. There was hemorrhage involving the renal pad of the left kidney and small hemorrhage of the left ligament of the inner pelvis. There were blunt force injuries of the vagina, anus and rectum. The injuries had been inflicted prior to death.

There were also light purple bruises slightly above the left eye and a one and one quarter inch maroon bruise on the upper mid-forehead which indicated a deep hemorrhage of this tissue section. In a nutshell, it was likely that someone beat the two-year-old baby and sexually assaulted her as well. The physical and sexual assault would have been painful and eventually, she bled out into the abdomen and died.

Preliminary Statements

Back at the station, Detective Olsen's partner was getting a preliminary statement from Jack, the mom's boyfriend. Jack stated that he had run across the street to get a pack of cigarettes when the child's mom arrived home from work to find her six year-old son lying down on the bed beside his sister. The little girl was not breathing. Jack was enraged that six year-old Andy could have hurt his sister so badly. He stated that the children had been in the room playing while he watched TV earlier in the day. Jack admitted that he had not checked on them for a couple of hours. Both children were reportedly fine when their mother left for work.

In the early part of the investigation, it became apparent that the children's mother, Janice, was mentally challenged. Past IQ testing had placed her in the mildly mentally retarded range. She held down a packing job at a manufacturing plant. In fact, instead of calling 911 from her home, when she noticed that her daughter wasn't breathing, she packed the child and her son into the car and drove to the nearest hospital for help. It was emergency room personnel who told her that there was nothing more they could do for the child.

Detective Olsen, himself, had spoken to Janice. She was inconsolable, blaming herself for letting Andy look after his little sister. She had picked up on Jack's story that somehow Andy had caused the death of his little sister. She did, however, indicate that Jack was her new boyfriend and she really didn't know much about him.

Jack had come into her life about three months ago when Janice's friend put an ad in the single's paper. She wanted Janice to meet someone and get out of the house once in a while. About one week after the ad ran, Jack called and left his name. Janice met him at a local nightclub. He was stationed at the air force base and seemed like a responsible guy. He had his own place off base and within two weeks they had moved in together. Jack stated that it would be easier for Janice financially if he could baby-sit the kids while Janice worked. Jack had even talked with her about marriage and he wanted to adopt the children. He seemed to especially like Janice's son, Andy.

Andy's First Interview

According to the neighbors, Andy was a boisterous six year-old who loved to play with toy soldiers. He was quick to warm up to most people. The same was true now. Police Officers had transported Andy to a children's program for a medical examination and a videotaped investigative interview. Eying the paper and crayons on a nearby table, Andy readily climbed into the interview chair, stating, "I want to color some pictures." The videotaped interview revealed the following initial questions and responses:

Interviewer: You want to color, Okay, let me pull the table over. ..

Andy: I want to color my own pictures...

Interviewer: Your own, okay...

Andy: I can draw...but you have to sit there and I'm going here.

As Andy began drawing, he got up and down from the chair and proceeded to move around the room. In an effort to get the child back in the chair, the interviewer stated, "I need you to sit down here...I heard something happened to you and I need you to tell me about that as best you can." The interview continued:

Andy: Tommy hurt me at school.

Interviewer: Who is Tommy?

Andy: He's a brown boy.

Interviewer: Is he your size or somebody bigger than you?

Andy: Some...one size bigger than me...I'm making a hat on the picture.

119

Interviewer: I think I'll color a picture too...

Andy: Here, you can use this paper but you can't use these crayons...

The interview continued with Andy focusing on coloring and intermittently responding to questions from the interviewer. Clearly, Andy was in control of the interview.

Taking Control Of The Interview

It is difficult to retrospectively evaluate interviews for ultimately the judgment to ask a particular question or not is the province of each interviewer. Andy was not an easy child to interview. Constantly moving about the room, he was difficult to keep on task. Like most young children, Andy was not the type of child that could do well in an interview room with a lot of distractions such as toys. His level of activity was a challenge to even the most experienced of interviewers. There are a number of ways to manage a child who has difficulty focusing and paying attention to interview questions.

If a child's activity appears to be the product of anxiety, offer the child something to hold in his hands. Objects that can be squeezed are helpful along with those that have smooth services such as polished rocks. If the child is still unable to sit still and focus on verbal tasks such as answering questions, offer drawing materials but use them to your advantage by requesting that the child draw something relevant to the investigation.

For children who have difficulty sitting, placing a colorful blanket on the chair or couch where they are seated is helpful. Choose a blanket with vertical stripes that can clearly be seen by the child. Once the child is seated, inform him or her that while talking, kids that sit here keep their feet right between the two lines on the blanket. Encourage the child to see if they are able to do the same. Most children rise to the occasion since they want to be able to accomplish the task. Limiting children's movement in this way allows them to focus on your questions. Consider the following interview segment from an interview with Andy once he was encouraged to keep his feet between the vertical lines on a blanket:

Interviewer: I talk with boys all day long. And I talk with boys who have a sister that died. I heard you had a sister and I need to know her name.

Andy: Sarah. Her got murdered.

Interviewer: Her got murdered...tell me what happened."

Andy: Eight times like this...eight times he punched her in the belly.

Interviewer: Eight times. Who punched her in the belly?

Andy: His name is Jack.

Interviewer: Where were you when Jack punched Sarah in the belly?

Andy: And he did the same thing to me but I never died.

Interviewer: He did the same thing to you?

Andy: And I was in her bedroom when he punched her.

Interviewer: So you're in the bedroom and what's the first thing that happened?

Andy: He put a pillow over my face and then he punched her belly.

Interviewer: And then what happened?

Andy: He punched her in the belly and then threw her.

Interviewer: And then what happened?

Andy: Even I couldn't talk or breathe.

Interviewer: You couldn't breath. I was kinda confused, if you had the pillow over your face, how could you see what happened to Sarah?

Andy:	She was crying like that and I turned around to see and him was doing this (punches self in the stomach)
Interviewer:	How come Jack punched your sister in the belly?
Andy:	Cause her touched the TV and Jack say "don't!" and her still did it.
Interviewer:	What did Jack hit Sarah with when he hit her belly?
Andy:	His fist.
Interviewer:	Where was mommy when Jack hit Sarah in the belly?
Andy:	Her was at work...and she got home and we went to the hospital.
Interviewer:	And then what happened?
Andy:	(jumps down from chair and starts to wander to the window to look outside).

For Andy, an extremely active child, this short sequence of questions and responses was highly productive. His activity level diminished once he began focusing on the task of answering questions. Note that early in the sequence of questions, Andy responded using the word, "murder." While use of the term needs clarification, with an active child, continue requesting information about what happened instead of immediately inquiring what the word means or where it was learned. While this clarification is important, the overall intent is to obtain a description of the acts that occurred versus the meaning of the event. Towards the end of the interview, attempt to clarify the use of overly sophisticated words. For example in Andy's case one could state, "you know when we first started talking you used the word murder. I'm wondering how you know that word" or "I'm wondering what makes you think that Jack murdered your sister."

The same principle holds true when interviewing individuals reporting other types of crimes. For example, when a child states, " I was molested" or an adult states, "I was raped" it is less effective to ask, "what does molested mean." Instead the interviewer encourages the child to produce a narrative with statements such as "you said you were molested - tell me what happened so I would understand."

Clarification at the end of the interview allows the investigative interview to flow better and limits digressions dealing with "definitions." Remember, at a minimum, the purpose of the interview is to find out what happened in as much detail using developmentally appropriate, non-leading techniques. There will be some highly active children, however, who are not able to attend to questions during an investigative interview. The focus of the investigation, therefore, shifts to the adults. In Andy's case, Detective Olsen had already begun a comprehensive interview of Jack.

The Interrogation of Jack

In his usual methodical manner, Detective Olsen had decided to thoroughly interrogate the mother's boyfriend. He had already run Jack through the NCIC computer for his criminal background and found no prior offenses. Detective Olsen, however, was prepared. He even had a copy of an old traffic ticket that Jack had received in Illinois while visiting his parents last year. Olsen wanted Jack to think he knew everything about him. Jack had come in voluntarily for the interview. Jack, however, was still the main suspect.

Detective Olsen knew that Jack was a military man. He had stayed in the military for the past seven years, comfortable with the regimen and rigidity that came with the job. Olsen knew that bolstering Jack's ego was the way to the truth. He began the interview praising Jack for taking care of this mother and her two children, stating, "you brought Janice and her two children in. They've had a hard life and you're trying to make it better. You and Janice had obviously talked about getting married – were you thinking about adopting the kids?" Jack replied,

> "We had talked about me adopting the boy –
> cause he would say stuff like, would you be my
> daddy and stuff like that. In fact from the get go,
> they were both calling me daddy but Janice was
> saying that it would not be a good idea for me to
> adopt the girl because she was on social

123

security and if I adopted her then she wouldn't get it anymore. Something along those lines so I would wait on the girl...you know, cause I loved that little girl...every now and then she would go back to calling me Jack, but I got her back saying daddy all the time..."

The interview continued, with Jack indicating that the little girl had not been herself the past couple of weeks. She had a cold and was always cranky.

Detective Olsen started out broadly, "was there anything that she did that really bothered you?" Jack replied, "well she was moody and cranky, always asking for her brother when he was gone to school but nothing really other than that." A more pointed question from the detective followed. "When was the last time that you ever slapped her...and by the way, get your foot off the table." Jack replied, "sure, sorry. Um, not that I can remember, I don't think I ever slapped her." The interview continued as follows:

Detective:	"Either you slapped her or you didn't."
Jack:	"Not that I remember – I don't think."
Detective:	Have you ever disciplined her?
Jack:	Well yes as a matter of fact I have.
Detective:	Tell me about that.
Jack:	Well yesterday, I remember yelling at her for playing with the TV set. I yelled at her to where she was scared and crying. I said, "don't play with that TV – don't touch it!"
Detective:	Is that when you slapped her?
Jack	I ...I um...I didn't – I don't know...
Detective:	Did her behavior upset you?
Jack	Yes it did.
Detective:	Did it piss you off?
Jack:	It frustrated me...I didn't know why she was upset or crying...but I never slapped her.
Detective:	We have to establish a couple of things here. One is you need to be a little more honest with me than you have been. And two, you need to be a lot more honest with me, Okay.
Jack:	In what ways cause I don't know...
Detective:	When was the last time you struck her?

Jack:	I don't know.
Detective:	Was it Wednesday?
Jack:	No
Detective:	Was it Thursday?
Jack:	No
Detective:	I'm asking you a real simple question, when is the last time you struck her…it's a simple question – when?
Jack:	"Okay, I've struck her – slapped her, um spanked her…but I don't want this to look like anything I have done…"
Detective:	Don't lie to me anymore – do you understand that?
Jack:	Yes sir.
Detective:	Let's talk man to man here. If you struck her, you struck her. So don't make yourself look like a fool by lying.
Jack:	Okay, she was probably playing with the TV set and I think I slapped her…her hands…
Detective:	Could you have hit her?
Jack:	It's a possibility but I didn't kill her…
Detective:	Is it possible that you hit her harder than you probably wanted to?
Jack:	Yes, and sometimes she zig zags when she tries to run away.
Detective:	How many times did you hit her?
Jack:	I don't remember.
Detective:	Was it more than twice?
Jack:	Yes.
Detective:	What time was it that you lost your cool this morning?
Jack:	It was about ten thirty in the morning. I was getting ready to take a shower and she was fiddling with the TV.
Detective:	And then what happened?
Jack:	I don't know – I just lost it…I just swung a couple of times…I didn't swing more than ten times…but I actually hit her about three to five times…you gotta understand now I'm very upset and I'm not taking into account how many times I'm swinging

	or hitting.
Detective:	Believe me Jack, I understand that. You had lost your cool.
Jack:	Yes, yes that is true...
Detective:	You could have hit her in the abdomen?
Jack:	Yes when she was trying to get away from me and she made um she fell down on the floor and I think I was just hitting in the direction that she was on the floor...and I hit in the direction that she was crying and she was crying...and then I got to the point where I realized this is no longer spanking a child, this is you know, beating and I love this child...I should have just spanked her once. I should have not even used a fist...You know...I think I need a lawyer. Maybe I need some legal representation or something...

I think we all get the picture here. The interview was terminated and no further questions were asked. Understandably, no information was obtained regarding possible sexual abuse of Andy's sister as documented by the medical examiner. The priority was to obtain information about the blunt force trauma to the abdomen that resulted in the child's death. The skillful detective obtained a confession from Jack. The investigation, however, was far from over. Andy's mother, Janice, offered the following pieces of information.

Information From Janice

Janice, a mentally challenged adult, stated that since her daughter's death, she moved from Jack's home to a small, subsidized apartment complex. She was currently working at a nearby McDonald's Restaurant. Janice was tearful throughout the interview, stating that she was worried about Andy. She had noticed bruises at times on Andy's face in the past but stated that Jack told her Andy was fighting at school. Janice also stated that she had seen bruises on her daughter's face in the past, however, she attributed them to some corrective eye surgery that the child had about a month prior to her death. Janice was asked if she had ever noticed anything else that Jack did which was "kind of unusual" to her. Janice responded as follows.

On several occasions Janice would awaken at night to hear her daughter crying. During these instances, Jack was missing from their bed. Janice would find him in her daughter's bedroom, "standing over her bed." Janice stated that on one occasion, she asked Jack what he was doing to which he replied, "What do you think. I'm changing her because she pissed all over me." During one of these incidents, Jack told her, "you better get up and look after your kids when they cry because if you don't, I'll end up killing them." At the time, Janice did not know how ominous the threat really was.

Janice denied any physical abuse to herself by Jack. She stated, that he frequently made her "feel bad" because he called her a "big, fat, welfare bitch." On the morning that her daughter died, the child was crying hysterically and did not want her mother to go to work. Andy wasn't feeling well so he stayed home from Kindergarten that day. And so it would be that Andy was potentially the only witness to the death of his sister.

In an effort to determine if Janice influenced her son, she was asked what she told Andy about the death of his sister. Janice replied, "the only thing I said was that Jack probably murdered your sister." Given Janice's limited cognitive abilities, she was asked if she understood what injuries were found on her daughter. Janice, replied, "no, I think she died from a bloated stomach."

Based on the information from Janice, along with Andy's earlier statement, Andy was asked the following questions in reference to possible physical abuse.

Interviewer: Did Jack ever do anything to you?

Andy: Yeh he slapped me.

Interviewer: What did Jack slap you with?

Andy: His hand and he said, "shut up" that's all and him… um he told me to say it was at school.

Interviewer: At school?

Andy: Yeh that I was fighting at school but I wasn't…but now I did. I got in trouble at school now.

Interviewer: You do?

Andy: Yeh. I don't know why but this kid made me mad

Interviewer: I see…well.

Once again, Andy got distracted. This time, however, the verbal task was switched to a drawing task. Andy was asked to draw where he was when something happened to his sister. In this particular case, there was prior discussion during the planning phase about using the police drawing to have Andy indicate where he was at the time of his sister's death. Architectural drawings, however, can be confusing to young children given their limited understanding of spatial concepts. For example, contrast the following police drawing with the one produced by Andy.

Figure 16. Layout of Residence Prepared By Police

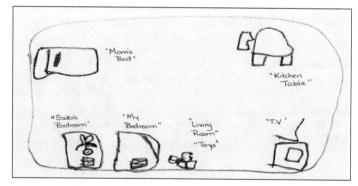

Figure 17. Andy's Drawing

If the police drawing had been used to have Andy point out where he was during the homicide, he might well have pointed to a spot that was not accurate. Note, however, the relative accuracy of his drawing compared to the police sketch.

Using Photographs of a Residence
While I do not advocate the use of crime scene drawings, neutral photographs of the crime scene location can cue recall for young, particularly active children. Neutral photographs are those that do not have any crime scene tape, evidence markers or investigators in the background of the photos. For the child who is easily distracted, limit your selection to three or four pictures.

Place the pictures in front of the child and ask him to identify the pictures. For example, if the crime occurred in a residence, ask the child to identify the various rooms. Generate some conversation about what happens in each room. Then ask children to identify where they were when something happened to the victim. Using a marker, have the child place an "X" on the photo to indicate where he or she was when the victim got hurt. Request the same information with regard to the victim's whereabouts.

If the child places him or herself in a location that does not permit visibility of the victim, feign confusion, stating, "Goodness, I'm confused. If you were over here, how did you see what happened to the (victim)?" This question generally produces a wealth of information about the sequence of the events. Alternately, the response may indicate that the child did not see what happened but may have heard or been told about the incident. A variety of clarifying questions can then be asked depending upon the circumstances of the case. Some investigators have inquired whether taking a child to the crime scene might be helpful, particularly for an active child who needs to move around.

Returning to the Crime Scene
The intent of returning to a crime scene would be to cue a child's recall or to more specifically identify what occurred during the homicide. My experience with this technique has not been positive. In one circumstance, a child was taken through a home where the dust used to collect fingerprint evidence was still on the walls. The residence was in total disarray. Apparently when the child entered the home, she took one look, turned around and said she didn't live

129

there. In another instance, a child was taken out to a remote area to assist investigators with identifying the location of a body. In route, she became distraught and began to hyperventilate. Rather than attempt these procedures, use neutral photographs of a residence or crime scene location to assist a child in providing an explanation. If photographs or drawings are used be prepared at times for criticism.

Pictures and Drawings

Given that you are using pictures to cue children's recall, there will be those who feel that the pictures, themselves, are suggestive. While I don't agree that neutral pictures are suggestive of facts about a crime, it doesn't hurt to examine the suggestibility of the child at the end of this task. One way to accomplish this is to feign confusion. For example, if a child has pointed to a place on a photograph earlier in the interview, one could select a different spot, stating, "Now I'm sorry. I forgot. Was this where you were when (victim) got hurt?" Most children will correct you, stating, "No, I told you I was over here." Such a reply is helpful in demonstrating this particular child is not suggestible.

If a child accepts the suggestion and does not correct you, pursue an explanation. For example, state, "I'm confused, or made a mistake. Earlier, I thought you said you were standing here." The child might feel intimidated and not want to correct an authority figure. On the other hand, if the child is suggestible, consider the information offered by the child with caution. Although Andy did not appear to be a suggestible child, there were those who criticized other aspects of his interview.

Criticisms of Andy

Some professionals felt that Andy was too "bubbly" while relating the aspects of his sister's death. Given that he was a highly active child, Andy's emotions were labile – laughing at something that caught his attention one minute and solemn during other parts of the interview. When criticisms about children's emotional presentations arise, direct evaluators to the content of the interview.

Andy was a six-year-old child who specifically reported that Jack inflicted blows to his sister's abdomen. At his age, he would not understand that these acts caused a lacerated bowel resulting in the death of his sister. His accuracy regarding the nature of the act actually enhances the quality of his statement. In addition, Andy would not yet understand that death is irreversible. Although Andy had been told that his sister was in heaven, he still looked for her when he came home from school. Why then, would one expect a high level of distress if Andy did not fully understand the complex situation that he witnessed?

Yet another criticism of Andy was that he could not fully recite his "ABC's" nor produce a lengthy narrative in response to the question designed to assess his language style. Although a child's inability to recite his ABC's tells us something about his environment and academic skills, it does not automatically mean that he or she is unable to tell us what happened. Reciting "ABC's" is a performance task. It comes with practice. Using it to determine a child's ability to relate an event is not appropriate.

An expert hired by the defense attorney suggested that Andy was an unreliable witness because he incorporated a fantastic element into his statement. During one of the interviews, Andy reported that he kicked and punched Jack, killing him so that his sister could run away. It is not uncommon for children who witness homicide to indicate what they would have liked to have happen, particularly acts that include saving the victim.[33] One can imagine the helplessness children experience when confined in a room with an enraged adult, inflicting injuries that kill.

If the concern about "unreliability" is related to the appearance of inconsistency between interviews, carefully examine the exact questions that were asked of the child in each interview. Review the videotape to determine if the child was even paying attention to the question or engaged in a different activity. In Andy's case, few questions related to the actual crime were asked of Andy during his initial interview. When the interview was structured so that he could keep his feet between lines on the blanket Andy was able to pay attention and answer several questions about the homicide. His greatest difficulty was with the sequence of events.

Highly distracted children who have difficulty attending to and organizing information may be more likely to leave something out of the sequence of events giving the appearance of implausibility. For example, a child may state, "Mommy was reading to us and Daddy hit her head on the cupboard." Assist the child who provides this type of response by stating, "Mommy was reading to you and what happened next?" Continue to assist the child in sequencing the event by inquiring "and then what happened very next" until the interactions have reached a logical conclusion.

Describing a sequence of traumatic events is a highly complex task for any child, and especially difficult for those with attention difficulties. Their problems, however, should not be mistaken for those of inaccuracy. Accuracy of information is best determined by examining evidence collected at the crime scene and through the course of the investigation. The following pilot project was a preliminary attempt to determine if some questions are better than others in eliciting accurate information about homicides committed by family members.

CHAPTER SEVEN

Children's Accuracy In Describing Homicide of a Family Member: *Preliminary Research Findings*

In 1997 some students and I set out to test the prediction that children's narratives, found in cognitive interviews about homicides, would provide the highest degree of accuracy about crime scene facts. Although early studies of cognitive interviews with adults resulted in findings of increased effectiveness compared with standard police interviews, more recent attempts to replicate findings have resulted in problems. Research conducted by Memon, Bull and colleagues found that the cognitive interview does not always facilitate recall.[34] Still others have indicated that there may be an increase in the frequency of errors committed during cognitive interviews.[35]

While some researchers indicate that the increase in error rates may be due to more questions being asked during cognitive interviews, others speculate that factors affecting memory in lab settings are different than those in real world contexts.[36] The ultimate aim in this research, therefore, was to examine if children could provide accurate information about the central elements of a homicide. If so, where in child witness interviews would information be reported most accurately? Since there were no studies that systematically examined this question, we hoped that our field-based research would contribute to knowledge about interviewing children in real-life contexts.

Method

Police agencies in two jurisdictions agreed to participate in the study. When a homicide investigation involved interviews of child witnesses, a modified cognitive interview protocol would be used. The frequency of children's responses to narratives would be examined. In addition, the types of questions that resulted in accurate information about a crime scene would be identified and analyzed. Only those cases that included a confession from the defendant, along with data that verified the child had been at the scene, would be included in the sample. Consent was obtained to examine the interview transcripts once all matters had been resolved in the criminal justice system. The sample, therefore, took several years to acquire.

Participants
Data were collected from forty-two children (23 male and 19 female). The children were identified as being present at the scene during the homicide of a family member. Children in this sample were between the ages of seven and fourteen with a mean age of eight years and two months. Children younger than seven years old were not included in the sample since they have limited language and metamemory skills. Eighty three percent of the children were Caucasian, nine percent Hispanic, six percent African American and two percent Native American.

Police in homicide investigations identified children for the study. Consent was obtained from legal guardians to examine the interview transcripts and case files once the criminal matters were resolved. The interviews were part of the ongoing criminal investigation and all children were considered for the sample if they met the study criteria of age. Two years after the interviews were conducted, only those cases that included a confession from the defendant were selected for review of interview transcripts. All case files were made available to the researcher following the criminal disposition of the case.

The Interviews
The interviews were requested by law enforcement as part of the ongoing investigation. All interviews were conducted immediately upon request of the police. Interviews occurred between two and twelve days following discovery of the body. The average delay in interviewing was four days. All of the interviews were videotaped.

The interviewer had over ten years of training in a modified cognitive interview technique. The modified cognitive interview protocol described in Chapter one was used as the interview protocol. The following modifiers were identified relative to each interview component.
- Rapport Building
- Neutral conversation was designed to establish comfort of the child as well as obtain a language sample.
- Obtaining a Narrative
  "I understand that something happened to your (victim). Think back to everything you remember and tell me as best you can what happened."
- Cued Recall Questions
  Based on information in the narrative one word was selected to cue the child.
- Direct Questions
  Who, what, where and how questions were asked.
- Neutral Closure

Once rapport was established, in an attempt to direct children to free recall, each child was instructed to report only what had happened. The account from the child was to be used later to develop cued recall and direct questions. If the child did not offer a narrative, direct questions were asked. When a direct question was asked, if the child responded, the interviewer followed with a request for a narrative. Children were informed that if they did not know the answer to a question that it was okay to say, "I don't know."

Coding and Scoring of Transcripts
All of the videotaped interviews were transcribed in their entirety. The transcripts were then coded and scored. The transcripts were examined for:
- frequency of response to the initial request for a narrative
- category of information recalled
- type of questions that resulted in accurate crime scene information.
The coding scheme for categories of information included:
- suspect identification
- location of the crime

- actions perpetrated against the victim
- identification of the murder weapon
- interactions such as conversation between defendant and victim
- motivation of the defendant

Research assistants then documented where in the interview information was found about each category. The questions were coded according to the following:

- open-ended
- cued recall
- direct questions

If information was provided in the free recall phase in response to the open-ended question, it was only scored during the cued-recall and direct questions phases if new information was added. Once the information was coded regarding where in the interview the response was located, data was compared with crime scene facts for accuracy.

Based on information in the case file, the child's recall was classified as:

- accurate
- error
- confabulation
- unknown

Accurate recall showed a match between the child's report and a fact in the case file. Error statements were coded if the child indicated that a detail was incorrect such as the color of a suspect's vehicle. Confabulations were identified if information was provided that could not possibly have occurred such as the description of a fantasy character committing the crime. If the case file did not include corroborating information about an aspect of the crime, the information was coded as unknown.

Prior to scoring the transcripts in this sample, the assistants independently scored ten other interview transcripts of children who were not included in this sample. The correlations of the two coders' scores are recorded in the following table.

Table 1. *Correlations of the Coders' Scoring*

Child's Recall	Types of Questions
Accuracy, r=.97 p<.001	Open-ended, r=.99 p<.001
Errors, r=.92 p<.001	Cued Recall, r=.97 p<.001
Confabulations, r=.99 p<.001	Direct Questions, r=.97 p<.001

Information About the Crimes

The majority of the children (55%) witnessed the homicide of their mother or step-mother. Six children witnessed the death of a sibling and five were present at the homicide of their father. The relationship between the children and the deceased is reflected in Table 2.

Table 2. *Relationship Between Children and the Deceased*

Relationship of Deceased to Child	Number of Victims
Mother	15
Step-Mother	8
Sibling	6
Father	5
Aunt	3
Uncle	2
Grandparent	2
Cousin	2

Note: The total number of victims is 43 as one child witnessed the homicide of both his mother and father during the same incident.

The types of injuries inflicted on the victims are recorded in Table 3. Many of the victims suffered several types of injuries. Most of the victims had bruises or scrapes. Guns and knives caused the most frequent life-threatening injuries. In two separate cases, the bodies had been dismembered.

Table 3. Types of Injuries Suffered By Victims

Injury	Number of Victims
Bruises and scratches	38
Gunshot wounds	14
Stabbings	12
Trauma to head	11
Trauma to abdomen	10
Retinal hemorrhages	7
Fractures	7
Injuries to genitals	5
Dismemberment	2
Other	2

Results

Frequency of Narrative Responses To Initial Open-ended Question

Out of the total sample, twenty-seven children (64%) offered narrative responses to the initial open-ended request for a description of what happened. Thirteen of the children (31%) responded to the open-ended question with only one sentence. Two children did not respond to the request for a narrative. One of these children was crying when she arrived for her interview. She continued to weep when the interview began.

Of the thirteen children who did not offer a narrative in response to the inquiry, ten had provided narratives when discussing neutral topics in the rapport building phase. Three children responded to the initial open-ended question with, "I don't know." Of these three children, two later provided information to the interviewer in response to cued recall or direct questions.

Categories of Information

The percentage of children who reported accurate information in specific categories is recorded in Table 4.

Table 4. Accuracy of Children's Reports in Specific Categories

Information Category	% Children Reporting	No. Children Committing Errors	No. of Children Confabulating	Accuracy Unknown
Suspect I.D.	95	0	1	0
Location	95	0	0	0
Violent Acts	90	1	1	0
Murder Weapon	86	2	0	0
Interactions	83	1	0	12
Motivation Of Defendant	69	4	0	8

Ninety five percent of the children reported the suspect's identity as well as the location of the crime. Only one child confabulated the suspect's identity, stating that "a lion" killed his mother. Ninety percent of the children reported violent acts that occurred to the victim. Only one child committed an error in the nature of the act and one confabulated that "a lion chewed up my mother." The murder weapon was identified by eighty six percent of the children. Two children incorrectly identified the weapon. Interactions between the victim and defendant were described by eighty three percent of the children. Many of the interactions were difficult to verify based upon the case file. Likewise, motivation for the homicide was not always found in the file, however, defendant confessions did offer some corroboration for children's descriptions of motivation. Sixty nine percent of the children offered an explanation about why the crimes occurred.

<u>Types of Questions That Resulted In Disclosure</u>
The following graph indicates the percentage of children reporting specific crime scene facts in response to the three categories of questions.

Graph 1. Questions Resulting In Specific Crime Scene Facts

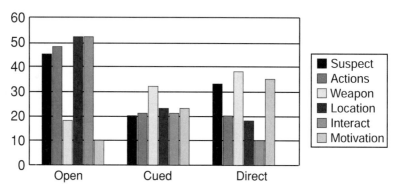

Suspect identification occurred most of the time in response to open-ended questions, however over one third of the children still required the direct question, "who did something to your (victim)? The violent acts committed against the victim were found largely in narratives, as were interactions such as conversation between the victim and defendant. Direct or cued recall questions were required in the majority of cases (72%) to obtain information about the murder weapon. The location of the crime was offered by over fifty percent of children in response to the initial open-ended request to tell about what happened. Motivation for the crime was not readily offered in the early narrative. Rather, the question, "do you know how come the (defendant) hurt your (victim)?" resulted in more information about motivation for the homicide. In addition, direct questions about conversation between the victim and defendant alerted children to reasons for the crime.

Summary of Findings
While the sample size in this study is small, the results do offer us some insight about interviewing children who witness homicide.

140

Overall, the findings indicate that children must be afforded a variety of opportunities to fully describe their experiences. While over half of the children provided narrative responses to the initial open-ended question, almost one third still required cued recall or direct questions to provide important information about the homicide.

Of the children who did not respond to the initial open-ended request, several had been exposed to extremely cruel and torturous crimes. For example, two separate children who witnessed dismemberment did not offer any narrative responses. Likewise, a child who witnessed the execution style killing of both his parents required cued prompts and direct questions throughout most of the interview. A variety of questions, therefore, are useful in interview protocols with children who witness homicide.

It is important to note that most of the child witnesses in this sample reported information with remarkable accuracy. Suspect identification was offered by ninety five percent of the children and only one child confabulated a response. This was a seven-year old child whose mother was dismembered. His explanation involved a lion killing his mother. Throughout the interview he appeared numb, still in a state of shock.

One might argue that suspect identification is easier in cases of family violence because the child most likely knows the defendant. Family violence resulting in homicide is a terrifying incident for a child. One could counter that fear and possible alignment with family members would result in children refusing to identify the suspect. It was evident that for one child, terror had resulted in his inability to provide much of any investigative information. The majority of children, however, were able to accurately provide suspect identification.

Likewise, location of the crime was accurately reported by all of the children who offered this information. Most of the homicides occurred in family residences, which increases the likelihood that children would be accurate about the location of the crime. Three of the children, however, accompanied the defendant to a different location where the body was disposed. Two of these children accurately described where the body could be found. The third child accompanied the defendant during the night making it difficult for him to describe the surroundings.

A significant number of children (90%) accurately described the violent acts that were inflicted on the victims. Most of these children described the specific acts in their narratives. This was considerably different than identification of the murder weapon, which frequently required the use of direct questions. For example, a child who provided the information, "daddy shot mommy" still required the question, "what did daddy shoot mommy with?"

Understandably, motivation for the crime was difficult for children to describe. In response to direct questions, sixty nine percent of the children offered an explanation for the defendant's behavior. Motivation included jealousy, drug deal retaliations, "accidents," being served with protection orders and/or divorce papers, family fights over money, alcoholism or drug use, and self-defense from another family member. The accuracy of the children's speculations was difficult to substantiate as not all of the defendants' confessions revealed the motivations for the homicides.

In conclusion, the majority of the school age children in this sample poignantly illustrated that they were capable of accurately describing central elements of a homicide that they witnessed. Although this study would have been more rigorous had there been more than one interviewer, a larger sample size, and multiple coders, preliminary findings show promise about children's effectiveness as witnesses when faced with frightening and dramatic events.

Although one cannot generalize the findings of this study to larger populations, these results do indicate that children can report information accurately in both narrative parts of speech and in limited responses to direct questions. Factors associated with the homicide, along with individual differences and the degree of distress manifested by the child are important for interviewers to consider when asking children to provide reliable evidence.

Different forms of violence produce diverse challenges for interviewers. For example, a child who witnesses several people killed in a bomb explosion may require different strategies for interviews and interventions than one who witnesses the shooting of a family member. Over the next decade, perhaps more field-based studies will examine both the capacities and burdens faced by child witnesses to violence. Of particular concern is the large group of children in this nation who witness chronic domestic violence. Children exposed to multiple episodes of violence require specialized interventions. Chapter eight discusses the vulnerabilities of children who routinely live with violence with their homes.

CHAPTER EIGHT

Children Who Witness Domestic Violence

"It is neither easy nor agreeable to dredge this abyss of viciousness, and yet I think it must be done, because what could be perpetrated yesterday could be attempted again tomorrow, could overwhelm us and our children..."

Primo Levi

Concern regarding children exposed to domestic violence has increased in the past decade as more evidence has substantiated the negative impact of witnessing abuse. Children can present with a host of behavioral and emotional problems due to witnessing violence in the home. The findings consistently bear out that children of battered women are more likely to be depressed and anxious.[37] Other difficulties such as aggression, evidence of lower school achievement and difficulties with social problem solving have also been identified.[38]

In order to provide effective interventions with children who are raised in violent homes, it is important to note that a substantial number of children are in close proximity to the violence. Many actually witness the infliction of injury as opposed to overhearing arguments or battering. Investigators who have specifically asked women where their children were during the violence found that in ninety percent of the cases, children are either in the same or next room.[39] This intensifies the helplessness experienced by child.

Other factors besides proximity to the violence affect the impact of domestic violence on children. Child factors such as cognitive abilities, coping skills, and temperament will impact the psychological adjustment of children in violent homes. Likewise, situational

143

variables such as the intensity and duration of the violence will affect children's mental health. Few of these variables have been extensively studied in the context of domestic violence. So how exactly does the witnessing of domestic violence exert an impact on children?

One model that helps explain the mechanisms that impact children includes both direct and indirect catalysts. Children's behaviors such as aggression can be the direct result of modeling parental behaviors.[40] Children copy what they see parents do. In addition, if a parent batters, there is an implication that since the behavior is acceptable to adults, it can also be acceptable if perpetrated by the child.

Indirectly, children's emotional and behavioral difficulties can be the result of emotional unavailability of parents who are victims or perpetrators of domestic violence.[41] A parent who is battered is likely to become depressed which will also limit the emotional availability of that parent to the child. Children with parents who are unavailable emotionally have more difficulty in relating to others. Parents who batter tend to have poor interactions with both adults and children. Lack of insight and impulse control by the batterer places children living in violent environments at risk for abuse as well. It is not uncommon for children living in high conflict homes to seek help from school personnel, nurses, peers or counselors. Children frequently accompany parents, mostly mothers, to domestic violence shelters where they typically present in crisis.

The immediate goal of crisis intervention with children who witness domestic violence is to provide for their immediate safety and reduce symptoms of distress. Once the situation is stabilized, the intent of treatment is to enhance a child's emotional security and improve his or her ability to relate to others and function competently. Counseling methods for traumatized children are found in chapter eleven. This chapter will address investigations and crisis intervention strategies using the case of the Connor family.

The Connor Family

Larry Connor, a forty-two year-old businessman, was married to forty year-old Helen for fifteen years. They had two children, ages three and twelve. Police had been called to their home several times in the past for domestic violence. The Connor's twelve year-old daughter made the latest 911 telephone call. The police dispatcher could hear Larry Connor telling the youngest child to pick up toys and throw them at his mother. Background noise that sounded as though someone was being struck was also heard. Crying, the twelve year-old caller begged for help cause "dad was hitting mom."

When police arrived at the home, Helen was curled up in a fetal position on the floor. She told police that an argument began when she told Larry she was finally leaving him for good. He replied that she couldn't take the car so Helen threw the car keys at Larry's head. Enraged, Larry threw Helen to the ground, yelling, "you're not gonna throw things at me." He proceeded to choke her telling her to "shut up." While Helen was gasping for air he punched her and hit her legs and head with a baseboard he pried lose from the floor.

When Larry heard police at the door, he cried out, "I'm not going to jail." Just as police entered the residence he dragged his daughter down the hall and barricaded the two of them in the bathroom. Larry screamed at police, "go ahead and shoot but the blood of my daughter will be on your hands." Larry had placed his daughter as a shield between himself and the bathroom door. Eventually the hostage negotiator talked Larry out of the bathroom. Although terrified, the child was physically unharmed. Larry was arrested and the children were taken to a local advocacy center for evaluation. Helen was transported to a nearby hospital.

At the hospital emergency room a physician documented the following:

> "...Patient states her husband beat her with a board and tried to strangle her...he has beaten her a couple of times before but she has stayed for the sake of the children...she is contused and bruised about the throat and across the clavicles bilaterally with a large bruise on the right anterior shoulder...she has approximately 8 significantly contused areas in the shape of a 2 inch wide by variable length injury from being beaten with a board on her left leg and approximately 3 injuries of a similar nature on her right thigh...I discussed at length with her the statistical likelihood of being injured significantly worse if not killed next time..."

After discharge from the emergency room, Helen and her children went to a domestic violence shelter. The following day, she

145

applied for and was granted an emergency order of protection against Larry. Tired of the battering, Helen also contacted an attorney and filed for divorce. Shortly thereafter, Larry sought custody of the children. He argued that Helen was unstable and an alcoholic.

As per the requirements of the domestic relations court, Larry and Helen were scheduled to attend conciliation court to see if they could "work out" their differences about the children. Mediation in custody disputes began in 1981 and continues to this day as mandatory in some states. Fortunately most courts now consider the Model Code on Domestic and Family Violence, which emphasizes the harmful effects of domestic violence on children. With the Connors, the level of violence and degree of control evident in their household made it unlikely that the parents could cooperatively decide visitations and exchanges of children without tension and discord.

At the initial conciliation court appointment, Helen was required to fill out a preliminary assessment form. She wrote the following:

> "I feel the children would be better off living with me because of the long history of domestic violence on Larry's part. He has beat me almost weekly for the past ten years. This last time he almost killed me. I thought we could either share holidays or alternate them. I don't know how this will work because he told me that if I ever took the children from him and got custody, he would hunt me down and kill me. He has threatened to leave the state with the children if the court orders that the children live with me...and then send someone back to finish off the job for him."

The court ordered that the children would live with Helen and have weekly visitation with their father. Exchanges of the children would occur in a neutral place by someone other than the parents. Following this preliminary order, Helen testified as follows during a domestic relations hearing on custody and visitation:

> "Larry said if I ever had custody of the children he would hunt me down, kill me and my family...and would do whatever it takes to get the children back. I know he will do it. It's just a matter of time. I don't want to keep the children away from their father – but I know he will

146

eventually kill me. Please place them with my
sister when that happens... "

Helen further testified that Larry had the potential to become
violent during the exchanges of the children. While the court
acknowledged that Helen's fear was real, weekly visitation was
ordered between Larry and his children. Holidays and vacations
would be split evenly between the parents. As you can expect, it
didn't take long before the local police department was called to
intervene. Larry had begun to stalk Helen.

After receiving custody of the children, Helen began to notice
Larry's vehicle parked outside of her workplace. At night she would
see him standing for hours on the front sidewalk outside of her
residence. The stalking behavior escalated and Larry began to leave
telephone messages for Helen even though the protective order was
still in effect. Larry's calls all had the same threatening tenor found in
the first message he left Helen:

> "...Helen pick up the phone. God damn it. Pick
> up the phone. I know you're not working cause I
> can see you through the blinds. Pick it up god
> damn it. I'm not going to play no more games
> Helen. I want my son. If you go to work I'm
> going to follow your ass and make you lose your
> fucking job. Now pick up the god damn phone.
> I'm getting fed up with this. If you come over
> here I'll bash your head in. I called to be nice and
> now you're going to play games with the fucking
> answering machine. Bring the cops and watch
> what the fuck happens. You ruined it all. If you
> don't pickup the phone in ten minutes you watch
> what happens you bitch. I gave you plenty of
> chances but no more. I want my kids now. You
> got ten minutes you bitch or I'm coming
> in there to bash your head in..."

When police responded to Helen's residence Larry was gone. A
report was taken and submitted to prosecutors for charging. Helen
waited for the court date to testify regarding Larry's violation of the
TPO. She was terrified that Larry would take her life. She also noticed
that her oldest daughter was becoming withdrawn. Reports from the
school indicated that the child would burst out crying in the middle of

147

class. Helen sought assistance from a local counseling agency. A crisis worker immediately saw the Connor children.

So how does one provide crisis intervention services to children who witness family conflict? What types of interventions are most effective in these situations? Let's start with the criminal investigation of domestic violence when children are present in the home.

Investigations Involving Children Who Witness Domestic Violence
Most states across the country now have mandatory arrest policies for domestic violence crimes. Every effort is made to identify the primary aggressor and avoid dual arrests. When children are part of domestic violence investigations, less consistency is evident among police department policies and procedures. Even report forms vary with regard to documentation of child witnesses to domestic violence. Unfortunately, many forms have no section at all to indicate the presence or absence of children during a domestic violence investigation, leaving the decision to include the information strictly up to the officer taking the report.

While there are many excellent report forms available for use by police departments, the Las Vegas Metropolitan Police Department (LVMPD) Domestic Violence Report form offers a concise yet comprehensive report of domestic violence. Between the years 2000-2001, LVMPD domestic violence unit investigated approximately 1,200 domestic violence reports per month that were forwarded by patrol officers. Large urban areas with high volumes of reports need a concise but comprehensive form to document domestic violence reports. The LVMPD domestic violence report form has several beneficial qualities.

First, the form is only one page long, so patrol officers can fill it out quickly before passing the information on for investigation by detectives. Second, the original report is attached to three carbon copies that are individually distributed to the domestic violence detail, the data collection repository for the state, and the victim. In some jurisdictions, the victim does not receive an original copy of the report. And finally, a section on the form indicates whether the persons involved in the incident have children. If so, their names and ages are recorded, along with whether they were present during the incident. There is also a separate section to document if a child made the 911 call to police. Courtesy of LVMPD, the form is illustrated below.

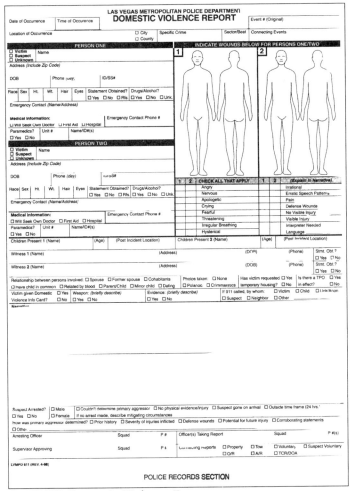

Figure 18. LVMPD Domestic Violence Form

If children were present during the domestic violence investigation and they are old enough to talk, any spontaneous utterances by children will be documented in patrol officers' reports. Follow-up videotaped investigative interviews are also recommended for each child.

Investigative Interviews

Individuals who interview child witnesses to domestic violence are advised to follow a protocol similar to the modified cognitive interview outlined in Chapter one. The interviewer develops rapport

149

with the child, attempts to obtain a narrative about the incident, and then clarifies the narrative with follow-up questions. Narratives from children who witness domestic violence tend to have similar characteristics. Since domestic violence is a crime that usually occurs more than once over a period of time, it is difficult for children to separate out the particular incident being investigated. This makes charging the offense difficult.

When children are able to give a narrative, the description may be a scripted account of violence in the home. In other words, when asked to explain what happened, the child describes the "usual way" that violence occurs. The following is an example of a scripted account of domestic violence, provided by a 7-year-old female during an investigative interview.

Detective: "Tell me what happened to your mother."

Sandra: "Well my dad was watching TV and drinking beer and then he got up and went to the kitchen. And my mom was washing dishes and he grabbed her hair and said those bad words like he always says and then he pushed her hard...like he always does it same...and then he always goes back to watch TV."

Statements such as, "he always does it the same" are indicative of scripted accounts. Clarification of specific incidents, placed in time frames, becomes the task of the interviewer.

Directing children to episodes of violence is important in order to delineate what violent acts and possible injuries occurred during a particular incident. Without such specific information in a criminal investigation, charging is difficult. For the child who has witnessed chronic violence, a blow to the victim's head that occurred days earlier may be just as vivid as kicking or shouting that prompted police to arrive at the scene during the day of the interview. If a child describes a head injury and the police report indicates kicking, the child's information may not be inaccurate, but simply the result of a blended account of events. A skilled interviewer will recognize scripted accounts of violence and direct the child to an episode in order to clarify the confusion.

Directing to Episode In Time Frames

One manner of directing the child to an episode in order to establish a time frame is to state, "I need to understand what happened here *today*." Another request that assists children in describing a specific episode is, " tell me about *a time that you remember the clearest*." And finally, "tell me as best you can what happened to your mom this *last time*" also directs a child to episodic memory.

Since the last incident of violence is most recent in the child's recollection, a time frame for the last event will be easiest to establish. When establishing time frames for incidents of domestic violence, the adult victim is the primary source of information. If corroborating information is sought from a child witness, important events in the child's life are used as anchors to determine if the violence occurred before or after the event. Birthdays, holidays and vacations are occasions that children generally remember. Other events to consider when attempting to establishing time frames with school age children are field trips, relatives visiting the home and sleepovers at friends. Television shows can also be used to determine when a violent act occurred. It is not uncommon for children to try and drown out family violence by turning on the television. Once specific episodes have been obtained from children, a series of direct questions can then be asked to clarify the information.

Direct questions in order to clarify information are designed based upon the unique circumstances of each crime. It is advisable, however, to ask all child witnesses to domestic violence the following questions at the end of the interview if the information has not already been offered:

1. Where on your (victim) did she get hurt?
2. How did that happen?
3. With what?
4. Did your (victim) get hurt with anything else?
5. Where on your (perpetrator) did he get hurt?
6. How did that happen?
7. What words was your (victim) saying when (perpetrator) (committed act child reported)?
8. What words was your (perpetrator) saying to your (victim)?
9. What did you hear?
10. Has anything ever happened to you?

In response to this last question, the Connor children described the stalking behavior of their father. Literature about stalking in the presence of children is rare. Clinicians, however, have heard accounts of stalking from adult survivors of domestic violence for decades. Several excellent forms have been developed by police departments to assist adult victims of stalking. Some of the clearest ways to record stalking incidents are offered in a packet by the San Diego County Stalking Strike Force.

Adult victims of stalking are requested to document times, incidents and additional information on easily understood forms. Police officers nationwide request victims to keep diaries of their stalker's pursuits, however, some victims are unclear how to record the incidents. The Stalking Incident Logs offered by the San Diego Strike Force provide victims with three separate forms to record incidents of harassment. Summaries of the forms are provided below.

STALKING INCIDENT LOG

Name of Target _____Name of Suspect _____

Date/Time_____

Description of Incident_____

Witnesses _____

Physical Evidence _____

Police Who Responded _____

HARASSING PHONE CALL LOG

Date/Time_____

Place Received_____

Comments _____

Tape-Recorded_____

DIARY NOTES TO RECORD THOUGHTS/FEELINGS

Date/Time_____

Diary Notes _____

_____

_____

_____

_____

Although I am not aware of any specific protocols for children who witness stalking, it is advisable to ask children about stalking incidents. Refrain from creating a sense of hypervigilance. Instead, inquire in a general manner about things that have been happening lately that might be frightening. Then, focus the topic and ask the child if they have seen or heard anything happen to the parent who is being stalked. Children who are aware of stalking behaviors have anxiety about what might happen in the future. Even though the batterer is no longer living with the family, a sense of safety has not yet returned. Crisis intervention methods can be used with children to stabilize situations and offer ways to manage their stress.

Crisis Intervention With Children Who Witness Domestic Violence

Police departments across the country are developing policies to ensure that survivors of domestic violence and their children receive crisis intervention services. In some jurisdictions, victim advocates are responsible for providing either the services or information and referrals to outside providers. It is important to note that crisis intervention is not therapy. Crisis intervention is a more immediate, problem-focused intervention.

Everly (1995) proposes the "SAFER" model of crisis intervention.[42] A summary of the model is found below:

S   Stabilization of the situation
A   Acknowledging the crisis
F   Facilitating understanding
E   Encouragement of adaptive coping
R   Restoration of independent functioning
      (or Referral for continued care)

153

Stabilizing the Situation

Stabilizing the situation requires that the physical safety of battered parents is an immediate priority. Safety planning generally includes assisting a survivor of domestic violence with an application for an emergency, temporary order of protection (TPO). While TPO's may be a first attempt at trying to keep families safe, the process of leaving a batterer places many women and children in imminent danger. For some, the only way to stay safe is to move away from the jurisdiction where the perpetrator resides.

Women who move now have the opportunity to take advantage of "full faith and credit ordinances" that are currently being adopted by many jurisdictions. These regulations ensure that TPO's issued by a jurisdiction other than where the victim resides will be honored and enforced by any court. Many women, however, are unable to move due to personal and financial reasons. Others are mandated by courts to live in the same state as the perpetrator if there are children in common who are visiting the offending parent. Safety planning, therefore, does not simply mean facilitating the survivor's application for a TPO.

Safety planning with battered women and their children can be a difficult process. Since safety plans are designed to decrease risk, they must be individualized. Risks such as life threatening injuries, death, finances, psychological impact and harm to one's children differ from one woman's life to the next. The timing and the manner of leaving a violent situation may be much different for one woman and her children in comparison to another. It is imperative, therefore to include the battered woman's perspective about her risks prior to developing a safety plan.[43] Jill Davies provides a comprehensive protocol for evaluating risk in her book, "Safety Planning and The Battered Woman." At a minimum, however, prior to developing a safety plan inquire of the individual:

1. What worries you the most right now?
2. What is the effect of leaving immediately?
3. What is the effect of staying?

Involve children in safety planning as well. Ask children what worries them the most right now. Instruct and practice with children how to dial 911 when any type of emergency arises. Be sure that an adult has packed a small bag with a change of clothes and some personal belongings of the child in case an emergency arises and the family needs to leave quickly. Include birth certificates and important papers in the bag. Assuming that safety plans are established, address specific domestic violence incidents with children.

Acknowledging the Crisis

Irrespective of what theoretical beliefs a counselor may have, it is undisputed that children who witness domestic violence must be provided an opportunity to describe the experience.[44] One reason for obtaining a full disclosure of the violence is to acknowledge the child's unique experience of the events. In addition, many children do not associate the witnessing of violence with distress symptoms that may follow the violent event. Specific information about the child's experience must be obtained in order to identify what is causing anxiety or distress.

Facilitate full disclosure of the experience in a child-friendly and safe environment. If disclosure is made in an unsafe environment, this can lead to even more stress for the child. The Connors twelve year-old daughter, used as a shield between her father and police, was asked to write out a description of her experience. The following is her account:

> "I got scared and he was hurting me...like my head was pressed against the door and I thought the cops would shoot through the door and I would die. I could hear my mom and my brother was in the living room and I heard a loud noise and I thought they were shot too. But I was glad that my brother wasn't in the bathroom with my dad cause... he was crazy. Just a little before he drug me down the hall he hit my mom with the board and there was blood everywhere. And when the cops finally got in and he put me up against the door he said shoot and I couldn't breath or nothing and then he just started crying and let me go out. And when I ran out my mom was still on the floor in the living room and he got handcuffed."

This account was a good beginning. The description included specific information and affective terms but more information was required about the personal meaning associated with the domestic violence.

Personal meanings of the violent incident need to be considered since they can preoccupy a child.[45] Preoccupation of thoughts or feelings can eventually lead to the development of symptoms. Personal meanings can be ascertained by asking children about the "worst moment" of the event. The question is intended to assess what aspect of the event was most troubling to the child. Helen Connor's daughter described the following as her worst moment:

> "It was right when my face pressed against the door and I couldn't breathe and I thought I was going to get shot and die."

About one week after this child went to live at the shelter, she began experiencing anxiety attacks primarily described as an inability to breathe. When she was finally able to disclose the worst moment of the violence, desensitization and relaxation techniques could eventually be used to assist in her recovery. During the third stage of crisis intervention, however, one could reduce the child's fear and anxiety by explaining signs and symptoms that may occur with a crisis.

Facilitation of Understanding

Explaining to children that their reactions are normal given what they have been through is important to calm their fears. Using analogies helps. For example, children understand that when one gets cut they bleed. Explain that when a child sees violence, the body reacts in other ways. Children do well with a "head to toe" explanation. Have school age children draw a picture of themselves and assist with labeling the kinds of symptoms that can occur. For example, one's head can ache after seeing violence. It is sometimes hard to pay attention in school. Eyes can shed tears. One's mouth can feel dry. The heart might feel like it is racing. Sweaty palms are common. One might have stomach aches. All of these are normal reactions to stress. Facilitating understanding of symptoms minimizes the cognition of helplessness that can develop from a child's inability to understand and control distress.

In the long term, if a child's sense of helplessness continues, he or she will be less able to deal with other stresses in life. Failure at overcoming tension associated with new events can eventually damage self-esteem. With self-esteem suffering, and an inability to deal with challenges in life, depressive features can develop. In order to help children manage their distress, the following approach may be useful.

Encouraging Adaptive Coping

Children can be taught basic stress management skills. Without assistance, they may try to calm themselves in an effort to alleviate the pain. One way that children relieve tension is to avoid anything that reminds them of the violent event. Avoidance of particular places, activities or persons is a way that children attempt to cope with trauma. Repetitive play in young children is another example of a defense from pain associated with recollection of a violent event. Avoidance in its extreme takes the form of dissociation, either during or following the domestic violence event.

Teaching children to manage stress will minimize the use of defense mechanisms such as avoidance. Breathing and relaxation techniques can be taught to children. Practice with children ahead of time so that the techniques can be used when anxiety manifests. In addition to breathing techniques, visualization can be highly effective with children. Individualized play or games can also be used to alleviate anxiety during times when children are describing their experiences of the violent event. For example, specific writing tasks, art or computer games, can help the child identify cognitions or thoughts about the violence.

If poor thought processes are evident during the crisis phase, reframe cognitions to reinforce positive or healthy thoughts. For example, authors Peled and Edelson offer a clear example of reframing a child's sense of helplessness into a situation of "acting smart" to avoid getting injured.[46] Reframed cognitions can gradually be reinforced over time. Reinforcing a variety of situations where children have mastered life's situations will not only enhance self-esteem but also slowly diminish learned helplessness. Most children in crisis are referred on for continued care.

Referral For Continued Care

It is recommended that children who witness domestic violence receive counseling following crisis intervention efforts. Counseling for seriously traumatized children is described in chapter eleven. Counseling beyond crisis intervention must address beliefs that children may have developed about the survivor and offender of domestic violence. Many children who repeatedly hear an aggressor denigrate the survivor or allocate blame for the beatings will repeat and eventually believe those statements. It is not uncommon to hear children state, "my mother deserved to be beat" or "if she just would have listened to him she wouldn't have got smacked." Since children love their mothers, these statements can create a sense of dissonance or conflict within the child. The agony associated with sorting out this dissonance can lead children to frustration and eventually aggression. Discussions about responsibility for violence and sex role stereotypes, therefore, become an important part of therapy.

Providing the child with an opportunity to talk with parents is an integral part of stress management. Parents can also offer important information about cultural beliefs, families and violence. It can be difficult for children to understand violence and control, particularly if children are caught between two cultures.

Providing Culturally Competent Care

Historically, the emphasis of mental health providers has been on psychological literature to guide counseling methodologies used with children who witness violence. The emphasis has been on the mind and cognitive therapies. A broader socio-cultural understanding of violence requires that we provide services to children in the context of their cultures and beliefs. If we do not work with children in a way that fits their culture, healing is unlikely to occur. In some cultures, talking about problems is not acceptable. In others, open expression of emotions is not allowed. Many cultures stress interventions that affect not only the mind, but the body and spirit. Harmony and balance are the desired outcomes.

The mind generally includes interventions that address cognitive processes. Thoughts, memories, feelings, self-esteem and defense mechanisms are considered when designing counseling activities that address the mind. While working with a child's thoughts and feelings, the body cannot be neglected. Current neuro-biological findings indicate that children who witness violence are affected not only psychologically but physiologically.[47] Since the stress of witnessing violence has such a tremendous impact on the body, bioenergetic therapies have been extremely helpful for children who witnessed violence. How the body responds to stress is important. Sleep, nutrition and physical exercise need to be incorporated into crisis intervention teaching. Finally, spiritual teachings or practices of a child's culture need to be included in responding to children in crisis.

Cultural adaptations can be made to all mainstream systems of care including crisis intervention and counseling. For example, several projects now address behavioral/mental health services for American Indian children. With Eagles Wings is a program offering wraparound services to children and families on the Wind River Reservation in Wyoming. *Sacred Child Project* is a strength-based project coordinated by the United Tribes Technical College in North Dakota. Tools such as storytelling, Talking Circles, the use of ceremony, rites of passage and kinship support are promising practices in the provision of services to children who witness domestic violence.[48] The programs shift care from a strict mental health model to involve families and communities. Interventions become holistic in order to address the overall impact of violence on a child. When providing services to children who witness domestic violence, ask yourself, "have I included techniques that will address the mind, body and spirit?"

CHAPTER NINE

Child Abductions: Victims and Witnesses

*"It's odd, I suppose, that when I think back over all
that happened in that terrible time, one of my
sharpest memories should be of some few moments
the day before everything happened..."*
Sue Miller

The Missing Children's Act of 1982 was largely a result of testimony about the staggering number of children reported missing in the United States each year. While the original testimony at U.S. Congressional hearings provided shocking statistics about the incidence of missing children, many types of investigative reports were included in the overall estimate. There are now several categories listed in the National Incidence Studies of Missing, Abducted, Runaway and Thrown Away Children in America (MISMART).[49] For purposes of data collection, the categories are:

a) **runaway**: missing child that has left home without knowledge/permission of guardians and has stayed away overnight;

b) **lost/injured or otherwise missing**: missing child due to one of these circumstances;

c) **family abduction**: child taken by parent/family either in violation of a custody order, failure to return child after a visitation or the intent to conceal the child from one who has a legal right to be with the child;

d) **thrown away**: child who is told to leave a household, has been away from home and not allowed back in or has been abandoned or deserted, and

e) **non-family abduction**: child taken by coercion or without authorization by a stranger/non-family member into a building or a vehicle of a distance of more than twenty feet, or the luring of a child for the purpose of committing another crime.

Irrespective of the investigative category, missing children pose unique, emotionally laden circumstances for families, law enforcement and others involved in the search, recovery, notification or reunification process. Investigations of missing children, therefore, involve complex interdisciplinary and volunteer efforts.

An array of articles, largely distributed by the National Center For Missing and Exploited Children provide guidelines for the general investigation of missing children. Individual police departments also have standard operating procedures when children are reported missing. Management issues, investigative checklists and a variety of resources are available for the many circumstances faced by investigators. In most of these manuals and documents, however, investigative interviews of child victims or witnesses are not specifically addressed.

Investigative interviews of child witnesses to abduction differ substantially from those of children who have been recovered. In addition, once children are recovered alive, reunification of children with families is often a difficult and complex process. The two families discussed in this chapter were chosen given the many issues faced by family members, investigators and counselors who participated in case resolution. The first investigation involved a family abduction.

Family Abductions

Conservative estimates by the U.S. Department of Justice indicate that about 350,000 family abductions occur annually in the United States.[50] Family abductions by their very nature involve multi-problem families. Authors Greif and Hegar[51] describe a family abduction as the ultimate breakdown in family functioning. The assortments of problems that precede a family abduction are varied.

Parents flee with children for a variety of complex reasons such as custody disputes, domestic violence, and child maltreatment or drug abuse. Allegations of abuse prior to abduction can be perceived or real. In addition to abuse, the reason for abduction could simply be disregard for court orders from a divorce that are not to a parent's liking. Therefore, a review of all information about family members who report missing children is important.

While court documents, counseling files, medical records or criminal histories are all necessary during an investigation, the deluge

162

of material can make one lose sight of the most important consideration, the child. While some child victims of family abduction are never recovered, others are found quickly, in places close to their homes. Some trek across various states or countries and are not recovered for years. The lives of these children become similar to fugitives. Always on the run, there is no stability in their existence. For the two girls in this next case, their plight was especially difficult. Victims of an international abduction, the children and their searching parent endured years of turmoil.

A Family Abduction

Lisa and Rob Foley married on the beautiful island of Kauai. Their first child, Jessica, was born in 1989. While the children's parents dispute many of the facts about their marriage, there is agreement that Lisa Foley left the marriage and returned on several occasions. Lisa, a United States citizen, stated that she sought an order of protection from courts in the United States due to domestic violence that officials in Canada were not investigating. Mr. Foley repeatedly denied the allegations, reporting that they were retribution from Lisa for a number of issues including his original reluctance to marry her.

Based upon continued turmoil, six months after the marriage, Mr. Foley initiated divorce proceedings in October 1990. The Court of Queen's Bench in Alberta, Canada awarded temporary custody of Jessica to her mother, Lisa, until litigation was resolved. Lisa, who had moved to the United States, was ordered to return to the jurisdiction of Canada by January of 1991 for resolution of the matter. While Lisa remained in the United States, Mr. Foley visited his daughter on several occasions. A second child, Jennifer was born in May, 1991. Lisa returned to Canada and resided for nine months with Mr. Foley and then obtained a residence of her own. The court case for custody of the children was still pending.

In May 1992, Lisa charged Mr. Foley with assault. Mr. Foley, who denied the allegations, successfully appealed the charges. During the assault investigation, a justice of the court required Mr. Foley to have supervised visitation with the girls. This interim order specifically prohibited either parent from removing the children from the Province of Alberta, Canada. At the recommendation of the visitation supervisor, in less than two months, Mr. Foley was granted unsupervised visitation of the girls. The hearing for permanent custody was pending.

163

Within the next several months, Lisa alleged that Mr. Foley slapped the oldest child in the face, causing bruising. Mr. Foley denied the allegations. The report was investigated by social services and found to be unsubstantiated. The social services file was closed. Five months later, Lisa alleged that Mr. Foley was touching the oldest girl inappropriately. She made her complaints to a children's hospital where the report was unsubstantiated by investigators. Mr. Foley again adamantly denied the complaints.

Mr. Foley continued to visit with his daughters awaiting the upcoming hearing for custody of his children. In May of 1993, Mr. Foley's adolescent son from a previous marriage suffered an unexpected and tragic death during a swimming accident. It was during this time that Lisa Foley contravened the provision of the court order and left the jurisdiction of Canada. She fled to the United States. She and the children were last seen entering a shopping mall in Canada during June of 1993.

When the girls did not show up for their regular visit, Mr. Foley began an extensive search in an attempt to find his children. He sought assistance from the Calgary Police Department, Child Quest International, Inc., and two separate private investigation firms. As time passed and the children remained missing, the Court of Queen's Bench in Alberta granted temporary custody of Jessica and Jennifer to Mr. Foley. Permanent custody was granted to Mr. Foley in October of 1994.

Listed as missing in countries throughout the world, leads regarding the girls had been called in from various jurisdictions including Nevada, Arizona, Texas, Missouri and Mexico. It was August of 1995, two years after the children's disappearance that yet another lead emerged.

The Children's Advocacy Center in Phoenix was originally located in an unassuming house surrounded with grass and trees. Personnel at the Center provided child abuse assessments and evaluations to a number of local law enforcement agencies. On August 8, 1993, a counseling student worked the front desk during the lunch hour. It was during this time that a man, identifying himself as Kenneth Horton, sought counseling for his three children. The student, happy to help, took down the following reason for referral on the intake form:

> "...5 year old child here from Missouri for one
> week summer visit with dad; Child's dad states

164

child's mother is a member of a satanic church; states child tells of horrendous stories about bruises and burns to her body; due to her affiliation he states can't make a police report because of danger to himself; states child told him mommy burned her but child won't tell it to anyone else; tells 2 stepsisters that she can't sleep in the same room as them because when she sleeps something comes out of her body and runs around the room; mom has custody but because child has an ear infection dad is keeping her an extra week; ...father has contacted the underground network to see about escaping from the country...current wife, is a stay at home mom...he is also seeking counseling for stepchildren, two girls ages 5 and 6...requesting counseling under an assumed name due to fear of reprisal from his child's mother and the satanic church..."

Mr. Horton would not leave an address or telephone number but indicated that he would call back to schedule an appointment for his girls. Upon return from lunch, the student informed staff of the unusual request from Mr. Horton. Uneasy with the request to treat children under assumed names, a Sergeant at the police department child crimes bureau was provided with the information. Four days later, a detective indicated that a felony arrest warrant was issued for Mr. Horton (alias) and his traveling companion who had abducted her two children from Canada. The children from Canada had been missing for over two years. Mr. Horton's five year-old daughter was also missing from Missouri for the past ten months. In all, a total of three children were listed as missing.

Mr. Horton was actually identified as Bradley Nilsson. Apparently he abducted his five year-old daughter from Missouri and joined Lisa Foley on the run with her two children. The following flyer from Child Quest International indicated to approach the pair with caution as Mr. Nilsson was in possession of a MAC-10 machine gun. He was also wanted for questioning in a homicide back east.

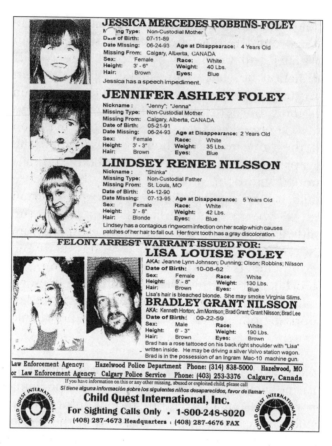

Figure 19. Child Quest International Poster

The student identified the man who sought counseling services as the suspect in the missing children's flyer. She also indicated that three children had been present in the Advocacy Center waiting area and they appeared to be the approximate ages of the missing children. Law enforcement related that the last sighting of the pair and the children had been in San Francisco, approximately one-month prior. Weeks came and went but Mr. Nilsson made no further contact with the Center. Law enforcement, however, mobilized their resources.

As per standard procedure, flyers were distributed to all local law enforcement agencies, hospitals, schools and counseling centers. Since investigators had information that Lisa, the suspect from Canada, had deep vein thrombosis, a medical condition of her legs, it was hypothesized that she might be visiting local hospitals. Police made extra efforts to deliver flyers and speak to emergency room personnel in each hospital located in the area. It wasn't until ten months later that Lisa Foley finally entered a hospital in Mesa, Arizona. Eight months pregnant, she was admitted with false labor pains.

A nurse, who recognized Lisa as the woman in the missing children's poster, called the Mesa Police Department. Lisa Foley was arrested at the hospital and transferred to a county medical center used by the local jail. In the hopes that Mr. Nilsson would arrive and lead officers to the children, undercover officers staked out the hospital. Within twenty-four hours, Mr. Nilsson visited Lisa and police tailed him to Mesa, arresting him during a traffic stop. Mr. Nilsson stated that he would show officers where the children were if he could get a deal. Officers refused, indicating that where children are involved, no bargain would be struck. Nilsson led them to a house anyway. Police entered, calling out the children's names.

Inside the home, police could find no sign of the children. They continued to call their names and search, finally deciding to check under the beds that were surrounded by bicycles and toys. The girls, under the beds, were hiding from police. They eventually crawled out and accompanied police to the Mesa Police Department Center Against Family Violence.

It was July 2, 1996 at 10:30 p.m. when the Foley girls were finally recovered. Almost a year had passed since they showed up at the counseling center. Now, police required interviews along with physical examinations of the children to determine their well-being. Upon visual inspection, there were no obvious signs of physical injury, so medical examinations of the children were scheduled for the following day. Their appearance, however, was testimony to their transient lifestyle. Their clothes were ripped and did not appear to be cleaned for some time. One child had torn socks and hiking boots without laces. Child Protective Services specialists were called to take custody of the children. Mr. Foley, the custodial parent in Canada was notified of the children's recovery.

When the children's father was contacted, he found it hard to believe that his children had been found. Like many parents of abducted children, his hopes had risen and fallen so many times, he was certain that they weren't in police custody. What made it more difficult was the mental health state of the girls, which made it impossible for them to talk with their father at this point in time.

Although the girls did not appear to have obvious signs of physical injury, their life on the run had resulted in bizarre perceptions about their father. The following interviews indicated their struggles.

Interviews of the Children

Given the late hour, only brief interviews were conducted with each girl. The first interview was with Jessica, the oldest child. Jessica stated that she was six years old and would soon have a birthday, and "that's when Brad is going to come and get us so we can be together again." The child was asked, "who is Brad?" to which she replied, "he's my daddy."

Jessica was asked if she had another daddy. She replied, "bad Rob...we're hiding from bad Rob who is the man that my mom divorced. Bad Rob is going to kill us and he hurt my mom." The interview proceeded as follows:

Interviewer:	How did Bad Rob hurt your mom?
Jessica:	I don't know.

Interviewer:	Did you see him hurt your mother with your very own eyes?
Jessica:	No, she told me about it.

Interviewer:	What did your mom tell you?
Jessica:	He hit her over the head with a hammer and rode over her legs with a motorcycle that's why she has those blue lines on her legs and sees the doctor...and he'll kill us and the new baby if he ever finds us.

Interviewer:	Did your mom talk with you about what you should do if you see your dad?
Jessica:	Yes...stay quiet for a while and then run away and then hide and find a phone and call Aunt Julie to come get us...that's why we can't go outside to play cause he might find us.

Interviewer:	Has your daddy Rob ever hurt you in any way?
Jessica:	No...but my mom said he did.

The interview continued with questions about where Jessica and her mother lived, how she had been treated and what her life was like. She was attending first grade at a local school but registered under a different name. She was not allowed to play outside for fear that someone might recognize her. She had traveled with her mother from state to state and into Mexico without staying long enough to make friends or finish school. She stated that she would have to repeat first grade because, "I didn't go enough days to pass school." Due to the late hour, the interview was soon terminated and Jessica's sister, Jennifer, was interviewed.

Jennifer stated that she attended preschool during the day and was living with her mother and daddy Brad. She stated, "my mom's name is Jeanie but her real name is Lisa. We can't call her Lisa cause bad Rob will find us and kill us." She was then asked, "Who is Bad Rob?" Jennifer stated, "he's not mine or Jessica's real dad, but I think he is but my mom said Brad is my real dad cause Bad Rob was mean to her and he's going to kill us and the baby if he finds us."

It was readily apparent that both girls had been repeatedly conditioned to believe that their father would kill them. Their father, on the other hand, knew nothing about the girls' current state of mind.

Perceived dangers about the searching parent are important aspects to clarify with children who are recovered from family abduction. A thorough analysis, however, must be conducted to determine if the fears are perceived or in fact real. In this matter, both children stated that they had never seen their father harm their mother. Nor did they have any recollection of him hurting them. Both girls independently stated that their mother told them about the violence.

In contrast to this situation, sometimes children actually have experienced violence prior to their abduction. Most children who developed language skills prior to the abduction can relate those incidents to you. In addition to questions about recollections prior to the abduction, questions must be asked of the child's experiences while on the run. It is important to obtain information about residences, schools and caretakers of children while on the run. One way to obtain this data is to work backwards in time to schools or daycares the child may have attended. If the child was not enrolled in a structured setting, have him or her tell you about a typical day. Ask children about what happened during the day from the time they got up in the morning until bedtime. Many children will relate a lifestyle in which they were continually in fear that someone might recognize them. Others may tell of abuse by individuals they were exposed to while on the run.

In a custodial abduction in another jurisdiction, a four year-old female was interviewed immediately upon recovery. She related that the man who cared for her repeatedly touched her privates. Her mother, attempting to arrange passage overseas, left the child in the care of a man who was identified by the underground network as a "safe house." During the abuse incidents, the child had no escape since she was not allowed outdoors during the daytime in the event that she would be seen. This particular child's recovery was incidental to a routine traffic stop. An alert patrol officer noted that the child's size and facial features matched a missing children's poster from a nearby jurisdiction. This child's hair color was different and her long locks had been cut into a much shorter style.

The situation described above also illustrates why it is critical to provide recovered children with a full medical examination as soon as possible after their recovery. Given the fugitive lifestyle of many abducted children, their nutritional status, dental care and basic needs are often gone unmet. All of these areas are important topics to be covered during interviews of recovered children. And lastly, it is critical to ask children about any instructions they received from the abducting parent regarding what they should do if captured by police. Information about children's plans if they are discovered is critical to ensure the safety of children once reunification is in process. While these preliminary assessments are conducted, keep the searching parent separate but informed about the process underway. Reunification can be a frightening and emotionally laden event, particularly if children were conditioned to believe that the searching parent is dangerous. This was the case with the Foley girls.

While the girls were being interviewed, Mr. Foley, still in disbelief that his children were actually in our presence, arranged transportation from Canada to Arizona. As requested, he brought a video of his last Christmas with the girls along with several family photos. Based on the girls' statements, the reunification would not be easy. But no one was prepared for just how difficult it would be.

When Mr. Foley arrived, the children were in the care of a foster family. The custody documents from Canada were verified and a hearing regarding the matter was scheduled for July 5, 1996. Of course, Mr. Foley immediately wanted to see his girls. He could not fathom that they were afraid of him. Distressed, he relayed, "not one day has gone by that I haven't looked for them." Mr. Foley, however, agreed to participate in whatever reunification process was best for his children. He just wanted to know they were alive and like other searching parents, he wanted to hold them. Mr. Foley readily expected the girls to come running into his open arms. What happened almost destroyed him.

The Reunification Process

Prior to meeting with their father, the children were shown videotapes and pictures of their life together in Canada. They viewed the images with a variety of emotions. The youngest, begged to see her father. She couldn't imagine that he had forgotten her birthday. The oldest girl, however, cowered behind a couch, refusing to come out. She cried, "my mom says that he's going to kill us. Maybe there are two Robs. Maybe this is one our mom didn't know about and there's another one out there who is going to kill us." We eventually came to an agreement. The children would accompany a detective and interviewer to the shopping mall. Jennifer, the youngest, could have lunch with her dad. Jessica could make her decision as the day went on.

While the girls were transported in one vehicle to the mall, a second detective transported Mr. Foley to the shopping center.

The girls tried on new outfits while the store attendant, offended by the odor and dirt on their old clothes, wanted to throw all of the articles in the trash. It is important to keep all clothing that children were wearing when they were recovered. Such items might yield evidence of abuse or assault. In this situation, the girls' mother later testified that the children were always well cared for. The clothing could prove otherwise.

Upon exiting the dressing room, Jessica stated that she and her sister needed to use a restroom. She whispered to her sister, "bathrooms always have telephones beside them. We can call Aunt Julie." Apparently, the instructions of her mother weighed heavily on her mind. Jessica was about to try and call her Aunt.

Both girls were accompanied to the bathroom at which point Jessica locked herself in a stall and refused to come out until her Aunt Julie was called. Coaxed by her sister, she eventually came out of the restroom. Given her panic, Jessica was informed that she did not have to see her father at this time. In contrast, Jennifer couldn't wait to see her dad.

171

It was one of those moments that you never really forget. A father, tears streaming down his face, hugging a child he had not seen for three years. Jessica, in a position to see the reunion hung back, watching it all. She turned, demanding to go back to the car. Since we anticipated Jessica's reluctance based upon her initial interview, Mr. Foley had been prepared for such an episode. We suggested that he make a short audiotape for Jessica, telling her that he would like to visit in the presence of the detective. Jennifer returned with the tape. After Jessica heard the tape, she remained adamant that she and her sister were instructed to run away. The girls conversed. Jennifer stated, "I saw daddy Rob. He doesn't want to hurt us – he wants to see you." Jessica ran upstairs and slammed the bedroom door, yelling, "No we're supposed to run away." Both girls were reassured that they could take their time and decide about visits the next day. Their father would be available for short, structured visits.

While Jessica's response may be confusing, it is not uncommon for abducted children to develop close ties with the abductor. Repetitive statements encouraging fear about the searching parent reinforce the bond. The longer a child is away, the more likely professional help is necessary. And the Foley girls had been missing for several years. Unfortunately, in the majority of recoveries of missing children, an average of fifteen minutes is spent on the recovery process. Little regard is given to the psychological or support services necessary for an effective reunification. You can see the difficulties associated with this reunification, now progressing into the second day.

Day two of the reunification process began similarly to the first with one small but important difference. Like the first day, Jennifer ran to see her father. This time, however, Jessica volunteered to see her father but only from a distance. Once in the parking lot of the shopping mall, she changed her mind and requested that her father come shopping with us. He readily agreed. During the walk through the mall, she tentatively began conversation. Was her room still pink? Did her grandma and grandpa still live by the water? What happened to her Winnie the Pooh Book? Eventually, there was a steady flow of conversation. The day ended well. The girls returned to the foster home where the stress of the past two days hit like a bombshell.

Once in the door, the youngest child who had been doing so well collapsed to the floor crying for her dad. She stated, "I don't know who my Daddy is. Why did Daddy Brad say that stuff? I want my Daddy Rob. Please don't leave me alone. I want my Daddy." Attempts to soothe the child were futile and eventually she sobbed herself to sleep. Jessica appeared equally confused.

The despair manifested by these children is important to consider, particularly since many advocacy groups assist women and children on the run. The psychological distress of children abducted by family members can be immeasurable. It is not only destructive but also cruel for children to live as fugitives. Children on the run have little opportunity to form healthy attachments, develop support systems or learn to cope with routine problems. They develop a sense of hyper vigilance, always looking over their shoulder, anticipating the worst. Their only survival mechanism is to run. And where could the Foley girls run to at this point in time?

Three days had now passed since the children were recovered. An emergency hearing had been set in Superior Court. Following an examination of the evidence, the Judge ordered that the girls be turned over immediately to Mr. Foley with the recommendation that he provide for the mental health needs of his children. The children's mother was taken into custody by a federal marshal who arrived with a warrant for her extradition to Canada. Brad Nilsson was also taken into custody and extradited back to Missouri.

Following the court's decision, the children were informed of the judge's decision. The girls were told that their mother was safe, had a bed, food and was being cared for. They would now be spending time with their father. Mr. Foley indicated that his preference was to return to Canada. Aware of the children's turmoil, however, he agreed to participate in further activities designed to ease the children's fears. Throughout the afternoon, the girls were prompted to recall positive aspects of their life in Canada. Eventually, the girls spoke about making snowmen, snow angels and visiting their grandparents. Mr. Foley gently participated in the conversation and spoke with the girls about the fun times they had back home. Jennifer soon relayed that she was ready to go home. Jessica continued to color, engaging in limited conversation. She did, however, pay attention to the pictures of airplanes and information provided about their trip home. The evening ended well.

The following morning, the girls were given coloring books and various activities for the plane ride home. They were accompanied to the airport where both girls got on the plane without any visible distress. Leaving their transient lifestyle behind, they made their way back to Canada. During follow-up telephone calls to their home in Canada, the girls stated they were having fun and getting to know their family again. There still remained major adjustments regarding structure and basic routines that most children of their age had previously learned to follow. Their dental hygiene and nutrition was so poor that intensive services were required for each. School and support services were necessary to help the girls catch up academically and socially. And there still remained the civil and criminal matters in the Canadian Courts.

The Courts in Canada eventually sorted out the masses of data regarding the children and their family. At the time of this writing, the girls are ten and twelve years of age. They live with their father and by most accounts are healthy and happy children. As their father states, although they are a joy, not all has been positive on their road to recovery. He wrote the following letter with the hopes that others may understand the turmoil that he, the girls and their extended family have endured. The letter is printed in its entirety without alteration.

Dear Tascha:

> Jessica and Jennifer are daughters of mine of my second; and *last*, marriage. Prior to Jessica being born, I was the proud father of two gorgeous daughters and a **great and loving son**. Jessica and Jennifer were abducted by their non-custodial mother when my son drowned just days before his graduation from high school. The abduction was a criminal act intended to hurt me at the worst of times and with no thought given to the resulting harm to anyone.

> I remember seeing my son lying in the morgue...just lying there without a mark on his body. I prayed to God that I would gladly give up everything I had if I could just get my son back.

> Weeks later; while still reeling from Steve's death, I had to deal with the thought of perhaps never seeing my youngest daughters again either. I swore to myself that I would do everything in my power to prevent that thought from becoming a reality. It took three years and three days to recover them and in the process I had spent a serious amount of money that I didn't entirely have.

Their total recovery took just about as long as did all of the burdensome expenses.

The truly sad thing in my life today is that when Jessica and Jennifer were returned to me in July of 1996, that event ultimately caused my relationship with both of my other daughters to all but end. Lana, now 28 and a lawyer had never wanted to even meet Jessica nor Jennifer. I have not seen her since the summer of 1995 when she visited me here in Calgary. My daughter Christa, now 21, and attending University had a great relationship with Jessica and Jennifer prior to their abduction but has not made any attempt to see them nor better the relationship since their recovery. Christa was last here during Christmas holidays in 1995. Today there is little if any communication between any of us. Lana and Christa have also stopped communicating with their grandparents – my parents.

I submit that they both feel *very* cheated. Lana has never wanted to accept Jessica as her sister. While Christa and Steve accepted both Jessica and Jennifer, Lana and Christa view them as costing way too much money to recover from their abduction. They have never taken an opportunity to understand and accept the harms-way that Jessica and Jennifer were in. Because of the expenses incurred, perhaps they feel cheated because their quality of life was diminished – thinking that they were not loved the same way because I never moved mountains for them. I am upset with them for the way that they think and act.

Life never returns to normal after the abduction of children. It charts a course that everyone is somehow guided by. Everyone's life that is somehow involved is affected in some way. Too often, it is a negative effect.

One of the positives from all that has happened, in addition to having two of my daughters in my daily life, is that it has brought my parents and I much closer. They have helped me a great deal and for that I am extremely grateful. It pleases me to see them be with and love their granddaughters.

I am finding it very easy to write about NOW without feeling sorry for myself about the past events. I would not have stated that a few years ago. My thoughts are only about the present and the future.

When writing, please do not alter the Childquest flyer in any way. You are permitted to use our real names. My children and I have nothing to hide from. Please always stay in touch.

Sincerely,

Rob Foley.

Mr. Foley's letter requires no further explanation. He has stated, however, that the girls' early experiences of violence and life on the run contributed to a number of problems with the girls that have largely been overcome, but still require constant patience and compassion. According to the ruling of the Canadian Courts, the girls' mother is no longer involved in the children's lives. Unfortunately, her actions led to a further series of losses for the children, she being one of them. Having spoken with her following the children's recovery, I am not certain that she will ever recognize her role in the stresses that they survived. While these girls were eventually reunited with their father, for another family, the searching is not yet over.

Missing and Endangered Child

January 2nd was the kind of lazy day that many enjoy after Christmas and New Year celebrations. Football games blared on televisions. Regulars, in the optimistic spirit of the New Year, watched the local team try and beat the Dallas Cowboys. Outside, in the Southwest, children played and rode their bikes.

It was late afternoon when two sisters finished playing at their friend's homes. When they made their way back home, the girls begged their mother for a couple of quarters to purchase some ice cream before the day ended. Their mom, visiting with cousins, gave the girls two quarters and they raced off to the corner in one last bike ride for the evening.

About 5:30 p.m., the youngest girl found the air chilly. Handing her quarter to her older sister, Mikelle, she turned back for home. Mikelle, eleven years of age, patiently waited for the ice cream truck. When the youngest girl stomped into the kitchen to play with the family dog, her mother realized that it was getting late. She directed the younger sibling to go and get her sister for supper. With the dog on a leash, the child walked out to the sidewalk outside of the family home. Only minutes had passed but when she peered down the street, there was no sign of her sister, Mikelle. In the middle of the road lay her sister's pink bike. She called for her sister. No response.

Picking up the bike, the child maneuvered it along with the dog, back home. Confused, she told her mother that her sister wasn't anywhere around. The girls' mother, concerned, told the child to go next door and see if Mikelle was at the neighbor's home. The neighbor boy, along with Mikelle's sister, walked around the block. Mikelle was nowhere to be seen. Within fifteen to twenty minutes of Mikelle's disappearance, her mother called police. Mikelle's father was also notified and rapidly made his way home. Mikelle did not show up that evening. A massive search was begun and police along with volunteers canvassed the neighborhood.

When going from door to door looking for a missing child, it is important that all personnel ask residents specific information. The inconsistencies that can arise when questions are not asked in a similar manner can be detrimental to a thorough investigation. Canvas forms offered by Nevada Child Seekers are one example of a lead sheet that is thorough and concise.[52]

While the case facts related to Mikelle's disappearance can not be presented here at this time, some suggestions based upon experiences in this matter may help others who need to interview children during the investigation of abduction. Several children in this case required investigative interviews. They included:

1. children at the residence where the girls played earlier in the day,
2. siblings of Mikelle,
3. the neighborhood boy who accompanied Mikelle's sister down the street,
4. friends of Mikelle from the neighborhood,
5. children from the neighborhood who were out playing during the day of the kidnapping, and
6. classmates of Mikelle who were her closest friends.

With school age children who are friends of the abducted victim, begin the interview with an open-ended style, inquiring about their relationship with the victim. Find out how often the child and victim

177

spent time together. When was the last time they were together? Most importantly, did the victim share any information that would have been a secret or perhaps that she was afraid to tell anyone else. Ask if the victim shared any diaries, personal journals or art with the classmate. Many of these items can provide a wealth of information.

When interviewing children who were in the neighborhood the day of the abduction, have children provide a narrative about what they did from the beginning of the day to its conclusion. Request that children provide a description of everything they may have seen, including persons who live in the neighborhood as well as those who had not been noticed before. Ask children to describe the vehicles parked or driving down the street during that day. In addition, ask if anyone has approached them or asked for their help at any time. Some abductors trick children into accompanying them by requesting their assistance in caring for animals or pets.

When interviewing the last child to have seen the victim, take the child on a reenactment of the events to replicate exactly what happened just prior to the abduction. With Mikelle's sister, it was helpful to videotape the walk so that one could determine how long it took for her to walk to the corner and then back home. Since most children are unable to accurately estimate time frames, the video is helpful because it can be timed. In addition, the video can be examined for residences, landmarks and vehicles in the immediate location from a perspective other than a map of the area or personal observation.

During the re-creation of the events, have the child explain exactly what he or she did. Complete a second walk using a video camera, inquiring specifically about what the child saw or heard as they were walking. In conclusion, offer support and crisis intervention services for all children who are involved in the investigation of a missing child.

Children throughout the community will be in need of services. Classmates of the child are faced with a reminder of the abduction on a daily basis when they view the child's empty desk at school. Children must be provided an opportunity to discuss their thoughts and feelings about the loss. Coping strategies can be taught to children in classrooms as well as to individual friends of the child. Family members must be provided regular and continuous support during their search. As you can see by the poster, Mikelle is still reported as missing.

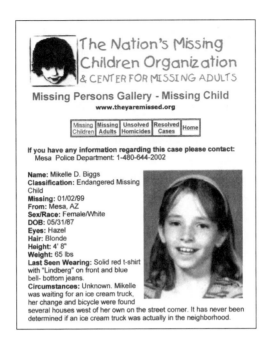

Figure 20. Missing Child

Until you are found Mikelle, the search will continue. One mother, whose child has not been recovered, described her life as a black hole years after the abduction. Depressed, she stated, "there is nothing I can do and nowhere I can go to get out of it. Unless my daughter is found, I surely will die here, deep in this blackness. When I see a glimmer of hope and reach up my hand, clasp onto it so that I can once again feel the goodness of humanity."

CHAPTER TEN

Charley & Sammy: The Quiet Children

"What is hell…it is the suffering of being unable to love."

T. Dostoevsky

January is one of the hardest months for the homeless walking the streets of large urban cities. Food and shelter are hard to come by since the cold led otherwise transient people to keep their spots at shelters and soup kitchens. Many sought refuge in smaller, outlying farming communities where churches and town folk were generous with meals and apt to offer shelter. That was how Joshua Harding happened to be in the small town of Goodyear.

Joshua, a pleasant man in his fifties, survived the streets for years. A Vietnam Vet who had fallen to hard times, he spent his days knocking back a few beers and reminiscing about the past. Every November, he headed towards the cotton fields and farm sheds that dotted the land. This year he headed back to his favorite town, 30 miles west of the state's capital city. He found a nice sheltered spot under the bridge within walking distance of town. For the next several months, this would be home.

On this particular morning, Joshua decided to get an early start searching through dumpsters for his breakfast. The morning air still had a chill and Josh could see his breath rise as he made his way into town. His first stop was at a dumpster just outside the strip mall that housed the town's only large grocery store, a pizza place and auto parts shop. He climbed inside and began to sort through the odds and ends in the bin. As he emptied out a plastic bag, he jumped back, startled at its contents. There lay a hand cut off at the wrist. His body trembled, and he wondered if he was having the shakes from the booze he consumed the previous night. Coming to his senses, he laughed, thinking surely this must be a plastic hand. He examined it more carefully. Feeling the vomit rising in his throat he dropped the hand and started screaming. A young boy stocking cans in the grocery rushed outside. In fear of the deranged man in the dumpster, he called the police.

Detective Funk was just finishing his morning coffee when the call came in about the homeless man in the dumpster. As he maneuvered the patrol car down the country streets, he marveled at the beautiful skyline. Once again he gave thanks for making the decision to leave his police job in the Bronx and finish out his retirement in this sleepy little town. During the past two years, he had come to know the townspeople well and he guessed Josh had come back for the winter. Josh was probably having flashbacks again.

As Detective Funk pulled up to the dumpster, he quickly recognized Josh. But somehow, today, he looked different. Tears streamed down his face. The elderly man was crouched on the pavement, pointing at the dumpster and mumbling incoherently about a hand. Funk peered in. There, resting on a piece of plastic lay a human hand. Funk looked back at Joshua. What had he done?

The detective eventually calmed the distraught man and heard Josh's version of coming across the hand during his early search for food. The detective radioed for some help. The scene was cordoned off and the task of sifting through the garbage for the rest of the body began. Inch by inch, the dumpster was searched. Boxes, left over pizza, and some crushed cartons were the only items found. So whose hand was this? And where was the rest of the body?

As Detective Funk packaged the hand, he observed that it was raggedly cut just above the wrist. Although this was noteworthy, his attention was drawn to the fingers. Each fingertip had been filed down and the pad of the thumb was peeled off. Someone went to a lot of trouble to conceal the identity of the victim. In shock, everyone headed back to the office. The small police department had no reports of missing persons. But adjacent to the town, the number of missing persons in the larger city was staggering.

For two weeks, Detective Funk waited for results on the hand from the state lab. When the hand was dropped off at the lab, the results did not appear promising. The technician's original opinion was that fingerprints would not be possible. DNA testing was still not implemented in most labs across the country. Identification of the victim would depend upon good police work.

Naturally, the "hand" made headlines and every psychic and visionary were flooding the telephone lines of the small department. Quietly, Detective Funk went about his business mapping out a 2 mile radius from the dumpster. His experience told him to start close to the point of the evidence and work outwards. He began interviews of every resident in the immediate area. Did anyone see anything unusual? Did anyone have any information? Everyone in town had their theories. They ranged anywhere from the Russian Mob to aliens dissecting body parts. Funk was looking for something a little more solid. Something more like a body.

For two weeks, he went without a lead and just when things look bleak he finally got a break. Living just a mile from the dumpster, Mrs. Jack, a seventy-one year old woman, was giving Funk an earful. She related her thoughts about the hand belonging to a woman who lived two doors down. She described the woman's husband as incredibly mean. "I could hear him screaming at her all the time. He'd scream at their little boy too. He was just a mean person." Now that she thought about it, Mrs. Jack hadn't seen the woman or her son for about the past two weeks.

Officers were familiar with the family mentioned by Mrs. Jack. They had been repeatedly called out to the 100 block of town for incidents of domestic violence. The family, John and Jenny Smith were new to the town, having moved in two months prior from somewhere out east. Neighbors were frequently calling police with allegations of drug use in the home or yelling and screaming coming from the house. Detective Funk recalled the complaints.

During one incident, a neighbor called Child Protective Services along with police. The Smith's eight year-old boy was frequently sitting alone at night on the edge of the neighbor's yard. He remembered the neighbor's exact complaint. "He was like Dennis the Menace. We were like the Wilsons. We were always telling him to get off the lawn."

Another old police report listed Cindy as the victim. Police had been called when neighbors heard John trying to get Cindy to buy him a six-pack of beer. She refused and neighbors could hear him hitting her. No one ever saw the abuse but everyone saw her bruises days after the fights. Both police and residents hoped the family would move out of town. Detective Funk had a sinking feeling as he walked towards the rear of the residence.

Around the back, a curtain in the house was left open. Peering through the window, it looked as though the place was abandoned. The back yard was thick with weeds and overgrowth. No signs of the woman or child. Jumping into the patrol car, he drove to the local elementary school.

School had only recently begun after Christmas break. Children were back from Christmas vacation for only a week but school personnel were familiar with the child in question. They identified him as Charley Smith. Charley's second grade teacher indicated that he had been such a behavior problem that most students stayed away from him. She had spent extra time with him before Christmas, making a card for his mother. And no, Charley had not come back to school since the Christmas break. During the past week Charley was absent. No one had called in to report him sick. School records listed an emergency phone number for the father's place of employment. Funk proceeded to check on the child's father, John Smith.

John was employed as a laborer at a local construction company. The construction supervisor indicated that John had not been to work since Christmas. Given the nature of the job, this was not unusual. The company's workers were transient and often left without notice. What was odd, however, was that the man left no forwarding address. The boss didn't know where to send John Smith's last check. People usually collect their pay before they move on. The construction supervisor agreed to call the detective if he heard from John. In the mean time, back at the station, officers tried to find out more about John Smith. Their search revealed one sister, living in Pennsylvania. Two days later a call came which led police to believe that John and his family had moved back east, most likely to Pennsylvania.

The construction supervisor, a local resident, was quick to call police when John Smith left a message with the secretary. Mr. Smith requested that his check be mailed to an address in Johnstown, Pennsylvania. It was the address of his sister. Detective Funk packed his bags. It was 1:00 p.m. in the dead of winter when the decision was made to fly to Pennsylvania. The plane was leaving in two hours. Police in Johnstown were alerted and expecting our arrival.

There's a camaraderie that exists between small town police departments. Officers go out of their way to help anyone from out of town. The same was true of Johnstown. In the midst of a brutal snowstorm, police in 4x4 vehicles were there to pick us up at the local airport and transport us to the hotel. It was midnight when we arrived and officers filled us in. Having staked out Mr. Smith's sister's home, officers had seen Mr. Smith and his son coming and going on a regular basis. They appeared to be living with her and the boy was registered at the local school. Police indicated that Smith's sister seemed to be an upstanding citizen. During the stakeouts there was no evidence implicating Mrs. Smith. None of the officers had faced the blizzard this morning to check out the house. As the snowstorm heightened into the wee hours of the morning, our group struggled with a plan.

There's a certain clarity that comes with adrenalin, coffee and concern about a child. Or so we chose to believe in this case. It was a premier plan and relied heavily on the knowledge of local law enforcement. Police in this area were very familiar with John Smith. A convicted felon, he had lived in the area several years ago. He also served prison time for a variety of charges. Prior to leaving the state, Smith was charged with a DUI. He never showed up for the hearing. There was an outstanding warrant for his arrest. At 2:00 a.m., Mr. Smith was arrested. He was booked into the local jail. Interviewing Charley would be much easier if Smith wasn't around. With any luck, Charley's Aunt would be cooperative. Perhaps the boy could tell us the whereabouts of his mother.

At 8:00 a.m., local police drove to the aunt's residence, explaining that police from another state wanted to talk with Charley. Charley's aunt complied and at 9:00 a.m., two officers, an adult female, and a child made their way into the detective bureau. The plan had worked so far.

The police department had one room equipped with video capability, however, there was no monitor room for detectives or officers to observe the interview. Detective Funk decided to interview Charley's Aunt during the interview of the child.

Charley's Aunt stated that her brother called from out of state the night of January 8, indicating that he was moving back to Pennsylvania. Her brother sounded upset and she inquired if everything was okay. Mr. Smith replied that his wife, Cindy, left him for another man. He was returning by bus to Pennsylvania with his son, Charley. He would be there in a couple of days.

Mr. Smith further elaborated that his wife called him from a payphone and said she wasn't coming back home. She told him where the car could be picked up and he found it parked behind the local grocery store. The Aunt said she told her brother he could come

185

and live with her only if he took care of the outstanding warrant for his arrest. On the phone, Mr. Smith agreed to those conditions. John and Charley Smith arrived in Pennsylvania on January 12th.

When Smith reached his destination, he carried two duffel bags with some clothes and toys for Charley and a bag full of papers. Among the papers was an unemployment check for Cindy that he asked his sister to cash. She refused his request, indicating that she would not do anything illegal. Mr. Smith and Charley stayed at her residence for the past three weeks. Charley's Aunt registered him in second grade at the local school where he had attended school since his arrival in Pennsylvania.

Detective Funk asked Charley's Aunt if the boy had said anything unusual to her or provided any information about his mother. She replied that Charley said his mommy and daddy had a fight in the kitchen. Nothing further was said. Concerned about his welfare, Charley's Aunt consulted school personnel about how he appeared in school. They reported that Charley was a quiet child who kept silent most of the day. Teachers would catch him staring out the window, "daydreaming" during class. Even during recess, he would sit silently at the corner of the playground. More visible problems, however, occurred at the Aunt's home.

First there was the problem of his restless sleep. Charley would wake at night in a panic, calling out for help. Second, he wandered the house repeatedly calling out the number 8. His Aunt reported, "over and over he keeps saying 8, 8, 8, and I don't know what he means." Problems were also beginning to be evident during Charley's interview.

Charley's Interview

Charley, pale and withdrawn, quietly seated himself in the interview room. Given his age, police stickers, cars and posters of motor cops caught his interest. During this rapport building phase, Charley was informed that we were here from the town where he lived in previously. Very specifically, he was informed that we were looking for his mom. Charley, silent, continued to paste stickers on a blank page. Switching to a neutral topic, Charley was asked if there was anything like his bike or things that we could ship from his old house since he came with relatively few items. In response Charley stated, "my dad said she ain't never coming back." Charley would not elaborate.

Since open-ended questions about what happened to his mom were not productive, Charley was asked where we could find his mom. He stated, "far from our house by the rocks. First you have to stop the car and get out. I was in the front seat." Again Charley became silent. In response to the question, "where was the last place you saw your mom, " Charley replied, "at the house...they were fighting...my mom and dad...and my mom got hurt." In response to "and then what happened," Charley reverted to his place of quiet. Charley was asked where he was when mom and dad were fighting and he stated, "at my friend's house." Clarification was obtained by stating, "I'm sorry I'm confused. If you were at your friend's how did you know what happened?" Charley replied, "it got dark outside so I went home and saw them in the kitchen." At this point, Charley started to perspire and panic spread across his face. His last answer was so labored it was clearly time for a break.

Charley, visibly relieved, went with a Dare Officer from his school to the police department lunchroom. It was difficult to decide how to proceed with a child who was considerably anxious, yet still giving limited but controlled answers to very important questions. One's options are similar to interviewing children who are crying.

1. Reassure the child's safety and teach him to take deep breaths in an effort to manage his anxiety. Proceed slowly, asking short questions.
2. Take a break and resume the interview when the child is calmer.
3. Stop the interview totally and rely on other investigative material.
4. Offer the child tasks other than talking that allow him to depict the events.

The last option appeared promising. When the interview resumed, Charley was offered a pencil and paper and provided the opportunity to draw what happened to his mom. He balked at the task and immediately stated, "I can't draw." Encouraging Charley was of no use. He immediately stated that he didn't feel like talking much anymore. The interview was terminated but Charley did agree to come back for a visit the next day. Police and his Aunt accompanied Charley back to her residence. She reassured officers that she would do nothing to impede the investigation. She also agreed to refrain from asking Charley any questions. A follow-up appointment was set for 8:00 the following morning.

187

After much brainstorming, it was decided that Charley would need a task that would require less effort. The task would require knowledge of what officers had found in Charley's old residence. While en route to Pennsylvania, officers had contacted the owner of the rental property and entered the home. The landlord stated that Mr. Smith called and said he was moving back east due to a family emergency. The landlord had cleaned the home and repainted the house. He stated that only one room needed repainting since it appeared that Mr. Smith had painted one wall in the bedroom. It was different than the original color. Officers were currently checking for blood evidence. We asked for photographs of the residence to be faxed to the Johnstown Police Department.

When the copies arrived via fax machine, the photographs were of little utility in cueing Charley's recall. The images were blurry and difficult to identify. The only alternative was to sit down and begin drawing. One by one, the furniture that was present in the photographs was drawn. Since the rental house had come furnished, the same items would have been in the house when Charley lived there. In addition, we drew a female, male and child figure. The items were cut out with the idea that Charley might be able to arrange them on a clean sheet of paper in order to assist him in telling us what he remembered. Where he placed the items might also reveal his recollection of the interior of the residence. If the items were placed accurately, the picture might corroborate his account of the events.

Charley appeared in good spirits when he arrived for his second interview. His Aunt, however, intercepted the Detective, frantic to talk with him outside of Charley's presence. She stated that her brother called from jail demanding to talk to Charley. She told him that Charley was in school but her brother was persistent. He told me to, "get my ass down there right now cause he can't talk about this on the phone." Charley's Aunt stated that she was afraid of her brother but willing to go and visit him. She wanted to know what happened to Cindy because she refused to believe that Cindy would leave without her son. She also said there was something else she hadn't previously revealed to police.

On several instances when the Smith family lived in Pennsylvania, Cindy, crying, had called and claimed that John accused her of seeing other men. John beat Cindy until she admitted that he was right. Cindy wanted her sister-in-law to know that the accusations were lies. The last time that the Aunt spoke with Cindy was on

188

January 4th. Cindy said she was getting ready to leave John for good.

While Detective Funk continued speaking with Charley's Aunt, Charley began his interview. He acknowledged that the information from his first interview was correct. His mom and dad had fought in the kitchen. He added that his dad punched his mom with fists by the stove in the kitchen. Charley said his dad then shouted at his mom, "get in the bedroom!" Charley followed his parents into the bedroom. At this point in the interview, Charley buried his head in his arms. He could not continue.

Charley was redirected to the box of cutouts on the table. He was instructed that he could use any of the items to place on a piece of paper so that we could know what the bedroom looked like. Charley sifted through the items.

The cutouts included a bed, TV, armchair, couch, table, chairs, stove, fridge, and coffee table. Although sparse, these were the only items in the house. The cutouts also included a female figure, male figure and child. Charley began to place items on the paper as he recalled them from his parent's bedroom. He placed a bed in the middle with a chair in the corner. On top of the chair he placed a TV. He then took a pencil and drew two lines, indicating that this was the doorway to the bedroom. He placed his name in between the two lines stating that he stood in the doorway and watched. Charley then took the female cut out and placed it on top of the bed, coloring in the left leg and right arm, stating, "this is the blood." He placed an "x" on the paper, stating "dad was here." A copy of the paper is below.

Figure 21. Charley's picture

Charley's placement of the furniture matched exactly to the items in the photo of the bedroom. Indentations remained where the bed had once been. Even the television was still precariously placed on top of the armchair. Using his picture as a reference, Charley stated that he went to the doorway of his parent's bedroom because of the fighting. He heard glass breaking and his mom yelling, "no." When he reached the doorway, he saw his mother laying on the bed and his father standing where he had drawn the "x."

Charley stated that the cut out of the female on the bed was his mother. The darkened areas he colored on the leg and arm of the cut out were blood. When asked if there was blood anyplace else, he replied, "it was all over my dad...and on the floor by the fridge." The blood out by the fridge was from his dad "punching and kicking" his mom. Blood was also streaked along the hallway wall leading to the bedroom and on the bedroom wall. When Charley's dad saw Charley in the doorway, he yelled and slammed the door shut. Charley did not hear his mother say anything after that point.

Charley was unsure how much time passed before his dad came out of the room. He did state, however, that he went to the living room and turned on a "Looney Tunes" video. It was about half over when his dad exited the bedroom. His dad went to the fridge for a coke and returned to the master bedroom. With a backward glance, Charley's dad ordered him to go to bed because they would be "getting up early in the morning." Charley slept on the pull out couch with the TV playing. Afraid of his father, he could not sleep.

In the morning, Charley found his father in the master bedroom disassembling the bed. The mattress and parts of the headboard lay on the floor. Charley stated that he helped his dad carry the mattress out into the garage. He could see blue bed sheets sticking out of a garbage bag into which his father threw his mom's purse and cigarette case. Two cans of yellow paint were in the bedroom. His father had painted one of the bedroom walls. There was no sign of his mother.

Charley's father told him that his mother left and was never coming back. He then directed Charley to help him carry some of the garbage bags out to the car. They carried about four or five bags and placed them into the trunk of the car. The first stop was at the dumpster by the grocery store. Charley stated that his dad threw one of the bags in there. Next, his dad drove along country roads and threw several bags out by some rocks away from the road. They returned home, finished cleaning up the house and left the next day on the bus to his aunt's house.

Most of Charley's answers were only one sentence long in response to direct questions. For example, elaboration about the car used to dispose of the body was not offered until specific questions were asked. The following interview sequence occurred after Charley said, "that's all...then we went to my aunt's."

| Interviewer: | I'm confused, what happened to your car? |
| Charley: | My dad called two men and they came and took it. |

| Interviewer: | Did you know the two men? |
| Charley: | No I never seen them before. |

| Interviewer: | What kind of a car was it? |
| Charley: | White Camaro. |

| Interviewer: | So the guys came to get the car and then what happened? |
| Charley: | That's all...then we came here. |

| Interviewer: | Did your dad do anything to the car? |
| Charley: | Yeh – we washed it at the car wash. |

| Interviewer: | Did it need to be washed? |
| Charley: | Yeh from the dirt and mud and rocks from where we were driving. |

| Interviewer: | Which car wash did you guys go to? |
| Charley: | It was somewhere in the city – I don't know the name. |

| Interviewer: | And then what happened? |
| Charley: | We took the bus here. |

| Interviewer: | Did you stop anywhere and get off the bus? |
| Charley: | No – they just let us get off to smoke but I stayed inside. |

| Interviewer: | Okay...anything else you can think of that is important that I may not have asked you? |

Charley: Nope.

Interviewer: Would you like to write a note to your old teacher or friends and say goodbye since you're in a new place now. We can take it back for you.

Charley: Yeh...my teacher, Mrs. Swanson...she was nice.

Charley's note was packed up to give to his previous teacher. It was determined that further interviews would probably not yield any additional information. The child needed to be in counseling which was arranged prior to our departure. It was now time for Charley to heal.

The interviews of Charley were conducted over the course of two days in four short (fifteen minute blocks) of time. While Charley was being interviewed on the second day, his Aunt, sobbing entered the police department. During a jail visit, John Smith told his sister that he killed his wife, Cindy. He then cut up her body and discarded the parts in various locations. John Smith stated he wanted to confess.

Mr. Smith admitted to killing Cindy in their home while 8 year-old Charley was watching T.V. He first beat Cindy in the kitchen and then stabbed her in the bedroom of their home. High on methamphetamines, John Smith dragged her into the bathroom where he cut up her body with a hacksaw and large knife. He packaged the pieces in plastic bags and threw them out in various remote locations while driving with his son in the front seat of the car. The date of Cindy's death was January 8th. Charley Smith had clearly committed the date of his mother's death to memory. The significance of the number eight now was obvious. As you can see by the headlines, John Smith's arrest came as no surprise to neighbors in his community.

Dismemberment arrest doesn't stun neighbors

By Dennis Wagner and Chris Moeser
THE PHOENIX GAZETTE

Neighbors usually are shocked to learn that the family next door was involved in

killing his wife and hacking her to pieces

In fact, residents were speculating for weeks that the dismembered hands found Jan. 8 in a Dumpster belonged to

hands.' "

"I could hear him screaming at her all the time," Betty Thornton, 71, said. "He was just a mean person. He'd scream at

Drive repeatedly to quell disputes. And at least one resident called detectives to share a murder theory.

Investigators sent fingerprints from the

Figure 22. Newspaper article

In addition to John Smith's confession, the state lab eventually matched a partial print on the severed hand to Cindy Smith. Blood evidence was found on the wall that Smith had painted. Although cleaned by Smith, blood was also detected on the kitchen floor and hallway. In spite of efforts to comb the area, no other body parts were found until months later. It was the sheriff's search team on horseback who stumbled on the torso of Cindy Smith while looking for another missing person. The rest of her body parts were never found.

In exchange for his testimony, Mr. Smith's only request was to get him out of the jail in Pennsylvania. At age forty three, his previous criminal record included thirty two counts of burglary, harassment and terroristic threats that had landed him in a Pennsylvania prison. Apparently, he had not made many friends. John Smith was eventually extradited to the jurisdiction of his crime where he pleaded guilty to second-degree murder. He was sentenced to twenty-two years in prison. Charley Smith was placed in foster care.

Given the horrific nature of this crime, telephone calls were made to follow-up on Charley's mental health. His Aunt stated that after the interviews were conducted, Charley seemed more at peace and spent most nights sleeping well at her home. His behavior over the next month, however, led her to turn him over to the state. He was eventually placed in counseling with a child psychiatrist. Much to everyone's amazement, Charley was discharged from therapy four weeks later. The summary report from the mental health clinic indicated that Charley was fine. He just needed to forget about what happened. Horrific events, however, just don't go away. Memories can torment children for years as you can see from the following summary about a child named Sammy.

Why Counseling Is Necessary

Prosecutors, preparing for sentencing in a vehicular homicide case, referred Sammy, a seven year-old boy, for an assessment. Sammy's mother, Wednesday Jordan, was the victim of the homicide. Two years prior, Wednesday was the passenger in a car carrying her two children, Sammy and Lisa. Sammy was five and Lisa was a toddler. The driver of Wednesday's car, a family friend, was drunk. The car crashed into another vehicle as well as a median and light post. Wednesday was killed instantly and the driver walked away unscathed.

Sammy and his sister were transported by helicopter to a nearby hospital and treated for minor injuries. Sammy, Lisa, and their grieving father, eventually went to live with Sammy's maternal grandparents. It was his grandmother that brought Sammy to the office.

Sammy's grandmother, Lynn, stated that prosecutors wondered if Sammy could testify at the upcoming sentencing of the drunk driver. When prosecutors met with Sammy, he remained silent, answering not one of their questions. Prosecutors, along with the grandmother were concerned about Sammy's mental health.

After her daughter's death, Lynn had scheduled Sammy for counseling. He attended a few sessions and counseling was terminated because the child was not discussing anything that happened. At home, however, Sammy refused to sleep in his own bed and woke frequently during the night. Every night he slept with his grandparents. To no avail, they had tried everything to get him back into his own bed. His father, lost in a world of grief, was little help. Often angry, he would yell at Sammy to "grow up" and listen to his grandparents. He felt Sammy was manipulating the household since his grades were fine at school. Sammy was a straight "A" student who caused no problems for teachers. In fact, he was one of their quietest students.

Being quiet was something that Sammy was good at. He drew no immediate attention to himself. If he did something wrong, his father would raise a fist or scare him by yelling. His mother, who protected him in the past, was no longer there. In fact, little did anyone realize, it was her image that often kept him awake.

During Sammy's initial assessment, he did not respond to any questions or casual conversation. He did not even speak his name. He did not respond to inquiries about cars, sports, bikes, family, pets or school. Sammy simply sat, appearing to pay attention to the questions but responding to nothing. He was not interested in drawing or painting. He sat quietly with hands folded in his lap. Sammy smiled occasionally and patiently waited to leave. After fifteen minutes of silence, Sammy nodded his head in agreement to a question about whether he would return for another visit.

It took several appointments before Sammy began to converse and engage in art activities. Eventually the topic of his mother's death was slowly introduced by starting from the periphery of the experience and working to the heart of the trauma. Of major concern was what Sammy was thinking about now. It appeared that something was preoccupying his thoughts to the degree that he could not sleep. Once Sammy felt comfortable and safe in the counseling environment, he offered some insight into his difficulty with sleep. Sammy was asked to draw what kept him up at night. He drew the following picture:

Figure 23. Sammy's Dreams

It was evident that Sammy still had intrusive recollections of the accident that occurred over two years ago. There were also other triggers that kept Sammy anxious and hypervigilant. One of these was the sound from the helicopter that air evacuated Sammy and his sister to the hospital. This information was obtained by asking Sammy to draw what he thought about when he was having a hard time paying attention at school. Sammy drew this picture:

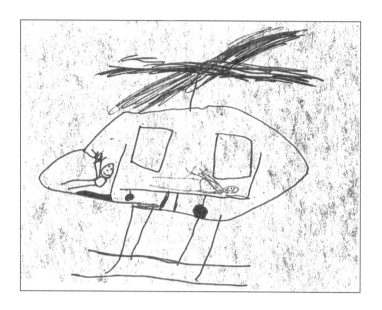

Figure 23. Sammy's Triggor Stressor

While these pictures appear to be the "heart of the experience," in fact they were peripheral to the core feature of the trauma. Upon impact, Sammy's mother was violently injured. Her neck was broken and she was partially decapitated. Everyone thought that Sammy was pinned under the seat and had not seen the body. Sammy, however, had crawled out from under the seat and witnessed the distorted image of his mother. This was one picture that he did not want to draw. Instead, Sammy was at the point in therapy where he could describe his horror. He was then taught to visualize his mother as he wanted her to look. Pictures of Sammy and his mother prior to her death were used to reinforce the positive images.

In order to reinforce positive aspects of children's lives, ask for descriptions of fun experiences the child had with the victim as well as with people who love and support him now. This task is important for a number of reasons. First, supporting positive images of the victim will eventually contribute to the replacement of the trauma images. Second, the counseling environment must not be perceived as simply a place that drags up painful memories. If this were the case, few children would want to come back for counseling.

For Sammy, one fond memory involved his mother cooking his favorite food, noodles. Over the course of time, positive images replaced trauma memories and Sammy was able to sleep in his own bed and concentrate better in school. It was a battle, however, to involve Sammy's father in counseling.

After his wife's death, Sammy's father quickly met an eighteen year-old female. Sammy's father was well into his forty's. The couple married and moved out of state, taking the children with them. Sammy's grandparents try to remain supportive of the children but the parents have limited their contact. Although Sammy had made incredible progress in counseling, the multiple losses of his mother, grandparents, school and friends eventually led to a host of behavioral problems. At the time of this writing he was placed on multiple medications, including anti-depressants. It is this type of outcome that counseling strategies attempt to prevent. Trauma specific therapies can help alleviate symptoms of stress and assist children in developing effective coping strategies. Chapter eleven offers some practical ideas for counseling children who witness violence.

Grief and Trauma: Counseling Children Who Witness Severe Violence

> *"I want to know*
> *if you will stand*
> *in the center of the fire*
> *with me*
> *and not shrink back""*
> Oriah Mountain Dreamer

Anthony, huddled in a corner at his daycare was overwhelmed beyond his capacity to cope. He had bitten his fingernails down until the skin bled. Gazing up from a flood of tears he wailed, "why won't my mommy come pick me up?" It had been three weeks since Anthony's mother died in a brutal homicide. He had attended her funeral and a class at his church on dying. Anthony, however, was four years old. His cognitive abilities weren't at the stage where he could understand that death was irreversible. All of the appropriate explanations in the world wouldn't change the fact that he didn't understand mommy was gone forever.

Anthony and His Family

On January 23, 1998, Anthony, his two sisters, their mother and her boyfriend, Dan, disappeared from the family residence. Friends who had shown up at the home for a baby shower found no one to be seen. Worried family members, aware of the couple's rocky relationship, reported the family missing. After an exhaustive appeal by the media, Anthony and his older sister were turned over to police one week later by a relative of Dan. The two children stated that Dan told them "mom took off with a boyfriend." At this time, Anthony and his ten year-old sister were taken into the care and custody of the state. One week later, Dan was detained by the border patrol while crossing into Mexico with the youngest child. Based upon a tip to the silent witness line, police discovered the children's mother buried in a shallow desert grave. Dan, who was also facing child sexual abuse charges, eventually pled guilty to murder and the children went to live with their maternal grandmother. Child Protective Services required an evaluation of the children and a plan of care.

Anthony displayed the immediate and intense suffering of many children who witness homicide. His ten year-old sister, at school when mom was bludgeoned to death with a brick, was also grief stricken. The youngest sibling, two years of age, would weep and cling to anyone who would hang on to her. Not surprising, since a toddler's need for attachment to a parent intensifies with high levels of stress. Comfort from her mother was no longer possible so she clung to substitute caregivers. The children's grandmother who had lost her daughter was equally distraught.

Since bereavement reactions vary based upon a number of factors such as the child's age, understanding of death, supportive networks, pre-existing or co-morbid conditions of the child, and prior relationships with the deceased, there is no specific pattern of symptoms that manifests when a child's parent dies unexpectedly. Add the helplessness and intense fear associated with witnessing a brutal death, and you have children presenting with an even more complex array of behaviors and symptoms. Such clients can present a daunting challenge for even the most experienced therapists. The following statement by a counselor indicates the complexity of the circumstances:

> "I have three children in my care that witnessed the murder of their most loved grandparents at the hands of their mother. Their mom is awaiting trial. The oldest child will be testifying, she was 11 at the time of the murder. The other children are 4 and 6. The 4 year old told me he went in the room and saw nana on the floor. It was a grizzly scene as they were beaten with hammers and stabbed in the neck. I have not found information to help me with these children...I am truly at a loss..."

The counselor is certainly not alone. Questions posed by mental health professionals counseling children who witness violence often include:

1) How does one obtain a full disclosure from the child?
2) How does one effectively identify triggers that remind a child of the trauma?
3) How does one assist a child to manage stress in light of everyday reminders of the trauma?
4) How does one deal with multiple losses related to change of households, schools and friends?
5) How can one facilitate the child's grieving when the unexpected and violent death occurred to someone the child knows?
6) How does one handle the competing dynamics of grief and trauma?

The last question perhaps poses the most difficulty for therapists since a bereaved child who witnessed homicide might suffer intrusive recollections, such as nightmares of a mutilated body. The tendency, therefore, would be to avoid remembering the deceased. If the victim is known to the child, in order to effectively grieve one must recollect and remember the deceased over time. With such dissonance, how does one effectively facilitate grieving without exacerbating symptoms of trauma? These are only a few of the dilemmas faced by those who provide crisis intervention and counseling services to children who witness violence. And most counseling methods have not been examined for their efficacy.

Conservative scientists who believe that only empirical data is trustworthy would suggest that few counseling techniques have been tested for effectiveness in alleviating the array of symptoms created by the intermingling of trauma and grief. The lack of research in this area is not surprising since well into the 1980's, the psychiatric community in general, believed that children did not suffer severe reactions to intense levels of stress. Today, there is sufficient evidence to indicate the contrary. With the staggering numbers of children who witness violence each year, the need for counseling is great.

It is estimated that each year, approximately ten million children in the United States witness family violence.[53] Although no current statistics exist on child witnesses to homicide, conservative estimates indicate that children witness at least twenty percent of homicides in urban areas.[54] Understanding posttraumatic stress, grief, and the impact of crises on the developmental tasks of childhood are important to design effective counseling strategies. A basic understanding of all three concepts is important, irrespective of the counselor's theoretical position.

Post-traumatic Stress In Children

According to the American Psychiatric Association (APA), traumatic events include those in which a child witnessed or experienced an event that involved actual or threatened death or serious injury to oneself or others.[55] The child's experience of the incident typically involved intense fear, helplessness or horror. Natural disasters can be catastrophic events for children but traumatic events caused by people result in more persistent and severe distress.

Psychic trauma may also depend upon the frequency of the event. In contrast to isolated events, repeated events such as domestic violence are known to cause severe psychic trauma in children. The diagnostic category that is used most often for children who develop symptoms in the aftermath of trauma is posttraumatic stress disorder, commonly referred to as PTSD.[56] There remains debate about whether posttraumatic stress is a psychiatric disorder with predisposing factors or whether the reaction is a normal one that occurs in response to abnormal stress.

The need for developmental stage-specific criteria to diagnose PTSD in children has also been discussed since those of varying ages display different symptom clusters.

There is general agreement, however, that young children may present with a disorganized, agitated state following a violent event. According to the APA (1994), most school age children and adolescents with PTSD develop symptoms that fall into the following general categories:

- persistent re-experiencing of the event
- avoidance of stimuli associated with the trauma
- symptoms of arousal

Re-Experiencing The Traumatic Event

Children can be plagued with memories of a traumatic event that include images, emotions, sensory impressions, behaviors, feelings or thoughts. Nightmares, night terrors, seeing images of the event during daily activities, repetitive play containing themes of the event and re-enactment of the trauma are all ways that children re-experience trauma. Any aspect of the traumatic memory can be re-experienced both during the day and at night. Intrusive recollections of the event can appear to the child during routine daily activities. This was the case for eight year-old Ray.

Ray's Intrusive Recollections

Ray was present during a shooting in his apartment living room. It was miraculous that he did not get shot since Ray's father, high on methamphetamines, fired twenty rounds from a gun. The father's girlfriend, struck by a bullet, died instantly. When SWAT arrived at the scene, it was Ray who eventually talked his father into turning over the gun. One month following the homicide, Ray's teacher reported that he sat and stared out the window during class time. Even when the teacher approached Ray's desk and spoke directly to him, he appeared to be in a dream state. Ray's mother, now the primary caretaker, stated that Ray would not sleep by himself, complaining of a fear of the dark and retribution from his father's girlfriend's family. He told his mother that he couldn't get a picture out of his head, but he was reluctant to draw the picture he was seeing. Ray also stated that he didn't want to talk about it.

During counseling, Ray appeared to be taxed by even the simplest requests. Starting out slowly, Ray was able to complete the following sentence:

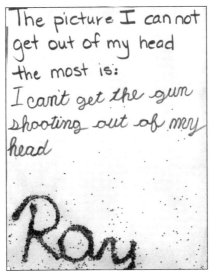

The picture I can not get out of my head the most is:
I can't get the gun shooting out of my head

Ray

Figure 25. Ray's Writing

This intrusive recollection was interfering with Ray's concentration and ability to complete class work. In an effort to address the problem, the teacher was requested to keep a chart with the circumstances and times that Ray appeared dazed. By charting the details it was determined that Ray appeared to be in shock when seated in only one classroom. Using simple and limited writing tasks in counseling, Ray was able to indicate that the noise and chaos of the shooting would flood his thoughts when he gazed out the classroom window. It was the blinds on the window that reminded Ray of the shooting. The blinds were the exact color of the ones at his old apartment.

Intrusive recollections or flashbacks are often caused by external or internal cues that remind the child of the stressful event. Although Ray identified the blinds on the classroom window as reminders of the shooting, not all children are able to identify a particular stressor in the environment. Adult observation is often necessary to corroborate the cue. Even if children cannot identify the triggers that produce stress, they still may experience physiological changes such as sweating, trembling, quickening of breath, hyperventilating or feeling like one's heart is racing. Children, therefore, may try to avoid people, places, thoughts, feelings or conversations related to the traumatic event.

Avoidance and Numbing

The stress and anxiety associated with remembering a violent event results in many children avoiding people, places or discussions of the violence. In counseling, it is important to determine if the child is avoiding discussion or simply unable to remember important pieces of information. When children are unable to identify aspects of the event, this may also lead to reluctance to participate in counseling. Determine which defense mechanism is operating by asking children if they don't remember or "just don't feel like talking about it right now."

If a child truly does not remember central features of the event, it becomes extremely difficult to identify cues that cause a flood of thoughts and physiological changes. Fragmented recollections are sometimes present when the child has experienced a state of shock. Such a state will often be accompanied by a sense of numbing and detachment from others.

Detachment or a numbing of emotions is often described by

children in the form of statements such as "I don't fit in anymore," "I have no friends," or "I just don't feel things the way I did before." Detachment and withdrawal resulting from trauma is often accompanied by a sense of a foreshortened future. This was particularly poignant with ten year-old Liza.

A Sense of Foreshortened Future

Liza's mother was murdered five days after Liza's birthday. The young mother was delivering a charity food box to the residence of a couple and their three children. Once Liza's mother entered the door, the male and female couple bound her with electrical cord and dragged her into the bedroom where she was sexually assaulted and stabbed to death. Her body was found by police, dumped behind the couple's home. The pair eventually confessed, stating that they were high on crack and wanted to steal some money. Liza's mother had $1.25 in her pocket. During the course of therapy with ten year-old Liza, she was asked about her dreams for the future. Her response was as follows:

> "I don't really think about it. I don't think I'll live to be sixteen so I don't think about driving a car. I don't think about what I want to be or anything like that"you know with all the crime out there, I just don't think I'll even make it to sixteen""

Like Liza, many children who witness violence express a sense of dismay about future events. This sense of disillusionment can appear as apathy to adults not familiar with the child's circumstances. Dismay can also be accompanied by self-destructive behaviors such as abuse of substances, self-mutilation, suicide attempts and starvation. While some of these behaviors can be a form of reenactment, they may also reflect a greater relationship between the trauma and somatization.[57]

Somatization and Inability to Modulate Arousal

Children who witness violence respond with alertness to their environment long after the danger has passed. In circumstances such as domestic violence, where the acts are chronic, children's bodies get used to the fight or flight response that is routinely required of them. Eventually, they begin to operate in a low-level fear response much of the time. Psychobiological findings indicate that continuous fight or flight responses can result in suppression or over-activity of the body's immune system, leading to a host of somatic and physical complaints. If children are in a chronic state of hyperarousal, evidence suggests that they lose their ability to identify and distinguish bodily feelings.

Symptoms of arousal are often relentless, and generally affect the child's sleep or concentration. Irritability, or a quickness to lose one's temper is often present. Children describe a sense of hypervigilance or "always being on the alert." Others manifest an exaggerated startle response. Children even vocalize that they feel "jumpy" for no identifiable reason. Young children may not be able to articulate the jumpy feeling but their behavior can reveal the startle response. For example, an exaggerated startle response was clearly evident in a preschooler who "jumped" every time a balloon popped at her daycare. She had heard and seen her mom shot with a .22 caliber handgun.

When children witness severe violence, extreme defense mechanisms may develop in order for a child to survive unbearable terror. Dissociation may occur during which time fragments of the violent experience split off from one's consciousness and sense of self. The connections between one's thoughts, feelings, sensations, images and behaviors about the violent event are shattered. In these extreme circumstances, therapies are designed to integrate the fragmented pieces and sense of self. In many of these instances, traumatic stress will intermingle with bereavement issues. Providers of care, therefore, require basic knowledge of how children mourn.

Grief

Like post traumatic stress, grief reactions in children depend upon multiple factors, including age, intellectual development, circumstances of the death and how current caretakers respond to the bereavement. Preschool children do not understand that death is irreversible. If a parent or sibling is the homicide victim, typically one sees apparent anxiety and distress through an increase in motor activity or agitated behavior. As time passes, and the deceased does not show up in the daily routine of their lives, children's anxiety moves into depression and eventually, the vacant eyes of despair.

Children like Anthony, not fully understanding their loss, rock themselves in the corner or engage in repetitive play in an attempt to soothe themselves. For example, children will take toys and strike them over and over with no end in sight. Typical of repetitive play, the activity never really goes anywhere.

For several weeks all Anthony wanted to do was "make mommy pictures" over and over to hang up in his room. Making "mommy pictures" consisted of pasting photocopies of his mother's picture onto pieces of white paper and drawing his 4 year-old version of hearts all over the paper. Anthony would cut and paste these pictures for hours at a time. With Anthony, the repetition appeared to be an attempt to master a helpless situation. Repetitive play occurs most commonly in young children with limited language capacity.

Children without extensive language skills may also respond to loss with altered bodily functions. For example, preschoolers who are already toilet trained may start bedwetting or may regress to infantile behaviors. An extreme example of altered bodily functions occurred with three year-old Katie. Katie witnessed the homicide of her ten year-old sister at the hands of her fifteen year-old stepbrother, Christopher. Police were called to the family home when the ten year old, a straight A student, did not show up for school. Law enforcement began a search for the missing child as well as her stepbrother who had left with the family car. Christopher, schooled in white supremacist dogma, eventually confessed to killing his stepsister because she was half African American in origin. Christopher threatened to kill Katie if she told anyone that he had stuffed the girl's body in a thirty-five gallon trashcan in the family yard.

Within one week of the slaying, Katie refused to walk, resorted to crawling and drank only from a baby bottle. She also became ill with continuous upper respiratory tract infections. Physicians indicate that illnesses are more common in bereaved young children, particularly if they have lost a parent. Physical complaints such as fatigue, loss of appetite and gastrointestinal problems, however, can also be seen in school age children who have lost a parent.

In contrast to preschoolers, school age children are somewhat better equipped to understand death and mourn for the homicide victim. Given their more developed cognitive skills, an understanding of death to the typical school age child can be likened to other types of harsh life circumstances. School age children need to experience the "reality" of the situation in order to fully comprehend the concept. For example, if a school age child is anxious about testifying in court, seeing the courtroom and having an explanation of the proceedings may diminish the anxiety. The same is true for death. Most school age children need to be able to understand the reality of death in order to mourn. In other words, they need to be able to see the deceased in the company of an adult who can explain the experience. Rituals such as funerals, prayer services or other ceremonies make the experience real for the child and are an important aspect to understanding death. The same is true for adolescents.

Adolescents are able to mourn and express feelings in a similar manner to adults. While there are no particular sequential steps in the grief process, in general, adolescents experience a numbing, shock or disbelief about the death. Sadness sets in and anger can be evident, either towards the deceased for leaving or towards oneself for "failing to help" a victim of violence. Although adolescents have the capacity to mourn, given their developmental stage, a desire for independence often results in withdrawn behavior and an attempt to "go it alone." This withdrawal can lead to extreme isolation. Occasionally, the withdrawal is a product of a posttraumatic identity in an attempt to organize one's life after a death in order to survive. These disruptions to the development of a child's sense of self can result in serious impairment. Counseling child witnesses to violence, therefore, inevitably requires one to understand developmental tasks of childhood and adolescence.

Developmental Tasks of Childhood and Adolescence

In his landmark text, Childhood and Society, Danish-American psychoanalyst, Erik Erikson, described eight stages of development in the human life cycle.[58] Five of these are applicable to children. Erickson believed that influences of individuals and the environment could affect the development of one's personality. Specific psychological strengths are most strongly affected during distinct stages of child development. Crises, such as witnessing violence or bereavement, at any stage of development must be successfully resolved in order to strengthen the capabilities of the child. Unsuccessful resolution may result in debilitating impairment related to the specific developmental task during which the crisis occurred. The younger the child, the more likely an impairment would occur since the child's sense of self has not yet reached the apparent character structure of a young adult. Chronic violence, such as that witnessed by children whose parents batter each other can involve disruptions throughout one's entire childhood. In order to understand how a child may be affected by violence, the developmental tasks for childhood and adolescence are outlined below:

Table 5. Erikson's Psychosocial Stages of Development

Age	Task	Important Event	Outcome
Infancy	Trust versus Mistrust	Caretaking/ Feeding	Trust versus mistrusts people and environment
Toddler	Autonomy versus Shame Doubt	Toilet Training	Pride in self versus doubt in one's abilities
Preschool	Initiative versus Guilt	Independence	Initiates activities versus inhibited
School	Industry versus Inferiority	School Success	Acquires skills versus feeling inferior
Adolescence	Identity versus Confusion	Peer Relations	Establishes "who am I" versus confusion

You can see that trauma and grief are crises that can affect the most fundamental tasks of childhood. Think of the toddler, Katie who witnessed the murder of her sister. She is now bedwetting and has regressed to bottle-feeding. Will she develop autonomy or a sense of shame and doubt about herself? Think of a bereaved school age child, whose academic work has declined and increasingly withdrawn behavior, has alienated friends. Will she experience skill mastery or a sense of inferiority? Since the developmental task of adolescence is identity versus role confusion, what type of identity will the adolescent develop when he repeatedly sees his father batter his mother? When violence is interwoven through childhood, counseling can assist children to successfully manage crises so that symptoms diminish, developmental tasks can be accomplished, and a sense of pleasure in life can eventually return. Prior to deciding upon counseling strategies, a thorough assessment of the child is required.

Assessment

As in most other circumstances, collecting data from as many sources as possible is important in the assessment of children who witness violence. The following form is offered as an example of preliminary information necessary for developing a plan of care for children who witness homicide.

INTAKE INFORMATION

Date: _____ Historian: _____

Child _____ Address: _____

DOB: _____ Phone: _____

Age: _____ Sex: _____ Race: _____

Special Needs: _____ Medications: _____

Legal Guardian: _____

Referral Source: _____

Pre-Event

Caretakers: _____

Siblings: _____

Address:_ _____

Daycare/School: _____Grade:_____

Performance at School:_____

Last apt. with a doctor: _____Reason:_____

Post-Event

Physical Placement:_____

Household/Shelter Members:_____

Location of Caretakers: _____

Placement of Siblings:_____

Daycare/School: _____Grade:_____

Performance at School:_____

Agencies Involved:

CPS: _____CPS Specialist:_____

Police Department: _____

DR#: _____Investigating Detective:_____

Attorneys: _____

Counselors:_____
Principal/Teacher_____
Physician: _____

Event:
Date:_____
Nature of Event:_____
_____
_____

Who found the body? _____
Child's Relationship To Deceased: _____
Location of Child When Police Arrived: _____
Spontaneous Utterances of Child: _____
To Whom:_____
Others At Scene: _____
Injuries to Deceased:_____
_____

Medical Examiner's Cause of Death:_____
_____

Suspect(s): _____
Relationship of Suspect to Child:_____
Current Status of Suspect:_____

Bereavement:
Was child told of death?_____ By Whom? _____
What was child told?_____
Type of services?_____ Date:_____
Child's Participation: _____
Mother's Religious Beliefs _____Father's_____

Current Status:
Appearance: _____
Appetite: _____
Academic Performance: _____
Social Interactions: _____
Sleep: _____
Affect: _____
Thoughts: _____
Behaviors:_____
Substance Use:_____
Other signs and symptoms: _____

Developmental Task of Childhood: _____

Most Immediate Concern: _____

_____

Expressed By: _____

Boychuk, 1997

This form is a starting point for collecting information relevant to trauma, bereavement and the child's growth and development. A more comprehensive history, relying upon multiple sources of information, will be required in each of the intake categories. As in other mental health assessments, the quality of the initial information will depend upon the reliability and amount of information provided by the historian. Even if the historian is a guardian who can provide extensive history, it is still important to obtain information from school, criminal justice, child welfare, medical and mental health professionals. A comprehensive assessment of the child's needs cannot be done in a vacuum. Emotions run high in circumstances involving children.

A grief-stricken relative may observe a child's behaviors differently than school personnel, coaches, or peers. Brief information given to you about the homicide may be considered differently once you have viewed the case file. And finally, child witnesses, themselves, will provide you with critical information. The more data you collect, the greater the likelihood that you will design the most effective counseling strategies for each particular child.

Counseling Strategies

Individual psychotherapy for children who witness violence must be based upon the intricate needs of each particular child. The immediate goal will be to assist the child and family to identify, manage and cope with distressing symptoms and thereby normalize the child's daily routine. First, address the symptoms that are most profoundly distressing for the child. These will differ with each child you see. At the risk of being overly simplistic, following the initial intake, ask yourself:

a)   What are the most distressing symptoms for the child?

b)   Are any of the symptoms/behaviors life threatening?

c)   What was the pre-existing condition of the child?

d)   What is the source(s) of each symptom?

e)   What theoretical models will guide my treatment?

f)   What strategies will I use for each presenting problem?

g)   Have I planned for care related to the child's body, mind and soul?

h)   How will I involve the family/caretakers in care?

i)   What are my plans for continuous assessment and evaluation of treatment?

In general, trauma-specific therapies require that children be able to remember, describe and process their experience in order to understand themselves and their world. This is most often referred to as "allowing a child to tell you their story." The problem lies in the fact that even after many children have "told their story," they manifest symptoms of hyperarousal or present with other somatic complaints. So how does one go about getting full disclosure?

Full Disclosure

A full disclosure requires one to collect, integrate and provide all fragments of memories related to a violent event. It can best be understood by examining the two basic forms of memory, conscious and unconscious.[59] Conscious memory, also referred to as declarative memory, stores information that can be stated or reported in narrative form. These include such aspects as facts, thoughts and emotions about the violent event. Sometimes, the level of terror is so intense, children fail to focus or attend to the facts or incoming stimuli. Instead, their memory contains perceptions, motor behaviors or body sensations related to the event. These bodily sensations are not possible for a child to articulate and are not extinguished by talking or processing information about the violence. Hence problems remain even with "telling of the story."

Over the years, specialized therapies have addressed body work and the field of bioenergetics has grown. Because of its specialized nature, I refer you to the works of Stanley Keleman[60] and Peter Levine.[61] The International Institute for Bioenergetic Analysis can also provide helpful materials for those interested in understanding the body-mind connection.[62] While body work is often necessary, one still must attempt to obtain a verbal disclosure from children.

Talking about violence is best done in a calm and safe environment. Children's experiences of discussing traumatic anxiety and overcoming it in a safe place reinforces that distress can be part of the past instead of the present. While most clinicians recommend that counseling begin with trauma versus grief work, this principle does not apply for all homicide cases. Children who witness homicide may present with severe symptoms that are the result of bereavement issues or dislocation given their placement in a new household. Interrupted sleep, eating and routine activities need to be examined carefully for the source of disruption. This was true of Heather, referred for counseling one day prior to the funeral of her mother.

Heather

Heather had lived with her mother and stepfather until her mother was fatally shot by police in a drug raid. The maternal grandparents offered their home as an emergency placement for Heather. Heather's mother, however, had become estranged from extended family for the past several years when she started making and dealing methamphetamines. The maternal grandparents were afraid to attend the funeral for fear of retaliation from Heather's stepfather, who was not yet apprehended. Instead of trauma work, the priority at this time was to prepare Heather for the funeral as well as arrange for transportation, and an adult to accompany her there. The session was spent identifying her favorite song, purchasing the music tape for the funeral, and preparing Heather for the services. Heather attended her mother's memorial services in the presence of a counselor and detective.

During the funeral, Heather approached the casket to say good-bye to her mother. She became instantly upset, stating how badly her mother's face looked. A significant amount of reconstruction had been done to the victim's face since she had been shot during the police raid. Like many teenagers, Heather was also upset at the clothes her mother was wearing in the casket, stating, "I know she wouldn't have wanted to wear that."

Less than a week after the funeral, Heather developed new symptoms. She started having nightmares about her mother's face. Much of the work that relieved Heather from the intrusive recollections focused on having her visualize how she wished her mother had looked and how she remembered her face from the past. For Heather, symptoms that developed from the bereavement services needed to be addressed before the trauma work related to the shooting. All symptoms, irrespective of their source, should be

214

carefully assessed to determine if they are life threatening. Such was the case with ten year-old Jenny, referred for counseling following the unexpected and violent death of her mother.

Jenny

Since her father was working, two women from a local church brought Jenny in for counseling. The family practiced a highly structured and rigid religion, and in some ways, the women had become "surrogate mothers" to this girl and her brother. The women felt that Jenny could not be helped by a counselor, particularly if the professional wasn't Christian. The women felt that prayer was the only road to Jenny's recovery. When Jenny arrived for her appointment, she weighed only forty pounds. The child had stopped eating entirely since her mother had been murdered.

Irrespective of any other problems, Jenny's physical health was of critical concern. She was referred to a pediatrician and started on multiple doses of pediasure in an effort to boost her nutritional status. Her weight, hydration, hemoglobin and electrolyte levels were monitored regularly. Although the seriousness of this situation was obvious, other children may hide acts designed to take their lives.

Suicidal gestures and acts are sometimes made in private. Suicidality, therefore, needs to be addressed with every school age and adolescent child who witnesses violence. It is most commonly seen with children and adolescents who feel they should have intervened or protected the victim during the violence. The topic can be readily addressed during counseling, particularly when aspects of the violent event are discussed. Addressing suicidality is an integral component of trauma-specific therapy.

Trauma-Specific Therapy

Trauma-specific therapy begins somewhat like an investigative interview in that children are presented with opportunities to describe their experiences of the violence. The difference is that one has time to elicit the information in smaller segments using more modalities that can slowly alleviate the child's distress.[63] Prior to eliciting the child's experience, teach the child deep breathing techniques, progressive muscle relaxation, and positive imagery. These are all helpful in demonstrating to the child that he or she can manage their distress. When children are able to describe violent events without overwhelming distress, their helplessness is diminished and sense of control is reinforced.

With school age and adolescent children who can give verbal accounts, have children describe what happened as best they can from beginning to end. Throughout the course of therapy, use other modalities, such as drawing, writing or movement to express the child's experience. Pictures often depict a much different aspect of the experience. Be creative in your efforts to understand the child's experience.

While drawing with colored pens is often appealing to younger children, in this technological age, other options are also available. Breanna, a twelve-year old girl used the computer to begin her counseling.

Breanna

On July 6, 1998, Breanna's father initiated a 911 call to police, reporting that his wife had shot herself in the head. When emergency personnel responded, they found twelve year-old Breanna outside of the home. The medical examiner and police documented that the gunshot wound was on the nose and there were soot deposits on the right side of the victim's face. Stippling was found on her right forearm, bruises under her chin, and red areas marked the center of her throat. The medical examiner indicated that death was not instant; rather, the victim had asphyxiated when her lungs filled with blood from the injury. In other words, she died a painful death, choking on her own blood. Breanna's father, a suspect at the time, was deceptive on two polygraphs administered by two separate examiners. However, there still was not enough evidence to arrest him for the crime.

In spite of initial difficulties with the investigation, detectives did not give up. An entire year was spent with a criminalist firearms examiner who assisted with an extensive recreation of the scene and several test firings with the revolver and ammunition. It was the expert's opinion that the gunshot wound could not have been self-inflicted and eventually, a jury found Breana's father guilty of his wife's murder. During the year prior to his arrest, Breanna lived with her father, a military man, described as highly controlling and hostile.

On the day of his arrest, Breanna was informed that her father was taken into custody. She was distraught, confused and upset that her only living parent was taken away from her. Breanna offered a sketchy and limited account of what occurred the night of her mother's homicide. Breanna stated that she was sleeping at the time her mom died. It was pretty hard to fathom that Breanna did not hear a .44 magnum fired in the next room. It became readily apparent that Breanna was not willing to implicate her father at any cost.

Breanna had difficulty talking about any type of emotions, in part, due to the highly controlled environment she had lived in during the past year. An honor student, Breanna did not want to write or draw but was willing to develop a book about her life using a PowerPoint computer package. Breanna began her account as follows:

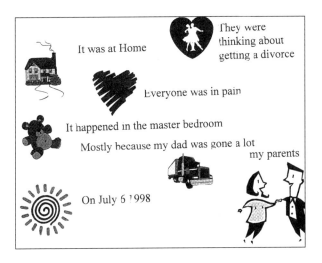

Figure 26. Breanna'a story

As you can see, Breanna's description began in fragments. Just as she was able to begin sharing her thoughts, a juvenile court judge ordered her placement with the paternal grandparents in spite of recommendations to the contrary from a court-appointed child psychologist, school personnel, counselors and child protective services specialists. The placement was in a different city and occurred just prior to the criminal proceedings involving her father. Breanna's therapy was discontinued and her paternal grandparents placed her in a church youth group.

The book that Breanna began to develop was designed to allow her to provide details of the violence and describe those aspects of her life that had changed. Depending upon the child's needs a variety of topics can be covered in the book. Many mental health agencies have limited budgets and supplies are scarce. These books can be developed using a simple three-ringed binder, white paper and plastic paper protectors. Some children elaborately glue lace and decorative items on the cover while others simply label the book.

Individualized Books Of Children's Experiences

Request that children label the book, "A Book About Me and My Mom" (victim of violence or deceased individual). Encourage the child to design the book cover in whatever manner they choose. The following are examples of book covers designed by two different ten year-old girls whose mothers were murdered:

Figure 27. Book Covers

The contents of a grief or trauma book are highly individualized and are based upon concerns that arise during counseling. Contents can include anything from the nature of restructured families to new school circumstances. For most children, however, the following issues arise at various times throughout counseling. Activities are planned around the following topics:

a) My Family
b) What Happened
c) Changes That Are Hard
d) Changes That Are Easy
e) My Body
f) Ways I Can Control Stress
g) Where My (victim) Is Now
h) Things I Have Never Asked But Want To Know

i)   Things I Miss About (victim)
j)   People That Love Me
k)   Things That Keep Me Up At Night
l)   School Days
m) What I Daydream About
n)   Things I Do Well
o)   Things I Can Do When I Get Upset
p)   Wishes For The Future
q)   Anniversary Pages Relevant To The Child and Deceased
r)   Behavior Modification Charts (With Stickers For Children Having Difficulty Concentrating, Remembering To Do Homework, Tasks, etc.)
s)   Leaving Counseling With Help From My Family

Each of the pages is designed to evaluate what the child is thinking or feeling in order to select an appropriate technique such as cognitive restructuring, desensitization or bioenergetic healing to address the presenting problem. Clearly, theoretical beliefs will guide the method used by the therapist to alleviate distress.

Eclectic methods involving cognitive restructuring, behavior modification, desensitization, story telling and holistic healing can be designed based upon writings and drawings of children. Art can provide valuable insight into cues that triggor either painful or pleasant memories for the child. Refrain from interpreting children's drawings, however, as there is too much room for error. Consider the following piece of art created by a ten year-old female whose mother was murdered by strangers:

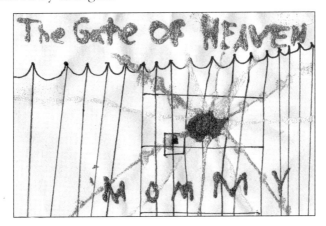

Figure 28. The Gate of Heaven

219

At first glance, the picture looks like the gates of heaven with the word mommy written in glitter pen. If one were guessing what the picture might mean, one might speculate that the picture was a representation of where this child thought her mother was. Instead, she explained the following:

> "I drew the gates of heaven cause that's where I think my mom is but I don't really know. I want to think she is there but what if when they were killing her – right before that she didn't believe in God and then she didn't go to heaven, or could she still go there?"

This particular piece of art generated questions the child had about God and the session offered her relief to know that her mom would be in heaven. Another way to obtain information that preoccupies children is to give them permission to discuss things they have never asked anyone else. An exercise that requests children to list "things I have always wondered about" gives children permission to inquire about immediate concerns that have not been verbalized. One nine year-old girl whose mother was the victim of a domestic violence homicide generated the following list:

I wonder:
1)   If she comes back to life will she forget about me
2)   If I will forget about her and nobody will tell me
3)   If my dog is O.K

This child's statements indicated her lack of understanding about the permanency of death. In spite of attending bereavement groups, she still thought her mother might come back to life. In addition, she was concerned about the fading memory she had of her mother's features. Displaying pictures of her mother helped alleviate some of her anxiety. Identifying fond recollections of a deceased victim of violence are important aspects of any child's counseling. The following list indicates one child's thoughts about her mother.

Figure 29. Things Liza Misses About Her Mom

Lastly, the importance of monitoring children on anniversary dates or those holidays that pay special tribute to the deceased are important. The following examples illustrate the difficulty that children may have on days such as Mother's Day, Father's Day, the anniversary of a parent's death and the first major holidays without the deceased. At one after school program, this nine year-old girl drew the following mother's day card. It stated, "On Mother's Day, mommy I made you a fuzzy poster. I am taking it to your grave."

Figure 30. Mother's Day Card

221

An adolescent, reflecting on her mother's homicide indicated the following anniversary dates were important to her.

My mom is at a Military Cemetery

see my mom on her
-BIRTHDAY
-CHRISTMAS
-ANNIVERSARY

Figure 31. Days To Remember

As the years pass, children will develop new concerns about the anniversary dates and other struggles with life. They will need different types of support.

Therefore, it is difficult to advocate pre-existing manuals for children to complete. Children's problems and symptoms don't follow an orderly table of context. Rather, general topics allow the therapist to individualize counseling and meet the needs of each child and family.

I also advocate that caretakers of bereaved children participate in counseling, particularly if they are related to the deceased. Relatives of crime victims often live in agony from day to day, while caring for children of the deceased. While their needs are equally great, their care is beyond the scope of this book. With counseling and support, they and the children they care for, can once again rejoice in the pleasures of life. An old therapy saying applies to counseling with children who witness violence just as with clients in other circumstances.

"Therapy is the boat across the river and we need to be sure that passengers eventually get off. "

CHAPTER TWELVE

Compassion Fatigue

After sharing the heart wrenching stories of children and families in this book, it would be remiss of me not to remind you of the strength, support, and resources you need to remain healthy and carry on. Whatever your role, volunteer, correctional officer, medical or mental health professional, police, advocate or human services worker, you are likely exposed on a routine basis to continued suffering and the results of cruelty. Your work requires tremendous emotional fortitude, which can drain your resources physically, emotionally and spiritually. At times you may have dedicated yourself so much to others that it feels like there is little energy left for yourself. Caring for oneself and others in a healthy balance is something most professionals strive for, but if you work with suffering individuals, families or communities, you are vulnerable to compassion fatigue.

The concept of compassion fatigue is relatively new, having emerged in the literature in the past decade. Compassion fatigue is "the emotional residue" from experiences with the suffering, particularly those suffering from the consequences of traumatic events.[64] It is substantively different from "burnout" which is generally associated with pressures in the workplace and can readily be healed by taking breaks or great vacations. Instead, compassion fatigue is a state of tension, or preoccupation with the trauma of clients – a kind of secondary posttraumatic stress.

Compassion fatigue manifests in a number of ways that are similar to post-trauma stress. Although the individual may not be traumatized by an event that was experienced, one absorbs the trauma through the experiences and disclosures of the client. Symptoms therefore, can include:

- re-experiencing the client's traumatic event through intrusive imagery, repetitive thoughts or nightmares
- avoidance of reminders of the client's traumatic experiences such as movies or material used in the course of therapy

- numbing or distancing from one's own feeling
- persistent arousal such as feeling overwhelmed or hypervigilant, making daily tasks and even minor decisions difficult to make
- physical or somatic complaints
- addictive or compulsive behavior including overwork, or self-medicating with alcohol or drugs
- disturbances of sleep,
- preoccupation with the safety of loved ones or oneself or the opposite counter-phobic behavior such as continually exposing oneself to danger
- increasing isolation from family, friends and colleagues
- driven behavior and an inability to relax
- disruption of cognitive schemas such as thoughts about how the world is or ought to be.

Checklists are now available to help individuals in assessing whether or not one is at risk for compassion fatigue. Much of the work in this area is being done at Florida State University Psychosocial Stress Research Program. Their instrument, currently under development, is not intended as a medical diagnosis but is simply a self- test. Try it out and determine what your risk level is.

Compassion Fatigue Self-Test
Consider each of the following characteristics about you and your current situation. Write in the number for the best response. Use one of the following answers:

1=rarely/never
2=at times
3=not sure
4=often
5=very often

1.___ I force myself to avoid certain thoughts or feelings that remind me of a frightening experience.
2.___ I find myself avoiding certain activities or situations because they remind me of a frightening experience.
3.___ I have gaps in my memory about frightening events.
4.___ I feel estranged from others.
5.___ I have difficulty falling or staying asleep.
6.___ I have outbursts of anger or irritability with little provocation.

7.___ I startle easily.

8.___ While working with a victim I thought about violence against the person or persons who victimized.

9.___ I am a sensitive person.

10.___ I have had flashbacks connected to my clients and families

11.___ I have had first-hand experience with traumatic events in my adult life.

12.___ I have had first-hand experience with traumatic events in my childhood.

13.___ I have thought that I need to "work-through" a traumatic experience in my life.

14.___ I have thought that I need more close friends.

15.___ I have thought that there is no one to talk with about highly stressful experiences.

16.___ I have concluded that I work too hard for my own good.

Items about your clients and their families:

17.___ I am frightened of things traumatized people and their family have said or done to me.

18.___ I experience troubling dreams similar to a client of mine and their family.

19.___ I have experienced intrusive thoughts of sessions with especially difficult clients and their families.

20.___ I have suddenly and involuntarily recalled a frightening experience while working with a client or their family.

21.___ I am preoccupied with more than one client and their family.

22.___ I am losing sleep over a client and their family's traumatic experiences.

23.___ I have thought that I might have been "infected" by the traumatic stress of my clients and their families.

24.___ I remind myself to be less concerned about the well-being of my clients and their families.

25.___ I have felt trapped by my work as a helper.

26.___ I have felt a sense of hopelessness associated with working with clients and their families.

27.___ I have felt "on edge" about various things and I attribute this to working with certain clients and their families.

28.___ I have wished that I could avoid working with some clients and their families.

225

29.___ I have been in danger working with some clients and their families.
30.___ I have felt that some of my clients and their families dislike me personally.

Items about being a helper and your work environment:

31.___ I have felt weak, tired, rundown as a result of my work as a helper.
32.___ I have felt depressed as a result of my work as a helper.
33.___ I am unsuccessful at separating work from personal life.
34.___ I feel little compassion toward most of my co-workers.
35.___ I feel I am working more for the money than for personal fulfillment.
36.___ I find it difficult separating my personal life from my work life.
37.___I have a sense of worthlessness/disillusionment/resentment associated with my work.
38.___ I have thoughts that I am a "failure" as a helper.
39.___ I have thoughts that I am not succeeding at achieving my life goals.
40.___ I have to deal with bureaucratic, unimportant tasks in my work life.

Scoring Instructions:
Make sure you have responded to ALL questions.
Next, circle the following 23 items: 1-8; 10-13; 17-26; and number 29.
Now ADD the numbers you wrote next to the items circled.
Note your risk of Compassion Fatigue:

26 or LESS – Extremely LOW risk
27-30 = LOW risk
31-35= Moderate Risk
36-40= HIGH risk.

Copyright, 1994, Florida State University Psychosocial Stress Research Program (Reprinted with permission)

While this test does not take the place of medical or mental health advise, it may provide you with some indicators about your vulnerability to compassion fatigue. Seek professional help if necessary or begin to carefully examine your lifestyle. Finding inner peace and healing compassion fatigue is not a one-time activity. It requires ongoing attention. Maryanna Eckberg[65], a pioneer in somatic psychotherapies, suggests some of the following ways to help you achieve a sense of balance.

1. Be grounded in your own body. In other words, be attentive to your breathing. Try this. Sit in a chair with both feet on the floor. When you inhale, put a little pressure on your feet. When you exhale, let up on the pressure and surrender to the exhale, making sure that you exhale all the air. Emphasize the exhale – breathing into the lower abdomen. Continue for a short time.
2. Be aware of how your body harbors stress. Use somatic interventions such as massages, body work, or regular exercise to ground yourself.
3. Detoxify your body with saunas or steam baths.
4. Eat healthy meals. Don't skip meals because you have "no time."
5. If you are feeling overwhelmed by a particular case, client, or situation, call someone immediately. It is crucial that you be able to talk with someone about this work and your experiences so that you don't begin to isolate yourself.
6. Participate in a variety of activities other than work related to trauma survivors. Write poetry, dance, read books or engage in personally satisfying creative endeavors.
7. Obtain support from professional activities where others can share with you their coping strategies.
8. Regularly evaluate how your work affects you and your relationships.
9. Meditate.
10. Have a spiritual belief system in place.

Above all, know that you are not alone. It is difficult to live with ease in a world where individuals inflict severe mental or physical pain upon each other. But we must always remember the resiliency of the human spirit – of both survivors and providers of care

for

"there will be paths through this forest and you and I will lose ourselves in the soft folds and curves of the ground. We will come to the water's edge and lie on the grass and there will be a small, unobtrusive sign that says - THIS IS THE REAL WORLD...AND WE ARE ALL IN IT."

—B. Traven

Epilogue

The girl's hands were poised perfectly on the ivory keys. Her father waited with anticipation for the melodious notes that stirred the hearts of audiences around the world. The girl, only twenty years old, paused for a moment to reflect on where she had been and where she was going. She thought for a moment about her childhood, with too many sleepless nights – too many dreams. The ache in her heart when her mother died had been great. At night, trying to console herself, she would chew on the corner of the quilt – methodically chewing all night long until her father finally took her for help. How she had struggled against counseling – trying to make sense of all those thoughts and emotions! But with rare courage and dogged determination she had taken risks. Even as a child, she knew she took them. It had not been without struggle. Through it all, she learned to embrace new people and new experiences. She found out that a good laugh could be more healing than a pill. And that one can have hopes and dreams and actually be joyous and happy! Instead of playing the piano, she picked up a pen and wrote:

> *"To all of you who may have suffered the heartache of a lifetime, I offer this...find someone who believes in you – even before you believe in yourself ...and strive for passion...for beauty, for life, and a world that is good..."*
>
> l.j.c., 2000

References

[1] See summary of research regarding the suggestibility of children by S. Ceci and M. Bruck, *Jeopardy in the Courtroom: A Scientific Analysis of Children's Testimony* (Washington, DC: American Psychological Association, 1995).

[2] See Gail Goodman, "Children's testimony in historical perspective," *Journal of Social Issues,* 1987, *40,* 9-31.

[3] Supreme Court of New Jersey, State V. Michaels, Decision, 136 N.J. 299; 642 A.2d 1372; 1994 N.J. LEXIS 504.

[4] See Mark Sauer, "Mending a Broken Trust," *San Diego Union-Tribune, (*December 17, 1995).

[5] See Geiselman, R.E., Fisher, R.P., MacKinnon, D.P. and Holland, H.L., "Eyewitness memory enhancement in the police interview: cognitive retrieval mnemonics versus hypnosis," *Journal of Applied Psychology,* 1985, *70,* 401-412.

[6] D. Schacter, "Implicit memory: History and current status," *Journal of Experimental Psychology: Learning, Memory and Cognition,* 1987, *13,* 501-18.

[7] See B.A.van der Kolk, " The body keeps score: Memory and the evolving psychobiology of stress," *Harvard Review of Psychiatry,* 1994, 1, (5), 253-65.

[8] See R. Fivush and J. Hudson, *Knowing and remembering in young children* (New York: Cambridge University Press, 1990).

[9] Interview protocols for child victims have been described by John Yuille, Ray Bull, Karen Saywitz, Kathleen Colbourn-Faller, Lucy Berliner, Debra Poole and Michael Lamb, Phil Esplin and B.W. Boat along with M.D. Everson.

[10] German psychologist Max Steller, along with John Yuille, David

Raskin and Phil Esplin, offered a modified cognitive interview protocol (unpublished) for children reporting sexual abuse in the mid 1980's. They were later joined in trainings by Steve Horowitz and Tascha Boychuk.

[11] M. Lamb and colleagues advocate the use of language samples prior to obtaining narratives about witnessed events. See M. Lamb, I. Hershkowitz, K. Sternberg, P. Esplin, M. Hovav, T. Manor and L. Yudilevitch, "Effects of investigative utterance types on Israeli children's responses," *International Journal on Behavioral Development*, 1996, 19, 627-637.

[12] When trying to remember one episode of an event that was witnessed many times, children and adults have trouble distinguishing one incident from another. See R. Fivush, "Developmental perspectives on autobiographical recall," in G.S. Goodman & B.L. Bottoms (eds.), *Child victims, child witnesses: Understanding and improving testimony* (New York: Guilford, 1993), pp. 1-24.

[13] See Boat, B.W. & Everson, M.D. "Use of anatomical dolls among professionals in sexual abuse evaluations," *Child Abuse and Neglect*, 1988, 12, 171-179 and Boat, B.W. & Everson, M.D. "Concerning practices of interviewing when using anatomical dolls in child protective services investigations," *Child Maltreatment*, 1996, 1, 94-104.

[14] See R. Bull, "Innovative techniques for the questioning of child witnesses especially those who are young and those with learning disability," in M. Zaragoza, J.R. Graham, G.C.N. Hall, R. Hirschman & Y.S. Ben-Porath (Eds.), *Memory and testimony in the child witness* (Thousand Oaks, CA: Sage, 1995).

[15] See J.H. Wigmore, *Evidence in trials at common law* (Boston: Little, Brown, 1974; originally published in 1904).

[16] See D. A. Poole and D. S. Lindsey, "Eyewitness reports of children exposed to misinformation from their parents," *Journal of Experimental Psychology: Applied*, 2001, 7, 129-154.

[17] See G.S. Goodman, J. Hirschman, D. Hepps and L. Rudy, "Children's

memory for stressful events," *Merrill-Palmer Quarterly*, 1991, 37, 109-158.

[18] See language and literacy skills of young children in David Dickenson and Patton Tabors, *Beginning Literacy With Language* (New York: Paul Brookes Publishers, 1999).

[19] See summary of research on fact/fantasy distinctions in S. Lepore, "Child Witness: cognitive and social factors related to memory and testimony," *IPT Journal*, 1991, 3, 1-35.

[20] See R. Fivush and J.A. Hudson, *Knowing and Remembering in Young Children* (New York: Cambridge University Press, 1990).

[21] See discussion of autobiographical recall by Fivush, R., & Hudson, J.A., *Knowing and Remembering in Young Children* (New York: Cambridge University Press, 1990).

[22] See Fisher, R.P., & McCauley, M.R. "Improving eyewitness testimony with the cognitive interview," In M.S. Zaragoza, J.R. Graham, G,C.N. Hall, R. Hirschman and R.S. Ben-Forth (eds.), *Memory and Testimony in the Child Witness* (Thousand Oaks, CA: Sage, 1995), pp. 141-159.

[23] Ceci, S.J., & Bruck, M. *Jeopardy in the Courtroom: A scientific analysis of children's testimony* (Washington, DC: American Psychological Association, 1995).

[24] See handouts from National College of District Attorneys (Training Manuals, 2000).

[25] Adapted from closing arguments of Kurt Altman, prosecutor extraordinaire.

[26] See J.S. Shaw and K.A. McClure, "Repeated post-event questioning can lead to elevated levels of eyewitness confidence," *Law and Human Behavior*, 1996, 2, 629-653.

[27] See J.H. Flavell, "First Discussant's Comments on What is Memory Development the Development Of?" *Human Development*, 1971, 14, 272-278.

[28] See J. H. Flavell, "Spontaneous versus verbal rehearsal in a memory task as a function of age," *Child Development*, 1966, 37, 283-299.

[29] See G.S. Everly and J. Lating (Eds.), *Psychotraumatology: key papers and core concepts in psychological trauma* (New York: Plenum, 1995).

[30] See C. Peterson and M. Bell, "Children's memory for traumatic injury," Child Development, 1996, 67, 36-42. and G. S. Goodman, G.S. Hirschman, D. Hepps, and L. Rudy, "Children's memory for stressful events," *Merrill-Palmer Quarterly*, 1991, 109-158.

[31] See R. Fivush and J.A. Hudson, (Eds.), *Knowing and Remembering in Young Children* (New York: Cambridge University Press, 1990).

[32] See H. Dent, "Experimental studies of interviewing child witnesses," In J. Dorris (Ed.), *The Suggestibility of children's recollections: Implications for eyewitness testimony* (Washington DC: American Psychological Association, 1991) 138-146.

[33] In sexual abuse cases, children also can incorporate fantastic elements in their account as a means of coping with the helplessness of the situation. See M.D. Everson, "Understanding bizarre, improbable and fantastic elements in children's accounts of abuse," *Child Maltreatment*, 1997, 2, 134-149.

[34] Memon, A., Wark, L., Holley, A., Bull, R., Koehnken, G. Eyewitness performance in Cognitive and Structured Interviews, *Memory,*1997, 5, 639-655.

[35] See Memon, A., Wark, L., Holley, A., Bull, R., & Koehnken, G. Reducing Suggestibility in Child Witness Interviews, *Applied Cognitive Psychology*, 1996, 10,
503-518.

[36] See Bull, T. Obtaining evidence expertly: the reliability of interviews with child witnesses in Expert Evidence: *The International Digest of Human Behaviour, Science and Law*, 1992, 1, 3-36.

[37] See E.M. Cummings and P. Davies, *Children and marital conflict:*

the impact of family dispute and resolution (New York: Guildford, 1994).

[38] See J. Graham and S.A. Bermann, "Family worries: assessment of interpersonal anxiety in children form violent and nonviolent homes," *Journal of Clinical Psychology*, 1996, 25, 280-287.

[39] See summaries of research by H. Hughes, "Research concerning children of battered women: clinical implications" *Journal of Aggression, Maltreatment and Trauma*, 1997, 1, 225-244.

[40] See F.D. Fincham,, "Understanding the association between marital conflict and child adjustment: an overview," *Journal of Family Psychology*, 1994, 8, 123-127.

[41] See Cummings & Davies in note one along with P.R. Shaver, G.S. Goodman, M.S. Rosenberg and H. Orcutt, "The search for a definition of psychological maltreatment," *Development and Psychopathology*, 1991, 3, 79-86.

[42] See G.T. Everly, and J.T. Mitchell, *Critical Incident Stress Management* (CISM): A new era and standard of care in crisis intervention. (Elicott City, MD: Chevron Publishing Co., 1997). Also see workbook used as handout by George Everly (CISM training, Las Vegas, Nevada, 2000).

[43] For a comprehensive protocol to develop safety plans with battered women see J. Davies, *Safety Planning With Battered Women* (Thousand Oaks: Sage, 1998).

[44] See R.S. Pynoos and K. Nader, "Children's memory and proximity to violence, " *Journal of Social Issues*, 1984, 28, 87-108.

[45] See discussion of persistent distress after traumatic events in L. Silveryn, J. Karyl, and T. Landis, "Individual psychotherapy for the traumatized children of abused women," In E. Peled, P. Jaffe and J. Edleson (Eds.), *Ending The Cycle of Violence* (Thousand Oaks: Sage, 1995), pp. 43-76

[46] See E. Peled, P. Jaffe and J. Edelson (Eds.), *Ending The Cycle of*

Violence (Thousand Oaks, CA: Sage, 1995).

[47] See P. Levine, "The body as healer: a revisioning of trauma and anxiety," *Somatics*, 1991, 13, 1, 18-27.

[48] See U.S. Department of Health and Human Services, *Promising Practices in Children's Mental Health*, Volume 1, (Washington DC: Center for Effective Collaboration and Practice, American Institutes for Research, 2000).

[49] See historical overview of measures enacted to assist missing children in Missing and Abducted Children: a law enforcement guide to case investigation and program management. (National Center for Missing and Exploited Children, Arlington, VA, 1994).

[50] See the National Incidence Studies of Missing, Abducted, Runaway, and Thrownaway Children in America. (U.S. Department of Justice, Office of Juvenile Justice Programs, 1990).

[51] See G. Grief and R. Heiger, *When Parents Kidnap: the families behind the headlines.* (New York: Free Press, 1993).

[52] Contact Nevada Child Seekers, Las Vegas, Nevada or LVMPD, Las Vegas, Nevada for copies of the form.

[53] See American Psychological Association. Violence and the family: Report of the American Psychological Association Presidential Task Force on Violence and the Family. (Washington DC: Author, 1996).

[54] Police who investigate homicides in urban areas estimate that at least twenty percent of their investigations of violence are witnessed by children (Informal discussions with homicide detectives in Los Angeles, Phoenix, and New York, 2000).

[55] See *Diagnostic and Statistical Manual of the American Psychiatric Association.* (Washington DC: Author, 1994).

[56] See R.S. Pynoos and S. Eth, "The child witness to homicide," *Journal of Social Issues*, 1984, 40, 87-108.

[57] See S. Keleman, *Somatic Reality* (Berkely, CA: Center Press, 1979) and P. Levine, *Waking the Tiger: Healing Trauma* (Berkely, CA: North Atlantic Books, 1997).

[58] See Erik Erikson, *Childhood and Society* (London: W.W. Norton & Co., 1950).

[59] See B.A. van der Kolk, *Psychological Trauma* (Washington, DC: American Psychiatric Press, 1987).

[60] See S. Keleman, *Your Body Speaks its Mind* (Berkely, CA: Center Press, 1975) and M. Eckberg, Somatic Psychotherapy in the Treatment of Posttraumatic Stress Disorder (Berkely, CA: North Atlantic Books, 2000).

[61] See P. Levine, The body as healer: a revisioning of trauma and anxiety. *Somatics*, 1991, 1, 11-19.

[62] There are various institutes of Bioenergetic Analysis throughout the nation. They focus on the mind-body connection and encourage interventions that are holistic. Faculty members at the The International Institute for Bioenergetic Analysis can offer resources.

[63] See methods for reducing stress in M. Eckberg, "A psychologist in El Salvador," *Bioenergetic Analysis: The Clinical Journal of the International Institute for Bioenergetic Analysis*, 1997, 8, 28-42.

[64] See C.G. Figley, *Compassion Fatigue: Coping with Secondary Stress Disorder in Those Who Treat the Traumatized.* (New York: Brunner/Mazel, 1995); Also see literature distributed online by the Florida State University Psychosocial Stress Research Program.

[65] See care of the caregiver in M.Eckberg, *Victims of Cruelty* (Berkely CA: North Atlantic Books, 2000) and E.W. Smith, P.R. Clance, and S. Imes, Touch in Psychotherapy (New York: Guilford Press, 1998); Also see J.W. Pennebaker, "Putting stress into words: Health, linguistic and therapeutic implications," Behavior Research and Therapy, 1993, 31, 339-548.

Recommended Books

American Professional Society on the Abuse of Children. (1997). *Code of Ethics*. Chicago: Author.

Cross, T, Earle, K., Echo-Hawk Solie, & H., Manness, K. (2000). *Promising Practices in Children's Mental Health Systems of Care*. Washington, DC: U.S. Department of Health and Human Services.

Dent, H. & Flin, R. (Eds.). (1992). *Children As Witnesses*. New York: John Wiley.

Eckberg, M. (2000). *Victims of Cruelty*. Berkley, CA: North Atlantic Books.

Fivush, R.& Hudson, J.A. (Eds.). (1990). *Knowing and Remembering in Young Children*. New York: Cambridge University Press.

Freyd, J.J. (1996). *Betrayal Trauma: The logic of forgetting childhood abuse*. Cambridge, MA: Harvard University Press.

Goodman, G.S. & Bottoms, B.L. (Eds.). (1993). *Child victims, child witnesses: Understanding and improving testimony*. New York: Guilford.

Levine, R. (1997). *Waking the Tiger: Healing Trauma*. Berkley, CA: North Atlantic Books.

Meloy, J.R. (2000). *Violence Risk and Threat Assessment*. San Diego, CA: Specialized Training Services.

Mohandie, K. (2000). *School Violence Threat Management*. San Diego, CA: Specialized Training Services.

Myers, J.B. (1998). *Legal Issues in Child Abuse and Neglect Practice*. Thousand Oaks, CA: Sage.

Poole, D.A. & Lamb, M.E. (1998). *Investigative Interviews of children*. Washington, DC: American Psychological Association.

Saywitz, K.J. & Elliott, D. (1999). *Interviewing children in the forensic context: a developmental approach*. Washington, DC: American Psychological Association.

Zaragoza, M., Graham, J.R., Hall, G.C.N., Hirschman, R. & Ben-Porath, Y.S. (Eds.). (1995). *Memory and Testimony in the Child Witness*. Thousand Oaks, CA: Sage.

Tascha Boychuk-Spears, Ph.D., RN has devoted most of her career to helping child victims of violence. Born in Canada, she received a doctorate from the College of Law and Social Sciences Justice Studies program from Arizona State University in 1991. For the past twelve years, Dr. Spears has interviewed or provided counseling to over 3,000 children who reported maltreatment. In 1997, with the Mesa Arizona Police Department and Arizona State University College of Nursing, she started a program for children who witnessed homicide. Dr. Spears has served as a consultant to law enforcement agencies throughout the nation as well as internationally on cases involving child witnesses to crimes. Her publications are on interview strategies with children. Dr. Spears is a recipient of the Arizona Office of the Attorney General Distinguished Service Award and the Phoenix Police Department Decade of Service Award. Dr. Spears currently teaches in the Department of Nursing at University of Nevada Las Vegas (UNLV).